graphis annual 75|76

Edited by Walter Herdeg

This is the 24th annual edition of a work that has been consistently called "a visual feast." This year's collection, from all over the world, continues its survey of graphics in advertisements, annual reports, booklets, book jackets and magazine covers, trade marks, letterheads, packaging, record covers, film and television and editorial design—selecting and beautifully reproducing what is happening in all design fields. Here is an endless source of ideas and a perfect "swipe file" for art directors, illustrators and designers, keeping them up-to-date as well as offering new ideas and solutions to graphic arts problems.

The Two Companion Annuals, Edited by Walter Herdeg:

GRAPHIS POSTERS

The International Annual of Poster Art

"The contemporary poster in its diverse usage for art, the stage, trade and industry and political propaganda, fills the need for many purposes," reports *Creative Signs & Displays*. "Technical advances have added to the richness and multiformity of the modern poster, which has risen to the position of an evolving art form." This new third edition offers visual evidence arranged in four major categories: *Advertising* posters, *Cultural* posters, *Social* posters, *Decorative* posters.

Published each year in early Spring.

PHOTOGRAPHIS

The International Annual of Advertising, Editorial and Television Photography

A document that records all change in objectives, techniques and taste, but also reveals—behind the professional aspects of advertising—how a changing economic situation affects the photographer. The 10th Anniversary edition of this widely used annual is, appropriately, divided into 10 sections: Advertisements—Booklets—Calendars—Packaging—Record Covers—Film/TV—Editorial Photographs—Magazine Covers—Book Covers—Annual Reports.

Published each year in late Spring.

Other Graphis Books, Edited by Walter Herdeg:

A new series in "Square Books" format (9-½" × 9-⅜") :

GRAPHIS / RECORD COVERS

GRAPHIS / DIAGRAMS

The Graphic Visualization of Abstract Data

In 9-½" × 12" format :

FILM AND TV GRAPHICS
Text by John Halas

GRAPHIS / ANNUAL REPORTS
Text by Richard A. Lewis

GRAPHIS / PACKAGING 2

Write for a complete catalogue :

VISUAL COMMUNICATION BOOKS

Hastings House, Publishers, Inc., 10 East 40th Street, New York, N.Y. 10016

graphis annual

75|76 graphis annual

The International Annual of Advertising and
Editorial Graphics

Das internationale Jahrbuch der Werbe-
graphik und der redaktionellen Graphik

Le répertoire international de l'art graphique
publicitaire et rédactionnel

Edited by: / Herausgegeben von: / Réalisé par:

Walter Herdeg

Walter Herdeg, The Graphis Press, Zurich

Distributed in the United States by
Hastings House, Publishers, Inc.
10 East 40th Street, New York, N.Y. 10016

Publication No 141   (ISBN 8038-2674-5)

Contents

Inhalt

Sommaire

Abbreviations

Abkürzungen

Abréviations

Cover design/Umschlagentwurf/Couverture: Erberto Carboni

■ EDWARD BOOTH-CLIBBORN was an art director for J. Walter Thompson when he first became involved in the activities of the emerging British Designers and Art Directors Association in 1962. For many years Executive Chairman of this organization and Chairman of the jury of its annual exhibitions, he has been able to follow the developments of British advertising and graphic design at close quarters, and from this vantage-point to survey the parallel evolution of graphics on the European Continent and in America. What he has seen in the last few years has not always gratified him, and as an open-minded and responsible critic with the good of the profession at heart, he has set down in our introduction a few thoughts that are worth pondering on.

■ EDWARD BOOTH-CLIBBORN war Art Director für J. Walter Thompson, als er 1962 erstmals in die Aktivitäten der sich bildenden britischen Designers and Art Directors Association einbezogen wurde. Er war jahrelang Geschäfts-führer dieser Organisation und konnte als Juryvorsitzender ihrer jährlichen Ausstellungen die Entwicklung britischer Werbung und Graphik aus nächster Nähe verfolgen und parallel dazu die graphische Entwicklung auf dem europäi-schen Festland und in Amerika überschauen. Was er in den letzten Jahren ge-sehen hat, erfreute ihn nicht immer. Als aufgeschlossener und verantwortlicher Kritiker, dem das Wohl seines Berufsstandes am Herzen liegt, hat er deshalb in unserer Einleitung einige Gedanken niedergeschrieben, über die es sich nach-zudenken lohnt.

■ EDWARD BOOTH-CLIBBORN était directeur artistique chez J. Walter Thompson lorsqu'il commença à participer aux activités de la Designers and Art Directors Association, alors au premier stade de son développement, en 1962. Depuis de nombreuses années, il est président en exercice de cette organisation, dont il préside aussi le jury annuel d'exposition. C'est ce qui lui a permis de suivre de très près le développement de la publicité et de l'art publici-taire en Grande-Bretagne et, parallèlement, celui de l'art graphique en Europe continentale et en Amérique. Le spectacle auquel il a assisté ces dernières années ne l'a pas toujours transporté d'aise, et c'est en esprit ouvert, en critique conscient de ses responsabilités et mettant l'intérêt de la profession au centre de ses préoccupations qu'il s'exprime ici.

Although the Editor's thanks to contributors is repeated in these lines from year to year, it is far from becoming a mere matter of form. The quality of every volume depends on the quality of the material submitted, and because we are aware of the considerable amount of work involved in preparing and sending in work, our indebtedness is annually renewed and this note of thanks continues to be written in a genuine spirit of gratitude.

Obwohl sich der Herausgeber in diesen Zeilen Jahr für Jahr bei den Einsendern bedankt, ist dieser Dank weit davon entfernt, nur Formsache zu sein. Die Qualität jedes Bandes hängt von der Qualität der Einsendungen ab. Da wir uns des beträchtlichen Aufwandes bewusst sind, der mit Vorbereitung und Einsendung von Arbeiten verbunden ist, erneuert sich alljährlich unsere Dankesschuld, so dass diese Danksagung stets in aufrichtiger Erkenntlichkeit geschrieben ist.

Bien que les remerciements que l'éditeur adresse à tous ceux qui ont contribué au succès du présent ouvrage se répètent d'année en année, ils ne sont pas de pure forme. La qualité de chaque édition dépend de la qualité des travaux qui y sont incorporés, et c'est bien parce que nous sommes pleinement conscients du travail considérable que représentent la préparation et l'envoi de ces œuvres que nous tenons à exprimer nos remerciements chaque année, dans quelques lignes inspirées d'un réel sentiment de gratitude.

Advertising in the 1980's — public nuisance or public servant?

One of the most interesting changes in advertising during the last year has been reflected in the way in which public-sector and non-profitmaking advertising have developed into an award-winning advertising genre in their own right. In Britain, for example, the Design and Art Direction Gold Award for 1975 went to a harrowing film publizising the need for fire prevention in the home; the Silver Award was presented to the Health Education Council for their work in promoting Britain's anti-smoking campaign.

There is no neat answer to why this change has come about, but there are one or two developments which give us some clues. Firstly, the country's public services and charities have increased their expenditure on advertising whilst many branded goods manufacturers have had to cut back their budgets. Secondly, today's youth has a much stronger social conscience than that of a generation ago.

The first point is bound to have some effect on the industry's attitudes to what advertising is all about.

The second point serves to remind us that far fewer young people from British universities and art schools find advertising an attractive industry in which to make a career. Their standards are new, and, perhaps, more idealistic, their hopes and fears different and, for many of them, success is more likely to be judged by personal achievement and self-fulfilment than by any purely financial or materialistic criteria.

Of course, young people are not entirely alone. Coupled with their opinion is that of many older people who have come to be critical of big business and the growing number of conglomerate companies with their widespread multinational connections. People no longer accept the falsification of truths or the misrepresentation of the real value of a product, and they therefore treat advertising with a strong degree of circumspection.

In many ways, of course, industry has responded well. But perhaps not well enough. In Britain, as in many other countries, there still remains a strong class distinction between the managed and the managers, the entrepreneur and the worker. In Britain this class barrier is maintained by some forms of advertising and mass media attitudes. This does much to prevent the progress vital to the nation's growth.

However, there is a general realization in most countries that something must be done to put an end to the blatant manipulation of the public's spending power, and that advertising should adopt a more informative role, one of public service. With this motive in mind, advertising may then also be used to bring about changes in the mistrustful attitudes held by those critical of the ways and means of industry.

Outside the advertising industry there are shifting patterns of trade. These too will affect advertising. For example, in the grocery business the world food situation will probably cause marketing organizations to re-assess their role and supermarket chains to regroup. Products such as bread, sugar and other essential foods which are dependent on bulk harvests from a few major supplying countries will cease to be sold competitively by manufacturers. Such a change can only be successful if the EEC can explain its importance. On the other hand, it is very important that changes like this should not contribute to blurring the separate national identities within the EEC.

Culturally, of course, there is already a blurring of identity, especially among the young. The "denim revolution" epitomizes this. But where, for the past four or five years, we have seen a uniform development that has its roots in the American working man's clothes and his dream of a free society with equal opportunities for all, we may now expect to see another revolution in style that owes its allegiance to the communal spirit and ideals of the Vietnamese peasant as the youth of today looks for identification with the oldest, most immutable civilizations we know.

In the light of all this the advertising industry must continue to re-define its attitudes so as to bring about the opening-up of communication between all sections of society. Society's strength lies in its intelligentsia; unless the advertising industry changes, it will never attract back this disaffected section.

While much has been done, there is still much to be done before we in Britain—and elsewhere—match the progress that is being made by those in the Netherlands such as Tel Design Group of The Hague with the GUN, who have been doing visual experimental work with posters in Bangladesh, and the Amsterdam-based advertising agency FHV/BBDO, whose concept of corporate communications goes beyond the normal role of an advertising agency to embrace all forms of interorganization-communication at every level.

It is in areas of this kind and with the same spirit of adventure that the advertising industry must adopt an attitude which is much more in line with public feeling and sympathy so that, in the years to come, advertising will be, and will be seen to be, much more of a public servant and much less of a public nuisance.

Until then we must expect it to remain the wasteful industry that it has come to be. Wasteful of talent and wasteful of resources. In the 1970's and 80's, waste cannot be condoned.

Edward Booth-Clibborn

Werbung um 1980 —
öffentliches Ärgernis oder Dienst
an der Öffentlichkeit ?

Eine der interessantesten Veränderungen in der Werbung spiegelte sich im letzten Jahr darin, wie sich Werbung auf dem öffentlichen und gemeinnützigen Sektor zu einem eigenständigen, prämiierbaren Werbegenre entwickelt hat. 1975 ging in England zum Beispiel der Preis in Gold für Design und Art Direction an einen erschreckenden Film, der für die Notwendigkeit vorbeugenden Brandschutzes in Haus und Heim warb. Der Preis in Silber ging an den Gesundheitsförderungsrat für seine Arbeit an einer englischen Anti-Raucherkampagne.

Warum es zu diesem Wandel kam, lässt sich nicht pauschal beantworten. Es gibt aber ein oder zwei Entwicklungen, die uns dafür einige Hinweise liefern. Erstens haben die öffentlichen Dienste und Wohlfahrtsverbände des Landes ihre Werbeausgaben verstärkt, während viele Markenartikel ihre Werbebudgets kürzen mussten. Zweitens hat die Jugend von heute ein stärkeres soziales Bewusstsein als das noch vor einer Generation der Fall war.

Der erste Punkt muss zwangsläufig Auswirkungen auf die Einstellung der Industrie gegenüber dem Sinn der Werbung haben.

Der zweite soll uns daran erinnern, dass es viel weniger junge Leute von englischen Universitäten und Kunstschulen attraktiv finden, in der Werbung Karriere zu machen. Ihre Massstäbe sind neu und vielleicht idealistischer, ihre Hoffnungen und Ängste sind anders, und viele von ihnen beurteilen Erfolg viel eher nach persönlicher Leistung und Selbstverwirklichung als nach rein finanziellen oder materialistischen Kriterien.

Natürlich stehen die jungen Leute nicht ganz allein. Ihre Meinung paart sich mit der vieler älterer Menschen, die dem Big Business und den engverflochtenen multinationalen Wirtschaftskonzernen nun kritisch gegenüberstehen. Die Leute akzeptieren nicht länger die Verfälschung von Wahrheiten oder das verdrehte Bild des wirklichen Wertes eines Produkts und bringen der Werbung ein starkes Mass an Vorsicht entgegen.

Natürlich hat die Industrie in vielerlei Hinsicht gut reagiert. Aber vielleicht nicht gut genug. Wie in vielen anderen Ländern, gibt es in England noch starke Klassenunterschiede zwischen Arbeitnehmern und Arbeitgebern, Unternehmern und Arbeitern. In England wird diese Klassenbarriere von einigen Arten Werbung und Einstellungen der Massenmedien aufrechterhalten. Dies trägt viel bei zur Verhinderung des für das nationale Wachstum lebensnotwendigen Fortschritts.

In den meisten Ländern macht sich jedoch eine allgemeine Erkenntnis breit, dass etwas unternommen werden muss, um der marktschreierischen Manipulation der Kaufkraft der Öffentlichkeit ein Ende zu setzen, und dass die Werbung eine informativere Rolle, sozusagen als Dienstleistung, annehmen sollte. Solchermassen motiviert, könnte die Werbung dann auch genützt werden, um einen Wandel der misstrauischen Einstellung jener zu bewirken, die Mitteln und Wegen der Industrie kritisch gegenüberstehen.

Ausserhalb der Werbeindustrie verändern sich Handelsstrukturen, was auch die Werbung beeinflussen wird. So wird zum Beispiel die Welternährungssituation im Lebensmittelhandel Verkaufsorganisationen veranlassen, ihre Rolle zu überdenken, und Supermarktketten zu Umgruppierungen bringen. Produkte wie Brot, Zucker und andere Grundnahrungsmittel, die von Massenernten einiger Hauptlieferländer abhängen, werden nicht mehr im Herstellerkonkurrenzkampf verkauft werden. Ein solcher Wandel kann nur Erfolg haben, wenn die EG seine Bedeutung bewusstmachen kann. Andererseits ist es sehr wichtig, dass derlei Veränderungen nicht zur Verwischung der einzelnen nationalen Identitäten innerhalb der EG beitragen.

Im kulturellen Bereich gibt es diese Identitätsnivellierung natürlich schon, vor allem unter der Jugend. Die "Jeans-Revolution" ist dafür ein gutes Beispiel. Wo wir aber in den letzten vier, fünf Jahren eine Uniform entstehen sahen, die auf der Kleidung des amerikanischen Arbeiters und seinem Traum einer freien Gesellschaft mit Chancengleichheit für alle fusst, können wir jetzt mit einer weiteren modischen Revolution rechnen, die auf Volksgeist und Idealen der vietnamesischen Landbevölkerung aufbaut, da sich die Jugend von heute mit den ältesten uns bekannten, strengen Kulturen zu identifizieren sucht.

Im Lichte dieser Entwicklung muss die Werbebranche weiterhin ihre Ansichten neu definieren, um Kommunikation zwischen allen Bereichen der Gesellschaft in Gang zu bringen. Die Stärke der Gesellschaft liegt bei ihrer Intelligentsia. Wenn sich die Werbebranche nicht wandelt, wird sie nicht in der Lage sein, die Abneigung dieses Gesellschaftsbereiches zu überwinden.

Obwohl schon viel erreicht worden ist, muss bei uns in England – und anderswo – noch viel getan werden, um mit dem in Holland gemachten Fortschritt gleichzuziehen, wo etwa die Tel Design Gruppe aus Den Haag mit GUN visuelle Experimentalarbeit mit Plakaten in Bangladesch geleistet hat und in Amsterdam die Werbeagentur FHV/BBDO beheimatet ist, deren Konzept korporativer Kommunikation über die normale Rolle einer Werbeagentur hinausgeht und alle Formen interorganisatorischer Kommunikation auf jeder Ebene umfasst. Auf Gebieten wie diesem und mit demselben Abenteurergeist muss die Werbebranche eine Haltung einnehmen, die viel stärker in Einklang mit Meinung und Wohlwollen der Öffentlichkeit steht, damit die Werbung in Zukunft mehr Dienst an der Öffentlichkeit und viel weniger öffentliches Ärgernis wird.

Bis es jedoch soweit ist, müssen wir damit rechnen, dass Werbung die verschwenderische Industrie bleibt, die sie geworden ist. Verschwenderisch im Umgang mit Talent und mit Geldmitteln. In den 70er und 80er Jahren ist Verschwendung jedoch unverzeihlich.

Edward Booth-Clibborn

La publicité de la décennie 1980 —
un fléau ou un service public?

L'un des changements les plus intéressants intervenus dans la publicité, l'année dernière, s'est reflété dans l'accès du secteur public et de la publicité non commerciale aux honneurs suprêmes. C'est ainsi qu'en Grande-Bretagne, la médaille d'or de Design & Art Direction pour 1975 a été décernée à un film poignant sur la nécessité de prévenir les incendies, de même que la médaille d'argent récompensait le Health Education Council, organisation nationale œuvrant dans le domaine de la santé publique, pour sa contribution à la campagne anti-tabac en Angleterre.

La raison de ce changement est difficile à cerner, mais l'observation de deux ou trois développements récents peut nous éclairer. Il y a tout d'abord le fait que les services publics d'intérêt national et les organisations de bienfaisance ont augmenté leur budget publicitaire, alors que nombre de fabricants de produits de marque se sont vus obligés de pratiquer des coupes sombres dans ce même budget. Ensuite, la conscience sociale de la jeunesse paraît bien plus développée que celle de ses aînés.

Le premier point aura nécessairement une influence sur l'attitude des industriels face à la publicité.

Le deuxième point nous rappelle le nombre désormais très réduit de jeunes gens issus des universités et écoles des beaux-arts et des arts décoratifs britanniques qui envisagent de faire carrière dans la publicité, qui a cessé pour beaucoup d'être une profession attrayante. Ils adhèrent à une nouvelle échelle des valeurs peut-être plus idéaliste; leurs espérances et leurs craintes sont de nature différente, et pour beaucoup d'entre eux, le succès est plutôt fonction du développement de la personnalité que de considérations et réalisations purement financières et matérielles.

Cette attitude n'est bien entendu pas l'apanage de la jeunesse. Nombreux sont ceux qui, plus âgés, critiquent le monde des affaires et le nombre croissant des conglomérats aux ramifications internationales. Le public n'accepte plus que la valeur réelle d'un produit soit déformée ou la vérité défigurée par une action publicitaire, ce qui le porte à ne plus accepter les messages publicitaires sans quelque réserve.

A beaucoup d'égards, l'industrie s'est adaptée à cet état de choses, mais peut-être pas assez. En Grande-Bretagne comme dans d'autres pays, il subsiste un fossé assez large entre employés et directeurs, ouvriers et chefs d'entreprise. En Grande-Bretagne, cette barrière sociale est entretenue par le biais de certaines formes de publicité et de certaines attitudes reflétées par les médias. Il en résulte un obstacle de taille au développement continu du progrès, qui est d'importance vitale pour la croissance de la nation.

Il existe toutefois une prise de conscience générale, dans la plupart des pays du monde, de la nécessité qu'il y a à mettre fin à la manipulation par trop éhontée du pouvoir d'achat de l'individu, et à confier à la publicité davantage un rôle d'informateur au service du public. Cette motivation nouvelle permettrait également de remédier à l'attitude de défiance propre à ceux qui critiquent l'action des industriels.

Hors de l'industrie publicitaire, les grandes structures d'échange commerciales sont en voie de transformation, ce qui ne manquera pas de peser sur les destinées de la publicité. C'est ainsi que, dans le commerce d'alimentation, la situation sur le marché mondial des denrées alimentaires va probablement amener les organisations de commercialisation à reconsidérer leur rôle, et les chaînes de supermarchés à se regrouper. Des produits tels que le pain, le sucre ou d'autres denrées vitales, dont l'approvisionnement dépend de l'abondance des récoltes dans un petit nombre de pays producteurs, ne pourront plus être vendus de manière concurrentielle par les fabricants. Un tel changement ne pourra être positif que si la CEE peut expliquer à ses citoyens l'importance qui lui revient. Il est par ailleurs essentiel que de telles transformations ne contribuent pas à effacer les frontières et identités nationales au sein de la CEE.

Sur le plan culturel, une telle confusion des valeurs nationales est naturellement déjà en cours, en particulier parmi les jeunes. La «révolution des jeans» en est un symbole. Mais alors que, ces quatre ou cinq dernières années, nous avons assisté à la diffusion d'un uniforme incarnant les vêtements de travail de l'ouvrier américain et son rêve d'une société libre offrant les mêmes chances à tous, nous pouvons nous attendre à présent à une nouvelle révolution vestimentaire et stylistique qui s'inspire de l'esprit et de l'idéal communautaires du paysan vietnamien, dans la mesure où la jeunesse d'aujourd'hui cherche à s'identifier aux représentants de l'une des civilisations les plus anciennes et les plus implacables du monde.

En considérant tous ces facteurs, l'industrie de la publicité doit continuer de repenser ses attitudes jusqu'à acquérir la démarche propre à établir la libre communication entre tous les compartiments de la société. La force d'une société réside dans son noyau d'intellectuels; à moins de se transformer, l'industrie de la publicité ne pourra jamais regagner à sa cause ce noyau qui s'est détourné d'elle.

Beaucoup de choses ont été accomplies dans ce domaine; il faudra pourtant en accomplir encore bien d'autres pour que nous puissions, en Grande-Bretagne comme ailleurs, assister à des progrès du genre de celui qui est effectué par exemple aux Pays-Bas par le Tel Design Group de La Haye, avec le GUN, par le biais de travaux visuels expérimentaux sous forme d'affiches au Bangladesh, ou par l'agence de publicité FHV/BBDO d'Amsterdam, dont la conception pour les communications d'une entreprise dépasse de loin le rôle d'une agence ordinaire pour embrasser toutes les formes de communication interorganisations, à quelque niveau que ce soit. C'est dans des domaines de ce genre et avec le même esprit d'aventure que l'industrie de la publicité doit adopter une attitude plus compatible avec le consensus général, les sympathies et tendances affectives du public, de manière à se profiler dans les années à venir bien davantage comme un service public et bien moins comme un fléau inévitable.

Jusque-là, il faudra s'attendre à la voir demeurer l'industrie du gaspillage qu'elle est devenue, gaspillant les talents et les ressources. Dans la décennie 1970 aussi bien que dans celle de 1980, le gaspillage ne peut plus être toléré.

Edward Booth-Clibborn

Index to Designers and Artists
Verzeichnis der Entwerfer und Künstler
Index des maquettistes et artistes

Index to Art Directors
Verzeichnis der Künstlerischen Leiter
Index des directeurs artistiques

Index to Agencies and Studios
Verzeichnis der Agenturen und Studios
Index des agences et studios

Index to Publishers
Verzeichnis der Verleger
Index des éditeurs

Index to Advertisers
Verzeichnis der Auftraggeber
Index des clients

■ Entry instructions will be mailed to anyone interested in submitting samples of outstanding graphics or photography for possible inclusion in our annuals. No fees involved. Closing dates for entries:
GRAPHIS ANNUAL (Advertising and editorial art): 15 December
PHOTOGRAPHIS (Advertising and editorial photography): 30 June
GRAPHIS POSTERS (International annual on poster art): 30 March
Write to: The Graphis Press, Dufourstr. 107, 8008 Zurich, Switzerland.

■ Einsendebedingungen können von jedermann angefordert werden, der uns Beispiele hervorragender Graphik oder Photographie zur Auswahl für unsere Jahrbücher unterbreiten möchte. Es werden keine Gebühren erhoben. Einsende-termine:
GRAPHIS ANNUAL (Werbe- und redaktionelle Graphik): 15. Dezember
PHOTOGRAPHIS (Werbe- und redaktionelle Photographie): 30. Juni
GRAPHIS POSTERS (Internationales Jahrbuch der Plakatkunst): 30. März
Adresse: Graphis Verlag, Dufourstr. 107, 8008 Zürich, Schweiz.

■ Tout intéressé à la soumission de travaux graphiques et photographiques est prié de nous demander les informations nécessaires. Sans charge de participation.
Dates limites:
GRAPHIS ANNUAL (art graphique publicitaire et rédactionnel): 15 décembre
PHOTOGRAPHIS (photographie publicitaire et rédactionnelle): 30 juin
GRAPHIS POSTERS (répertoire international de l'art de l'affiche): 30 mars
S'adresser à: Editions Graphis, Dufourstr. 107, 8008 Zurich, Suisse.

Editor, Art Director, Designer: Walter Herdeg
Assistant Editor: Stanley Mason
Project Manager: Josette Leuenberger
Art Assistants: Klaus Schröder, Wilfried Maret, Peter Wittwer, Otmar Staubli, René Sahli

1

Magazine Advertisements

Newspaper Advertisements

Zeitschriften-Inserate

Zeitungs-Inserate

Annonces de revues

Annonces de presse

Of men and greenbacks.

If you market to men, you should know (a) that median annual income of GRIT adult males is about equal to the national average, while (b) small-town cost of living—real estate, taxes, entertainment, commuting, all that—is slightly lower

than a bullfrog's belly.

If you market to men, that adds up to greenbacks aplenty at America's grass roots. For power tools. And power boats. And guns and fishing rods and a long list of other products which, says TGI, GRIT men want

and will pay for.

If you market to men, three out of four GRIT adult males won't see your ad in Sports Illustrated. And nine out of ten won't see it in True.

If you market to men, you need a little GRIT.

Big frog in small towns GRIT
THE NATIONAL SMALL-TOWN WEEKLY
Home Office: Williamsport, Pa.; Branch Offices in New York, Chicago, Detroit   West Coast: Wheeler/Newell, San Francisco; Snyder/Clarkson, Santa Monica

1

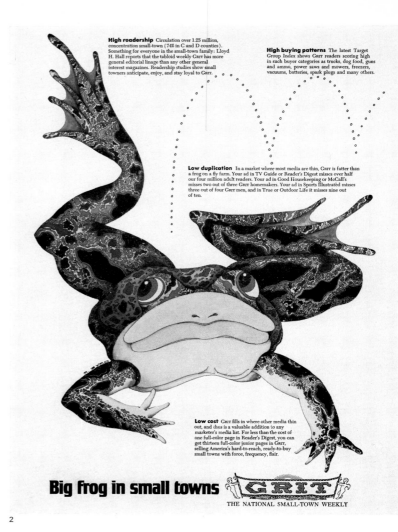

High readership Circulation over 1.25 million, concentration small-town (74% in C and D counties). Something for everyone in the small-town family: Lloyd H. Hall reports that the tabloid weekly GRIT has more general editorial linage than any other general interest magazines. Readership studies show small towners anticipate, enjoy, and stay loyal to GRIT.

High buying patterns The latest Target Group Index shows GRIT readers scoring high in such buyer categories as trucks, dog food, guns and ammo, power saws and mowers, freezers, vacuums, batteries, spark plugs and many others.

Low duplication In a market where most media are thin, GRIT is fatter than a frog on a fly farm. Your ad in TV Guide or Reader's Digest misses over half our four million adult readers. Your ad in Good Housekeeping or McCall's misses two out of three GRIT homemakers. Your ad in Sports Illustrated misses three out of four GRIT men, and in True or Outdoor Life it misses nine out of ten.

Low cost GRIT fills in where other media thin out, and thus is a valuable addition to any marketer's media list. For less than the cost of one full-color page in Reader's Digest, you can get thirteen full-color junior pages in GRIT, selling America's hard-to-reach, ready-to-buy small towns with force, frequency, flair.

Big frog in small towns GRIT
THE NATIONAL SMALL-TOWN WEEKLY

2

1–3 Magazine advertisements with full-colour illustrations from a series intended to promote the family weekly *Grit* as an advertising medium with an unusually large readership in small towns. (USA)
4 Full-colour trade press advertisement for quality hoses made by *B.F. Goodrich* for a wide variety of applications. (USA)
5 Colour advertisement in a financial magazine about the stock transfer services offered by a bank, the Cleveland Trust. (USA)
6 Magazine advertisement in blue and white shades for *Royal Gate* vodka. (USA)
7 Black-and-white magazine advertisement for *Head Start,* a hair conditioner containing special vitamins and minerals for healthy hair growth. (USA)

1–3 Mehrfarbige Zeitschriften-Inserate aus einer Werbekampagne für das Familien-Wochenblatt *Grit* als Inseratenträger mit grossem Leserkreis in amerikanischen Kleinstädten. (USA)
4 Fachpresse-Inserat im Mehrfarbendruck für Qualitätsschläuche mit vielfältigen Anwendungsmöglichkeiten, hergestellt durch die Firma *B.F. Goodrich.* (USA)
5 Farbiges Inserat in einer Finanz-Zeitschrift, in dem die Cleveland Trust Bank ihre Dienste für den Transfer von Aktien anbietet. (USA)
6 Zeitschriften-Inserat, das in Blau-Weiss-Tönen für *Royal Gate* Wodka wirbt. (USA)
7 Zeitschriften-Inserat in Schwarzweiss für *Head Start,* ein spezielles Haarpflegemittel mit Vitaminen und Spurenelementen für gesunden Haarwuchs. (USA)

1–3 Annonces de revue avec illustrations en couleurs. Ces exemples figurent dans une série promotionnelle pour l'hebdomadaire de famille *Grit* qui se propose en tant que moyen de publicité qui est beaucoup lu dans les petites villes. (USA)
4 Annonce de revue professionnelle en couleurs pour les tuyaux de qualité *Goodrich* qui se prêtent à des fins les plus diverses. (USA)
5 Annonce en couleurs qui présente les services de transfert d'actions offerts par une banque. Campagne publicitaire dans les revues économiques. (USA)
6 Annonce de magazine en teintes bleues et blanches pour une marque de vodka. (USA)
7 Annonce de revue en noir et blanc pour une préparation capillaire spéciale contenant des vitamines et des minéraux favorisant la croissance des cheveux. (USA)

ARTIST / KÜNSTLER / ARTISTE:

1 Ray Domingo
2 Robert Byrd
3 Charles Santore
4 Elwyn Mehlman
5 Theo Rudnak
6 Cliff Spohn
7 Gene Wilkes

We may have one of the last systems that thrives on transfers.

First it was the streetcars, then the busses and now even many banks look askance when you ask them about transfers. But our Corporate Trust Department welcomes stock transfer agent business.

Years ago we made a commitment to the manpower and equipment we knew would be necessary to provide the kind of information corporations now need in tremendous volume. That's why we can provide really complete statistical information for each of your shareholders, and we're glad to do it.

So, if you think you should know more about what your shareholders are doing, maybe you should know more about what we are doing. Call Daniel L. Frederici, Vice-President, Corporate Trust Department, at (216) 687-5702 and ask him about a transfer. Or, write to him at 900 Euclid Ave., Cleveland, Ohio 44101.

When you're out to do big things, it's nice to have a big friend.

CLEVELAND TRUST

Advertisements / Inserate / Annonces

5

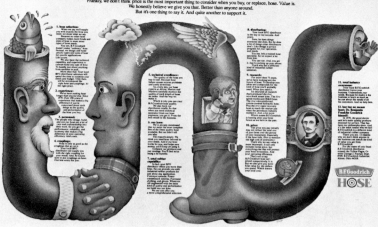

How to be a big frog in small towns.

GRIT is the one national publication that deliberately woos the great small-town market.

Which is why millions of small towners each week read GRIT thoroughly, regard it highly, and

— when they're asked — respond to it enthusiastically.

So ask them.

Make your good media plan better by adding GRIT. You'll add balance. You'll give your selling

story a powerful bullhorn in a major market where other media are but a distant chorus.

Best of all, you'll do it all for very few greenbacks indeed.

THE NATIONAL SMALL-TOWN WEEKLY

Home Office: Williamsport, Pa.; Branch Offices in New York, Chicago, Detroit West Coast: Wheeler/Newell, San Francisco; Snyder/Clarkson, Los Angeles

3

4

ART DIRECTOR / DIRECTEUR ARTISTIQUE:

1–3 Elmer Pizzi
4 Petter Thoen
5 Larry Pillot
6 Suzzanne Gillaspie
7 Don Gill

AGENCY / AGENTUR / AGENCE – STUDIO:

1–3 Gray + Rogers Inc.
4 Griswold-Eshleman Co.
5 Lang, Fisher, Stashower, Inc.
6 FCB-Honig
7 Workshop

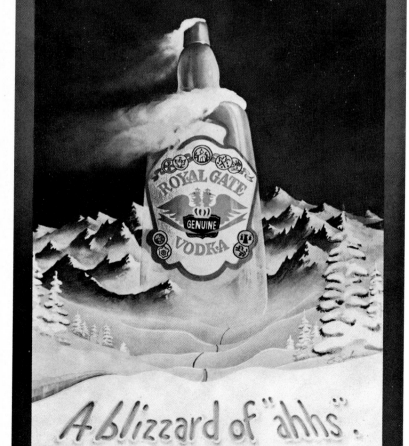

6

Nobody can get a new head of hair out of a bottle.

But Head Start, a special vitamin & mineral compound formulated for hair care, can supplement what you should be getting.

A well balanced diet.

Major nutritionists have known for some time that hair needs special vitamins and minerals to be healthy. Without a balanced diet your hair could be starving to death. Dying. And how many of us eat well balanced meals?

Major government surveys show that not many of us do. Not with hectic schedules, processed foods and preservatives that preserve, but

destroy food value.

So, we developed Head Start for hair, which contains a special vitamin and mineral compound not found in your regular multi-vitamin pills.

Head Start can help arrest your balding and improve existing hair.

Head Start is an excellent hair conditioner. It builds body, along with your diet, naturally. From the inside out.

So, if you've started losing your hair, use your head.

Try Head Start. It works.

It's the second best thing to a transplant.

HEAD START. FOR THE MAN WHO WOULD RATHER CUT OFF HIS HEAD THAN GO BALD.

Use Head Start under the guidance of a professional hair stylist. He can help you. We just help him.

Head Start, the vitamin and mineral compound for hair is formulated by Cosvetic Laboratories. Copyright® 1972

7

27

8

9

10

11

12

When things get you down, think of "Salmon with Sauce."

13

14

15

16

17

ARTIST / KÜNSTLER / ARTISTE:

 8 Rick Meyerowitz
10–12 Willi Rieser
13–17 Seymour Chwast

ART DIRECTOR / DIRECTEUR ARTISTIQUE:

 8 Barbara Schybeck/Dick Calderhead
10–12 Ernst Herzog
13–17 John Sapienza

AGENCY / AGENTUR / AGENCE – STUDIO:

 8 Calderhead, Jackson Inc.
 9 J. Walter Thompson Co., Ltd.
10–12 Advico-Delpire
13–17 Van Brunt & Co.

uno, due, tre... tanti giri di bontà
Girella Buondì Motta.

Girella, un nuovo "centro" della linea Buondì Motta

18

19

18 Full-colour magazine advertisement for *Levi's* hard-wearing jeans for boys, made of tough *Avondale* fabric. (USA)
19 Magazine advertisement in full colour for a *Motta* Swiss roll. (ITA)
20 Double-spread magazine advertisement for *Guinness* beer with lettering consisting of typical figures by the artist and costume designer Erté. (GBR)
21, 22 Complete double-spread magazine advertisement and detail of the artwork (in flat colours) for the psychotropic drug *Thorazine* made by SK & F. (USA)
23 Magazine advertisement for a film (This Agreeable Game for Two). Figures in brown and pink shades. (BRA)
24 Announcement of a programme on PBS Television dramatizing the marital life of Henry VIII in six episodes. The programme was sponsored by the Mobil Oil Corporation. (USA)

18 Mehrfarbiges Zeitschriften-Inserat für die strapazierfähigen *Levi's* Knabenjeans aus ebenso strapazierfähigem *Avondale*-Material. (USA)
19 Das farbige Zeitschriften-Inserat wirbt appetitanregend für *Motta*-Biscuit-Rouladen. (ITA)
20 Doppelseitiges Zeitschriften-Inserat für *Guinness*-Bier. Die Buchstaben in Form von Figuren verraten die Hand des Künstlers und Kostümentwerfers Erté. (GBR)
21, 22 Vollständiges, doppelseitiges Zeitschriften-Inserat und Detail für *Thorazin*, ein psychopharmakologisches Präparat. Flach aufgetragene Farben. (USA)
23 Zeitschriften-Inserat für einen Film («Dieses angenehme Spiel zu zweit»). Figuren in braunen und rosa Tönen. (BRA)
24 Ankündigung eines Theaterprogrammes in sechs Folgen im PBS-Fernsehen über das Eheleben Heinrichs VIII. Unter dem Patronat von Mobil Oil Corporation. (USA)

18 Annonce de revue en couleurs pour une marque de jeans extrêmement résistants, faits d'*Avondale*, une étoffe aussi résistante. (USA)
19 Annonce de revue en couleurs pour les bûches *Motta*. (ITA)
20 Annonce de revue double page pour la bière *Guinness*. Les caractères reprennent des figures typiques d'Erté, artiste et dessinateur de costumes bien-connu. (GBR)
21, 22 Annonce de revue double page et détail de l'illustration (en couleurs à plat) pour un produit psychotropique de Smith, Kline & French. (USA)
23 Annonce de magazine pour un film (Ce jeu plaisant pour deux personnes). Figures en teintes brune et rose. (BRA)
24 Avis d'une station TV qui présente un programme en six épisodes traitant de la vie conjugale d'Henri VIII. Ce programme a été patronné par la Mobil Oil Corp. (USA)

21

22

IT'S ALWAYS BEEN GOOD TO LOOK AT.

20

VIDYA PRODUÇÕES CINEMATOGRÁFICAS apresenta

Carlo Mossy
Dilma Loes

em

ESSA GOSTOSA BRINCADEIRA A DOIS

produtores associados:
KIKO FILMES
DI MELLO P.C.
CONDOR FILMES
E. A. CURY ADM. PART.

com **Vera Fischer**
Andrews di Negri
Teresa Trautman
Cleia Simões · Lídia Mattos
Cláudio Oliani
direção: **Victor di Mello**

23

Divorce Henry VIII style.

For Henry VIII, a queen was also a pawn.
Something he could use to breed political alliances and heirs for the Tudor dynasty.
The difficulty was getting from one wife to the next.
Starting tonight on PBS, Masterpiece Theatre brings you the first episode of The Six Wives of Henry VIII.
Six superbly acted dramatizations (seen in their entirety for the first time on American television), starring Keith Michell, with Alistair Cooke as your host.

The Six Wives of Henry VIII
9PM Channel 13
MASTERPIECE THEATRE

Mobil

24

Advertisements
Inserate
Annonces

25

26

27

25 "Come and sit at table—then take it with you." Ad from a campaign for a furniture supermarket. Black and white. (SPA)
26 Newspaper advertisement announcing a special travel supplement of *The New York Times*. (USA)
27 Announcement in the trade press of a display of *Timme's* imitation furs in a New York hotel. (USA)
28–32 From a series of small advertisements with the slogan "Playing with commas" for the modern brand *Polidraga*. Black and white. (ITA)
33, 33a, 34 Two space promotion advertisements and detail of the artwork in actual size for the magazine *Bunte*, which claims to present the pleasant aspects of life. (GER)

25 «Kommen Sie, setzen Sie sich an einen Tisch – und nehmen Sie ihn mit nach Hause.» Inserat aus einer Werbekampagne für einen Möbel-Supermarkt. (SPA)
26 Zeitungs-Inserat, das eine spezielle Reise-Beilage der *New York Times* ankündigt. (USA)
27 Fachpresse-Inserat, das eine Ausstellung von *Timme's* Imitations-Pelzen in einem New Yorker Hotel anzeigt. (USA)
28–32 Aus einer Serie von Kleininseraten mit dem Slogan «Spiele mit Kommas». Schwarzweiss. (ITA)
33, 33a, 34 Vollständige Inserate und Detail im Format 1:1 für die *Bunte* als Inseratenträger, ein Magazin, das sich rühmt, dem Leser die heiteren Seiten des Lebens zu zeigen. (GER)

25 «Assieds-toi à la table – et puis, prends-la avec toi.» Annonce figurant dans une campagne publicitaire pour un supermarché de meubles. Noir et blanc. (SPA)
26 Annonce-presse pour le supplément de vacances de la *New York Times*. (USA)
27 Annonce de revue professionnelle pour une exposition de fourrures synthétiques présentée dans un hôtel newyorkais. (USA)
28–32 D'une série de petites annonces pour *Polidraga* (slogan: «le jeu des virgules»). (ITA)
33, 33a, 34 Annonces d'une série promotionnelle et détail de l'illustration pour la revue *Bunte* qui prétend ne présenter que les aspects positifs de la vie. (GER)

28

29

30

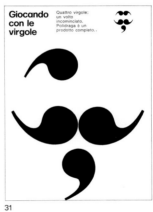

31

32

ARTIST / KÜNSTLER / ARTISTE:

25 Julio Arruga Martinez
26 Gene Maggio
27 Jackie Geyer
28–32 Rinaldo Del Sordo/G. Berlinghieri
33–34 Richard Hess

DESIGNER / GESTALTER / MAQUETTISTE:

26 Arnold Kushner

ART DIRECTOR / DIRECTEUR ARTISTIQUE:

25 Miguel Rogla
26 Andrew Kner
27 Rob Lopes
28–32 Rinaldo Del Sordo

AGENCY / AGENTUR / AGENCE – STUDIO:

25 Publicidad Vila International
27 Levine, Huntley, Schmidt. Inc.
28–32 Studio Giob
33–34 Robert Pütz GmbH & Co.

Advertisements / Inserate

33

33a

37

38

35

36

McGregor Socks

39

35, 36 Complete magazine advertisement and detail of the artwork in actual
size for *Essochem* inner liners for tubeless tyres, which will prevent loss of
pressure by air leakage. (GBR)
37, 38 Black-and-white trade press advertisements from a series for the Con-
versational Voice Terminal Corporation, which makes machines for taking
orders by phone and thereby prevents losses due to human fallibility. (USA)
39 Magazine advertisement for *McGregor* socks. (CAN)
40, 41, 41a Details of the illustrations and complete magazine advertisement
for a line of *Levi's* jeans, shirts and jackets that match each other. (USA)
42 Colour advertisement placed in the medical press for the *Roche* pharmaceutical *Bactrim* for use against bacterial infections, especially of the respi-
ratory and urinary tracts. (SWI)
43 Black-and-white advertisement placed in the medical press by Lederle
Laboratories, makers of *Incremin* with an iron syrup that is so palatable that
children will readily take it. (USA)

before

40

after

41

41a

42

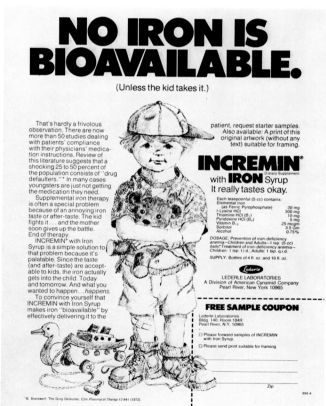

43

35, 36 Vollständiges Fachpresse-Inserat und Ausschnitt 1:1 für schlauchlose Autoreifen, die innen mit Chlorobutyl von Esso Chemicals Ltd. ausgekleidet sind und darum keine Luft verlieren. (GBR)
37, 38 Zwei schwarzweisse Inserate aus einer Kampagne in der Fachpresse für telephonische Bestellungsaufnahme-Apparate. (USA)
39 Zeitschriften-Inserat für Socken von *McGregor*. (CAN)
40, 41, 41a Detail-Ausschnitte und vollständiges Zeitschriften-Inserat schildern in Farben die Geschichte eines Mädchens, das dank *Levi's* assortierten Blusen, Jeans und Blousons innert kurzer Zeit seine ganze Garderobe durch eine neue ersetzen konnte. (USA)
42 Farb-Inserat in der Fachpresse, das für *Bactrim* wirbt, ein Produkt von *Hoffmann-La Roche* für die Behandlung von bakteriellen Infektionen des Respirationstraktes und der Harnwege. (SWI)
43 Schwarzweisses Inserat über die Vorzüge von *Incremin*, einem schmackhaften eisenhaltigen Sirup gegen Anämie bei Kindern und Erwachsenen. (USA)

35, 36 Annonce de revue complète et détail de l'illustration en grandeur originale en faveur d'un revêtement pour les pneus sans chambre qui est absolument étanche à l'air et garantit une pression constante. (GBR)
37, 38 Annonces noir-blanc tirées d'une série publiée dans la presse professionnelle pour un appareil qui permet d'enregistrer les commandes téléphoniques pour ainsi éliminer des fautes et malentendus. (USA)
39 Annonce de journal pour des chaussettes *McGregor*. (CAN)
40, 41, 41a Détails des illustrations et annonce de revue complète pour une gamme de jeans, de chemises et de blousons *Levi's* en couleurs assorties. Avec peu d'argent on réunit un grand choix de vêtements. (USA)
42 Annonce en couleur pour *Bactrim* de *Roche*, un produit pharmaceutique pour le traitement des infections bactériennes, surtout des voies respiratoires et urinaires. Campagne publicitaire dans les revues médicales. (SWI)
43 Annonce en noir et blanc pour un sirop ferrugineux contre l'anémie. Ce sirop est si savoureux que même les enfants le prennent sans mot dire. (USA)

ARTIST / KÜNSTLER:

44, 45 Clark L. Robinson
46–50 Tomi Ungerer

ART DIRECTOR:

44, 45 Clark L. Robinson
46–50 Robert Pütz

AGENCY / AGENTUR:

44, 45 Clark L. Robinson, Inc.
46–50 Robert Pütz GmbH

Your customer has had about all she can take. Brighten her day. Give her a good look at the meat she's buying.

It hasn't been easy
on your customer lately.
Inflation. Phase Four. The Beef
Shortage. She feels like she's been
through the mill. So the guy who does
something nice for her is going
to be remembered. That could be you!
If you package your meat in the new
Super Vue® Meat Trays,
the ones with windows,
from Diamond International.

Super Vue is what she's been asking
for. A tray that *really* lets her see
what she's getting. Top and bottom.

She'll like Super Vue Trays
because they're made of wood
and are bio-degradable.
And because our supply of wood
is constantly renewing itself

Super Vue Trays can help conserve
our dwindling petroleum reserves.

Super Vue is what you've been
looking for, too.
A tray that breathes to keep
your meat looking fresh longer.
One that saves you money by reducing
down-grading and re-wrapping.

Put a little psychology to work
in your meat department.
Show your customers what
they're getting.
That'll give *you*
an extra
competitive
edge.

DIAMOND INTERNATIONAL CORPORATION
Fiber Products Division, 733 Third Avenue, New York, N.Y. 10017

44

A broken egg may not seem like much to you – but it can cost you a customer.

You have a lot of other things to
worry about. An egg probably
doesn't seem too important.
But the economics of packing
economy may be working
against you. If you're packing
in flimsy, light-weight
packages you may be losing
more than just eggs — you may
be losing customers.

Your dissatisfied customer probably won't bring a broken egg
back to you (after all, he'd use more gasoline than the egg's
worth at today's high prices), but he may start buying his eggs
in a market that has good packaging. And once he has his foot
in their door you don't know where he'll end up.

That's why we think you'll agree that
good egg packaging is more important
than ever. At Diamond International
we've always had a thing about
protecting eggs. We've developed
Pillopost® to give the very best
protection available. And for
customers who want to see what
they're getting we designed Super Vue®.

You owe it to yourself
to look into them.

DIAMOND INTERNATIONAL CORPORATION
Fiber Products Division, 733 Third Avenue, New York, N.Y. 10017

45

DAS HAUS bringt mehr Coupon-Rücklauf,
denn jede Schere stürzt sich drauf.

Aktive Kontakte sind die besten.

48

44, 45 Double-spread black-and-white advertisements from a series placed in the trade press by Diamond International Corporation, here promoting window trays for meat and protective packages for eggs. (USA)
46–50 Examples of the artwork and one complete advertisement from a space promotion series, all in full colour, for *Das Haus,* a home magazine that claims to bring more coupon returns because "any pair of scissors will jump on it". (GER)

Advertisements
Inserate
Annonces

46

47

49

50

44, 45 Zwei doppelseitige, schwarzweisse Fachpresse-Inserate von Diamond International Corp. für durchsichtige *Super Vue*-Verpackungen – z.B. für Fleisch und Eier –, die dem Detaillisten helfen sollen, seine Kundschaft zufriedenzustellen. (USA)
46–50 Vollständiges Farbinserat und vier Bildausschnitte aus einer Werbekampagne für *Das Haus* als Inseratenträger im Sektor Bauen und Wohnen. Die Schere symbolisiert die vielen Coupons, die von den Lesern ausgeschnitten und eingesandt werden. (GER)

44, 45 Annonces double page en noir et blanc pour une marque d'emballages transparents spécialement conçus pour étaler et protéger des articles de charcuterie et des œufs. Exemples tirés d'une série parue dans la presse professionnelle. (USA)
46–50 Exemples des illustrations et annonce complète figurant dans une série promotionnelle pour une revue spéciale qui prétend rapporter plus de coupons de réponse, car «les ciseaux s'y lancent pour les couper». En couleurs. (GER)

37

Our weighty
argument for Ethrel:
Recoverable yields
average 3 tons/acre more.

51

Ethrel can have your young
apple trees carrying their own
weight a year or two earlier.

52

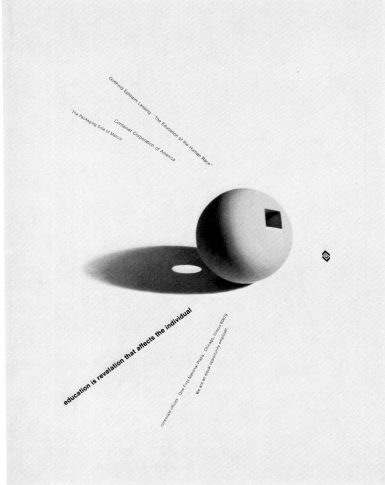

Gotthold Ephraim Lessing: "The Education of the Human Race"

The Packaging Side of Marcor

Container Corporation of America

education is revelation that affects the individual

corporate offices One First National Plaza Chicago, Illinois 60670

We are an equal opportunity employer

53

ARTIST / KÜNSTLER / ARTISTE:

51, 52   Colopy Dale
53   Steve Keller
54—56   Tomi Ungerer

ART DIRECTOR:

51, 52   Anthony V. Leone
53   Bill Bonnell III
54—56   Robert Pütz

AGENCY / AGENTUR / AGENCE:

51, 52   Lewis & Gilman Adv.
53   Container Corporation of America
54—56   Robert Pütz GmbH & Co.

Es ist gut, den Regenbogen im Haus zu haben.

55

51, 52 Large advertisements with colour illustrations in the trade press for a plant regulator made by Anchem Products, Inc., here for tomatoes and apples. (USA)
53 Black-and-white advertisement from a long series for the Container Corporation of America, here with a quotation from Lessing. (USA)
54—56 "The rainbow helps in low-pressure periods." —"It's good to have the rainbow in the house." From a series of magazine advertisements for *Siegwerk* printing inks (symbolized by a rainbow). Fig. 56 shows the artwork of Fig. 55 in actual size. (GER)

51, 52 Grossformatige Fachpresse-Inserate mit Farb-Illustrationen für *Ethrel*, ein neues chemisches Pflanzenmittel, das eine grössere Ernte z.B. von Äpfeln und Tomaten bewirken soll. Hersteller ist die Anchem Products., Inc. (USA)
53 Schwarzweisses Inserat aus einer langen, andauernden Kampagne der Container Corporation of America, hier mit einem Lessing-Zitat. (USA)
54—56 Aus einer Reihe farbiger Zeitschriften-Inserate für *Siegwerk*-Druckfarben mit dem Regenbogen als Symbol. Abb. 56: Bildausschnitt in Originalgrösse. (GER)

51, 52 Annonces avec des illustrations en couleur pour un nouveau produit biologique pour les plantes, ici pour les tomates et pommes. D'une revue professionnelle. (USA)
53 Annonce en noir et blanc tirée d'une longue série pour la Container Corporation of America, ici utilisant une citation de Lessing (USA)
54—56 «L'arc-en-ciel aide à survenir les périodes de basse pression.» — «C'est bien d'avoir l'arc-en-ciel à la maison.» D'une série pour les encres d'imprimerie *Siegwerk* (symbolisés par l'arc-en-ciel). Fig. 56: illustration grandeur originale. (GER)

Im Tief hilft der Regenbogen.

Wenn ein Drucker mal ein Tief hat, dann ist es oft ein Farbproblem. Der Regenbogen hilft.

Siegwerk hilft mit den Druckfarben für den Qualitätsdruck.

Siegwerk hilft mit den Druck-

hilfsmitteln für den Qualitätsdruck. Zum Beispiel mit den Wischwasserzusätzen, Siegwerks „Grüne Welle": Vom universellen Wischwasserzusatz bis zur „Grünen Welle für spezielle Fälle", Siegwerks problemgerechte, praxisbe-

währte Spezial-Wischwasserzusätze. Mehr über Druckfarben und Druckhilfsmittel vom Regenbogen-Service für das Hoch nach dem Tief.

SIEGWERK-FARBENFABRIK
52 Siegburg

54

56

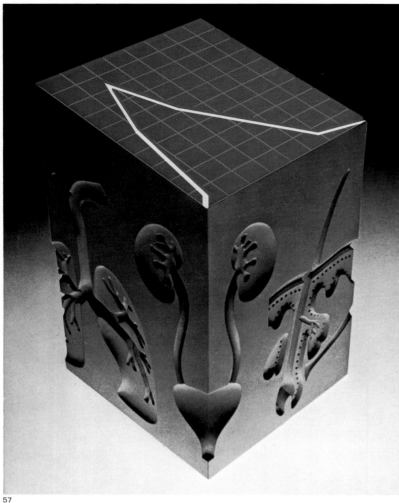

57

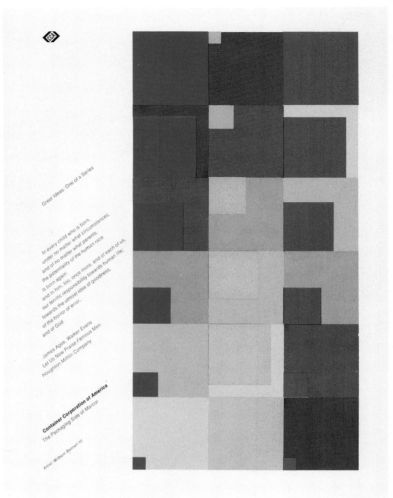

59

from Beecham Research:
a new broad-spectrum antibiotic
with rapid absorption
and exceptionally high serum levels

new
Amoxil t.i.d. dosage
(amoxicillin)

58

Frankenstein
THE TRUE STORY
JAMES MASON • DAVID MCCALLUM • AGNES MOOREHEAD • MARGARET LEIGHTON
MICHAEL SARRAZIN • MICHAEL WILDING • SIR JOHN GIELGUD • JANE SEYMOUR
SIR RALPH RICHARDSON • LEONARD WHITING • NICOLA PAGETT • CLARISSA KAYE
PART 1 TONIGHT 00:00 PM NBC CHANNEL 00

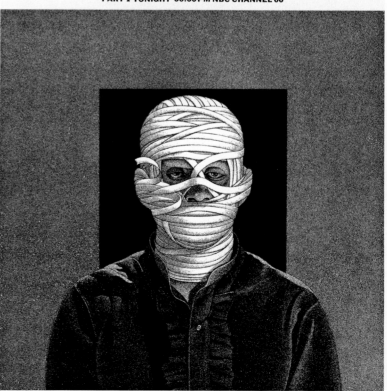

ARTIST / KÜNSTLER / ARTISTE:

57, 58 Lou Bory/Herb Loebel (Photo)
59 Bill Bonnell III
60 Maya Stange ASG
61 John Coletti
62 Wilfried Maret
63 Wilson Mc Lean
64, 65 Randolph Enos

ART DIRECTOR / DIRECTEUR ARTISTIQUE:

57, 58 John Geryak
59 Bill Bonnell III
61 Jerry Berman/Gene Icardi
62 Wilfried Maret
63 Dolores Gudzin
64, 65 Murlin Marsh

AGENCY / AGENTUR / AGENCE – STUDIO:

57, 58 Kallir, Philips, Ross, Inc.
59 Container Corporation of America
60 Institut Dr. Friesewinkel
61 Berman Icardi, Inc.
63–65 National Broadcasting Co.

63

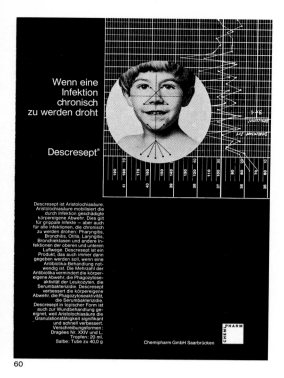

60

61

62

57, 58 Colour page and corresponding spread of an advertisement in the medical press for an antibiotic made by Beecham-Massengill Pharmaceuticals. (USA)
59 Magazine advertisement from the famous Container Corporation series quoting great ideas. (USA)
60 Advertisement in medical magazines for an antibiotic. Black and white. (GER)
61 Advertisement from a campaign in the trade press for *Crown Zellerbach* papers, here for newsprint. (USA)
62 Black-and-white advertisement for *Varian* measuring, testing and computing equipment. (SWI)
63–65 Black-and-white advertisements for two late programmes on NBC television. (USA)

57, 58 Farbseite und vollständige Doppelseite in der medizinischen Fachpresse für *Amoxil*, ein neues Antibiotikum mit Breitspektrums-Wirkung. (USA)
59 Aus einer Reihe von farbigen Zeitschriften-Inseraten der Container Corporation of America mit grossen Zitaten. (USA)
60 Fachpresse-Inserat für ein *Chemipharm*-Antibiotikum. (GER)
61 «Keine Nachricht ist schlechte Nachricht.» Fachpresse-Inserat für *Crown Zellerbach*-Zeitungs- und andere Papiere. Schwarzweiss. (USA)
62 Inserat in Schwarzweiss für *Varian* Mess-, Test- und Computer-Geräte. (SWI)
63–65 Schwarzweiss-Inserate für zwei Spätprogramme, ausgestrahlt vom NBC-Fernsehen. (USA)

57, 58 Page en couleur et annonce double page correspondante pour un antibiotique. Campagne publicitaire dans les revues médicales. (USA)
59 Annonce de magazine présentant des grandes idées. D'une longue série de la Container Corporation of America. (USA)
60 Annonce tirée d'une revue médicale pour un antibiotique. En noir et blanc. (GER)
61 Annonce d'une campagne publicitaire pour les papiers *Crown Zellerbach*, ici pour les papiers de journaux. (USA)
62 Annonce en noir et blanc pour une marque d'ordinateurs, d'appareils de mesurage et de contrôle. (SWI)
63–65 Annonces en noir et blanc pour deux programmes de nuit d'une station TV. (USA)

64

65

Advertisements
Inserate
Annonces

41

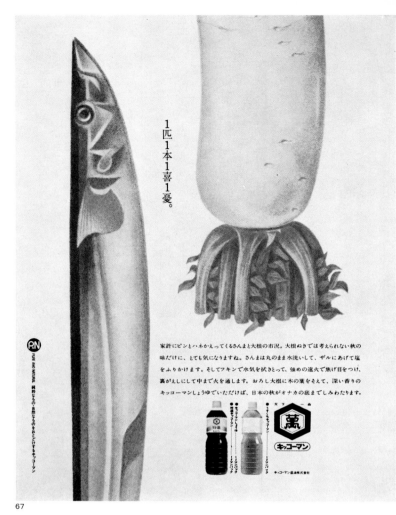

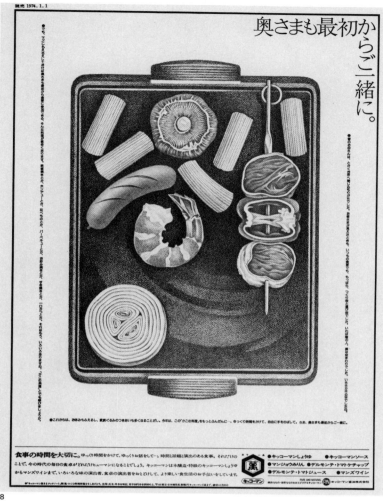

68

ARTIST / KÜNSTLER / ARTISTE:

66–68 Tadashi Ohashi
69, 70 Klaus Getreu
71, 72 Makoto Wada

DESIGNER / GESTALTER:

71, 72 Yoshihiro Saito

ART DIRECTOR:

66–68 Tadashi Ohashi
69, 70 Alan Telfer-Layton
71, 72 Minoru Takahashi

AGENCY / AGENTUR / AGENCE:

69, 70 Slesina-Bates
71, 72 AZ, Inc. Advertising

66, 67 Full-colour magazine advertisements from a long and continuing series for soya sauces made by Kikkoman Shoyu Co. Ltd. (JPN)
68 Full-page black-and-white newspaper advertisement for *Kikkoman* sauces. (JPN)
69, 70 From a series of black-and-white magazine advertisements for *Mercury* outboard motors with various power ratings. (GER)
71, 72 Black-and-white newspaper advertisements (full page) for *Kagome* preserves. (JPN)

66, 67 Farbige Zeitschriften-Inserate aus einer sich über längere Zeit hinziehenden grossen Werbe-kampagne für Soya-Saucen, hergestellt von Kikkoman Shoyu Co. Ltd. (JPN)
68 Ganzseitiges Zeitungsinserat in Schwarzweiss für *Kikkoman*-Saucen. (JPN)
69, 70 Aus einer Serie von schwarzweissen Zeitschriften-Inseraten, welche die Vorzüge von *Mercury*-Aussenbordmotoren verschiedener PS-Stärken beschreiben. (GER)
71, 72 Schwarzweisse, ganzseitige Zeitungsinserate für *Kagome*-Konserven. (JPN)

66, 67 Annonces de revue en couleur figurant dans une longue série pour les sauces soja de Kikkoman Shoyu Co. Ltd. (JPN)
68 Annonce de journal en noir et blanc pour les sauces *Kikkoman*. (JPN)
69, 70 D'une série d'annonces de revue en noir et blanc pour des moteurs hors-bord à différents chevaux-vapeur. (GER)
71, 72 Annonces de journaux en noir et blanc pour des conserves *Kagome*. Pages entières. (JPN)

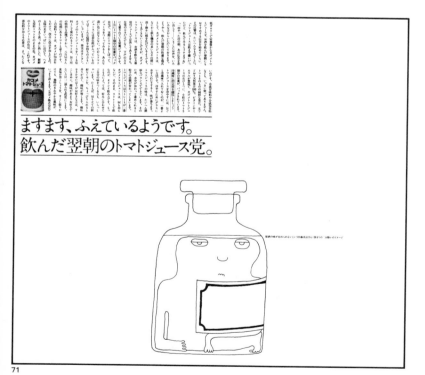

71

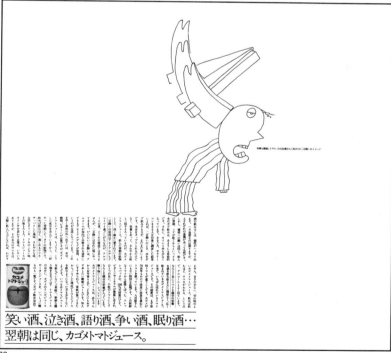

72

Advertisements / Inserate / Annonces

73

74

73 Full-page newspaper advertisement listing the 43 points that are checked in every *Avis* car before it is passed to the hirer. Black and white. (SWI)
74 Full-page newspaper advertisement in colour for *Orlando* wines explaining the advantages of the various types of corkscrew. (AUL)
75 Full-page newspaper ad for *The New York Times* as a "low-cost luxury". (USA)
76, 77 Detail of the drawing and double-page newspaper advertisement with a competition for children, who are asked to draw, construct or embroider a bird as a contribution to the protection of the environment. (NLD)
78 Newspaper advertisement in colour about financial seminars organized for the members of a youth club attached to the *First American* bank. (USA)

73 Ganzseitiges, schwarzweisses Zeitungs-Inserat, das die 43 Punkte aufzählt, die bei jedem *Avis*-Fahrzeug geprüft werden, bevor es dem Kunden übergeben wird. (SWI)
74 Farbiges, ganzseitiges Zeitungs-Inserat für *Orlando*-Weine, das die Vorzüge der verschiedenen Typen von Flaschenöffnern erläutert. (AUL)
75 Ganzseitiges Zeitungs-Inserat für die *New York Times* als «einen Luxus zu niedrigem Preis». (USA)
76, 77 Ausschnitt und vollständiges, doppelseitiges Zeitungsinserat mit einem Wettbewerb, das die Kinder auffordert, einen Vogel zu zeichnen, zu konstruieren oder zu sticken als Beitrag zum Vogelschutzjahr. (NLD)
78 Farbiges Zeitungsinserat über Seminare zum Studium von Finanzfragen, organisiert für die Mitglieder eines der *First American* Bank angeschlossenen Jugendclubs. (USA)

73 Annonce de journal sur page entière énumérant les 43 détails qui sont contrôlés chaque fois avant qu'une voiture *Avis* est louée. Noir et blanc. (SWI)
74 Annonce de journal sur page entière pour les vins *Orlando*. Elle explique à fond les avantages des différents tire-bouchons. En couleur. (AUL)
75 Annonce de journal pour le *New York Times*, un «article de luxe bon marché». (USA)
76, 77 Détail du dessin et annonce de journal sur double page pour une compétition s'adressant aux enfants: on leur demande de dessiner, construire ou broder un oiseau pour ainsi contribuer, eux aussi, à la protection de l'environnement. (NLD)
78 Annonce de journal en couleur en faveur de séminaires économiques organisés pour les membres d'un club de jeunes attaché à une banque. (USA)

ART DIRECTOR / DIRECTEUR ARTISTIQUE:

73 M. Willuweit
75 Andrew Kner
76, 77 Herman Gerritzen
78 Chet Sailor

AGENCY / AGENTUR / AGENCE – STUDIO:

73 Adolf Wirz AG
76, 77 Prad B.V.
78 Noble Dury Advertising Agency / Creative Source Design Studio

44

75

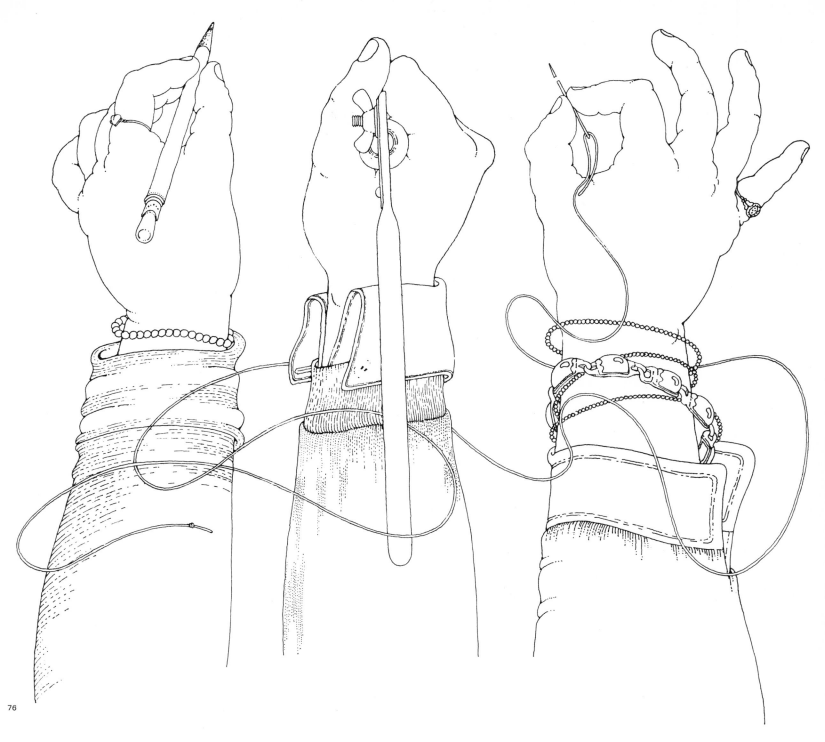

76

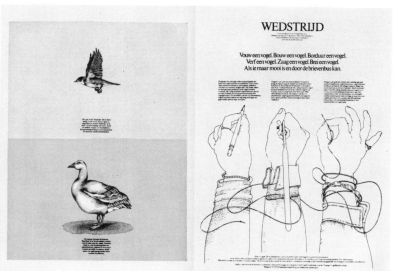

77

78

ARTIST / KÜNSTLER / ARTISTE:

73 Renato Farinoli
75 Bill Basso
76, 77 Mariet Numan
78 Bobbye Cochran

DESIGNER / GESTALTER / MAQUETTISTE:

75 Peter Schaefer

Advertisements / Inserate
Annonces

79

80

83

São Paulo está chamando os tarzãs de praia para enfrentarem uns leões de verdade e outras aventuras.

Uma das atrações de São Paulo é o Simba Safari. Um parque enorme com leões e outras feras soltas, vivendo muito à vontade como se estivessem na selva.
Pegue a sua Jane, vá passar um fim de semana em São Paulo e dê umas voltas de carro entre as feras. E esses leões nada têm a ver com aquele da anedota.
Num fim de semana em São Paulo, você pode encontrar outras aventuras.
Visite o bairro japonês. Dê uma voltinha no Metrô. E os restaurantes? Pode escolher: russo, alemão, espanhol, mineiro holandês, português, baiano, húngaro, gaúcho, chinês, japonês.

Você vai conhecer museus. Se quiser.
O Teatro Municipal de São Paulo tem espetáculos todo santo dia. Ballet, música erudita, jazz, música pop, peças teatrais de grande montagem, dentro do Programa de Expansão Cultural da Prefeitura.
E à noite, amizade, deixe o sono pra depois.

Muito samba, shows, boates, teatros, cinemas - pra que dormir cedo?
Num fim de semana em São Paulo, você vai ter muito o que fazer, muito pra ver, muito pra comprar.
Quem gosta de procurar lojas cheias de novidades e pechinchar preços, vai achar São Paulo uma festa. Butiques com mil bossas e ruas daquele jeito da rua da Alfândega com centenas de lojas.
E sabe de mais uma? Os hotéis estão dando descontos.*
Você não vai se arrepender de perder um domingo de praia. Pode ser até que chova aqui. E se estiver frio em São Paulo, taí a chance pra você usar aquele casacão maravilhoso que depois da viagem à Europa, nunca mais saiu do guarda-roupa.

SECRETARIA DE TURISMO E FOMENTO DA PREFEITURA DO MUNICÍPIO DE SÃO PAULO
SINDICATO DE HOTÉIS E SIMILARES DE SÃO PAULO

Are you looking for a better fit?

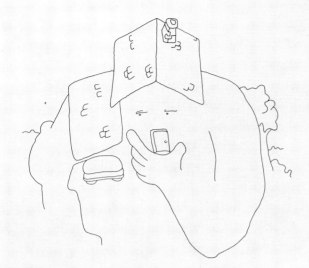

Los Altos Foothills
Own one of the last new homes in Los Altos. Select from individually designed, elegant 3-5 bedroom, 2-3 bath homes with all the amenities included for gracious living. Choose from a wide selection of architectural styles in this prestigious location. Call 961-1441.

$81,665 to $125,000

Alamo Orchards
DII presents 16 custom designed homes in the beautiful country community of Alamo. Alamo Orchards features 4 bedroom, 2-3 bath homes with the special DII exclusive "Epicurean Kitchen." Close to Walnut Creek and BART. Call (408) 275-8430 or 961-1441.

from $82,000

Villas de San Alma
Twenty-six beautiful villas and exclusive Palo Alto combine to create a superb new community. Designed by John Brooks Boyd Associates, AIA, these 3 bedroom and 3 bedroom with study, 2-2½ bath, lot line homes feature interior courtyards. Call (408) 275-8430 or 961-1441.

from $59,950

 Visit all three DII communities. A sales office is located at 2601 Stonehaven in Los Altos. For further information, call 961-1441. Projects of Dividend Industries Inc. Presented by Town and Country Properties.

81

WHEN AT&T WANTS TO TALK TO 42 MILLION ADULTS, THEY DON'T CALL THEM ON THE PHONE.

It used to be that corporate advertising ended up only in business publications. Consumerism has caused corporate advertisers to rethink that strategy. More and more see their corporate purposes better served by speaking out to the general public.

This more aggressive approach to corporate communication favors TV Guide magazine. Consider the values we bring to such advertisers as AT&T.

One is coverage, plain and simple. Run an ad in any issue of TV Guide magazine and you've got an audience of some 42 million adults. Run a six-time schedule, and you jump the net reach to over half of all U. S. adults.

Another is readership. Of our total magazine, of your advertising. Dollar for dollar, an ad in TV Guide generally gets a better reading than the same ad in Digest or any other major magazine.

If what you have to say in your corporate message can benefit from the broadest possible coverage and predictably high readership, you could surprise yourself in TV Guide.

WE'RE BIG. WE'RE EFFICIENT. WE GET READ. YOU GET READ.

82

Voici notre chef de fabrication.

Chez Kiri, il n'y a que de vrais professionnels du fromage.
Il le faut, quand on se mêle de faire un fromage impeccable pour les gosses.
Nos professionnels, ce sont les vaches. Kiri les trait et, moins de 24 heures plus tard, ajoute au bon lait frais qui garde un maximum de qualités nutritives, de la crème de lait toute aussi fraîche.

Et puis, il l'emballe le tout dans une chouette boîte colorée.
Doux, moelleux, léger... et plein de forces, le petit fromage Kiri se fait adorer des gosses.
C'est gai de travailler avec des collaborateurs compétents.

kiri
à la crème-met room

Kiri à la crème.
Le fromage trait hier pour les gosses.

Un produit

84

Advertisements / Inserate / Annonces

2

Booklets

Folders

Catalogues

Invitations

Programmes

Broschüren

Faltprospekte

Kataloge

Einladungen

Programme

Brochures

Dépliants

Catalogues

Invitations

Programmes

ARTIST / KÜNSTLER / ARTISTE:

85 David Franek
86, 87 Niels Diffrient/Alvin R. Tilley/Joan C. Bardagjy
88–90 Andrés Puech
91–93 Ian Dalton
94 Michael Wade

DESIGNER / GESTALTER / MAQUETTISTE:

94 Glenn Tutssel

ART DIRECTOR / DIRECTEUR ARTISTIQUE:

85 David Ashton
88–90 Andrés Puech
91–93 Barrie Tucker
94 Glenn Tutssel/David Lock

AGENCY / AGENTUR / AGENCE – STUDIO:

85 Ashton-Worthington, Inc.
86, 87 Henry Dreyfuss Assoc.
88–90 C.P.A., S.A.
91–93 Tucker & James
94 Lock, Pettersen

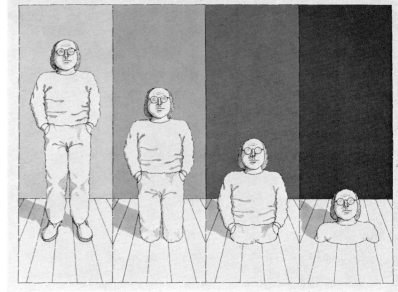

85

88

89

91

92

Booklets / Prospekte / Prospectus

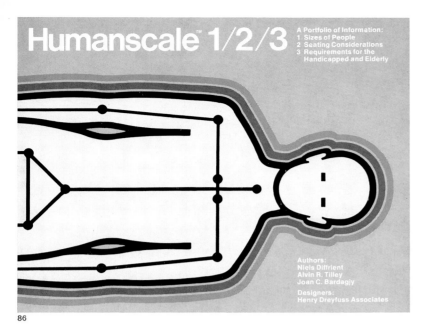

Humanscale 1/2/3

A Portfolio of Information:
1 Sizes of People
2 Seating Considerations
3 Requirements for the Handicapped and Elderly

Authors:
Niels Diffrient
Alvin R. Tilley
Joan C. Bardagjy

Designers:
Henry Dreyfuss Associates

86

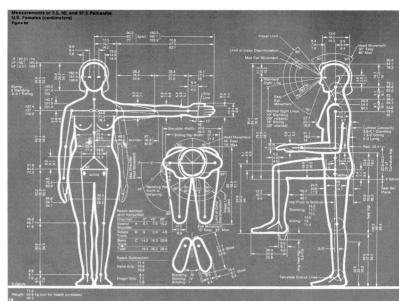

Measurements of 2.5, 50, and 97.5 Percentile
U.S. Females (centimeters)
Figure 8d

87

85 Page from a booklet about stress published by Sinai Hospital Auxiliary, Inc., Baltimore. (USA)
86, 87 Cover (figure in two reds and yellow on silver) and page (white on red) from a booklet on human proportions for furniture designers, published by the MIT Press. (USA)
88–90 From a series of cards about *novigama* anti-tetanus injections. Full colour. (SPA)
91–93 Double spread and two pages in full colour referring to stress and vertigo respectively, from a *Sandoz* booklet on disorders and their remedies. (AUL)
94 Colour cover of a folder about a new liquid nitrogen container made by Union Carbide U.K. Ltd. Red lettering, yellow ground. (GBR)

85 Seite aus einer Broschüre über Stress. Schwarzweiss. (USA)
86, 87 Titelblatt (Figur in zwei verschiedenen Rottönen und Gelb auf Silber) und Seite aus einer Broschüre für Möbel-Designer über die menschlichen Masse. (USA)
88–90 Aus einer Serie von Karten über *novigama*-Antitetanus-Injektionen. (SPA)
91–93 Doppelseite und zwei einzelne Seiten über Stress einerseits und Schwindel anderseits, aus einer *Sandoz*-Broschüre über Beschwerden und deren Behandlung. Farbig. (AUL)
94 Farbiges Titelblatt einer Broschüre über einen neuen Behälter für flüssigen Stickstoff. Rote Schrift auf gelbem Grund. (GBR)

85 Page d'une brochure traitant des différents aspects du stress. Noir et blanc. (USA)
86, 87 Couverture (figure en deux rouges et jaune sur argent) et page (blanc sur rouge) d'une brochure pour les designers de meubles. Elle a pour sujet les proportions de l'homme. (USA)
88–90 D'une série de cartes publicitaires pour des injections anti-tétanos. Polychrome. (SPA)
91–93 Page double et deux pages en couleurs se référant au stress et au vertige respectivement. D'une brochure traitant des différents aspects de désordres et leurs remèdes. (AUL)
94 Couverture polychrome d'un dépliant publié en faveur d'un nouveau récipient pour l'azote liquide, fabriqué par Union Carbide U.K. Ltd. Typo rouge sur fond jaune. (GBR)

90

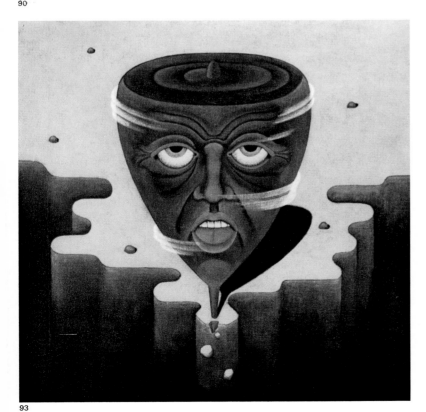

93

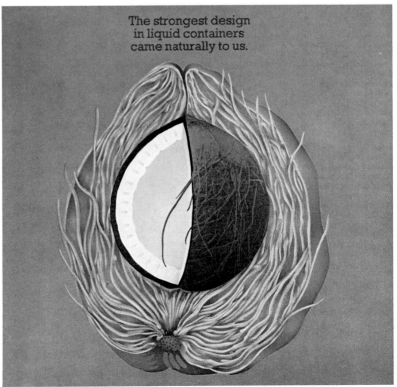

The strongest design in liquid containers came naturally to us.

94

ARTIST / KÜNSTLER / ARTISTE:

95–97 Enric Huguet
98 Alan J. Klawans
99 Felix Müller
100 Franco Bertarelli/Veniero Bertolotti
101, 102 Bob Paganucci

ART DIRECTOR / DIRECTEUR ARTISTIQUE:

95–97 Enric Huguet
98 Alan J. Klawans
99 Felix Müller
100 Veniero Bertolotti
101, 102 Bob Paganucci

AGENCY / AGENTUR / AGENCE – STUDIO:

95–97 Estudi Huguet
98 Smith Kline & French Labs.
99 Felix Müller
100 Studio 4
101, 102 Geigy Pharmaceuticals

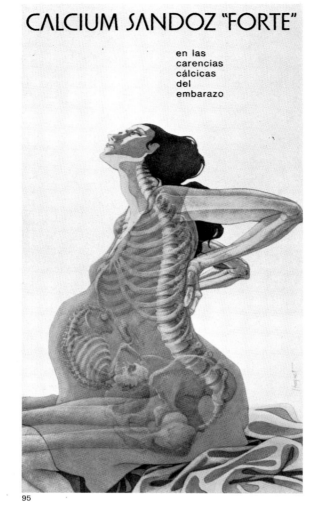

CALCIUM SANDOZ "FORTE"

en las
carencias
cálcicas
del
embarazo

95

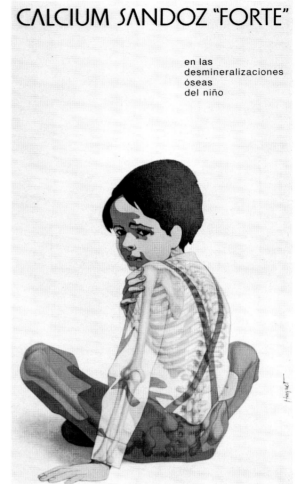

CALCIUM SANDOZ "FORTE"

en las
desmineralizaciones
óseas
del niño

96

95–97 From a series of cards about a *Sandoz* product to combat calcium deficiency, here in expectant mothers, children and the aged. Figures in full colour. (SPA)
98 Cover of a folder on *Ornex*, an SK & F treatment for colds. Black and red. (USA)
99 Cover of a booklet for schoolchildren issued by the Bremen public health authorities. (GER)
100 Card about a *Wander* pharmaceutical against colds and allergies. Face in full colour. (ITA)
101, 102 Covers of folders about the antidepressant *Tofranil*, now available in a single daily dose. (USA)

95–97 Aus einer Kartenserie über ein *Sandoz*-Produkt gegen Kalziummangel bei Schwangeren, Kindern und Älteren. Farbige Figuren. (SPA)
98 Titelblatt eines Prospektes über ein Produkt gegen Erkältungen. Schwarz und rot. (USA)
99 Titelblatt einer Broschüre der Bremer Gesundheitsbehörde für Schulkinder. (GER)
100 Karte über ein *Wander*-Präparat gegen Erkältungen und Allergien. Gesicht farbig. (ITA)
101, 102 Titelblätter von Prospekten über das Antidepressivum *Tofranil,* jetzt in Tagesdosen erhältlich. Farbig. (USA)

95–97 D'une série de cartes publicitaires pour un produit *Sandoz* contre la déficience de calcium, ici avec référence aux femmes enceintes, aux enfants et aux gens âgés. Figures polychromes. (SPA)
98 Couverture d'un dépliant pour *Ornex,* une préparation contre les refroidissements. Noir/rouge. (USA)
99 Couverture d'une brochure du service de santé de Brême, s'adressant particulièrement aux étudiants. (GER)
100 Carte publicitaire pour un produit pharmaceutique contre les refroidissements et allergies. (ITA)
101, 102 Couvertures de dépliants pour un antidépresseur, vendu en doses journalières pour mieux répondre aux exigences des patients. (USA)

For cold sufferers with fever...

98

Monika und Heiner fragen ihren Schularzt

99

Booklets / Prospekte
Prospectus

CALCIUM SANDOZ "FORTE"

en las
osteoporosis
en personas
de edad
avanzada

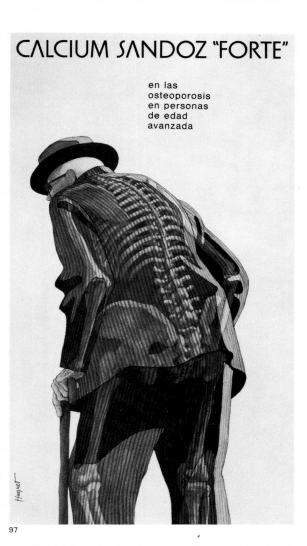

97

TRIAMINIC
PEDIATRICO
gocce orali

duplice azione

☐ sintomatica della rinite comune

☐ preventiva della
sinusite e dell'otite media

(WANDER)

risolve la congestione nasale

100

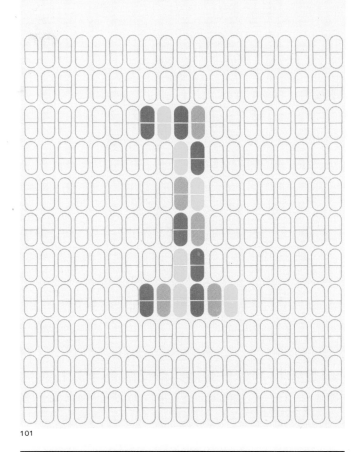

101

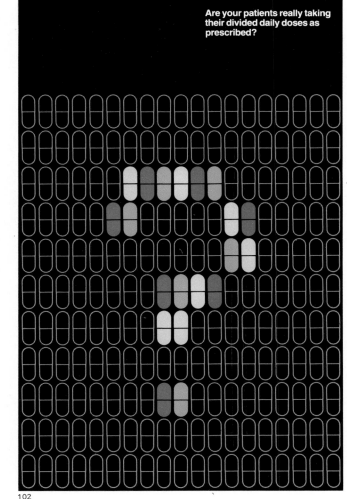

102

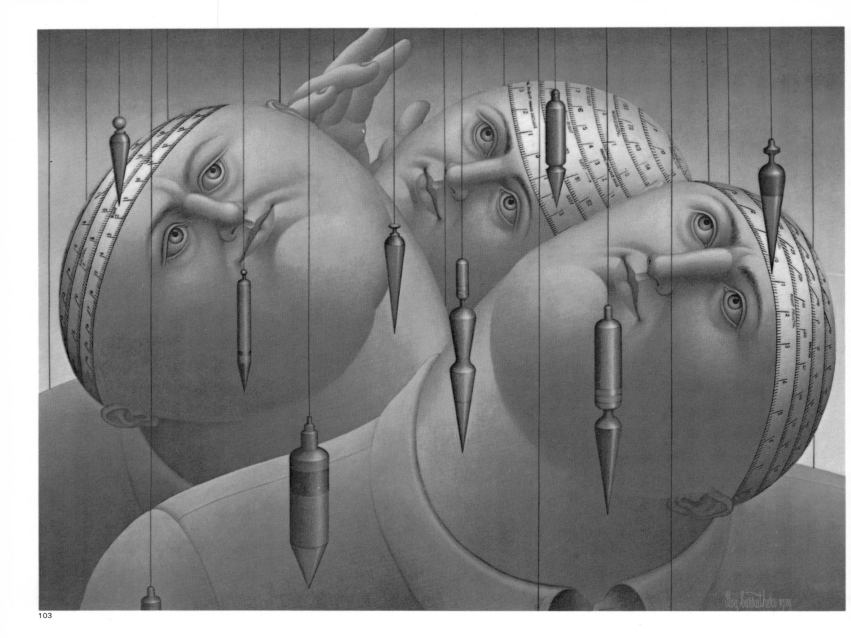

103

ARTIST / KÜNSTLER / ARTISTE:

103 Roy Carruthers
104 Gervasio Gallardo
105 Gilbert L. Stone
106 Charles Santore
107 Ferenc Pintér
108, 109 Mark English

ART DIRECTOR / DIRECTEUR ARTISTIQUE:

103–106 Anthony V. Leone
107 Bruno Vicki
108, 109 Frank Wagner

AGENCY / AGENTUR / AGENCE – STUDIO:

103–106 Lewis & Gilman Adv.
107 Intercon Italiana
108, 109 Sudler & Hennessey, Inc.

104

105

**Booklets / Prospekte
Prospectus**

103–106 From a series of large mailers about a *Roerig Pfizer* product against vertigo, which is interpreted by a different artist on each card. (USA)
107 Colour cover of a folder about *Control* for the treatment of anxiety. (ITA)
108, 109 Colour covers from a series for a *Pfizer* pain-relieving drug in which various philosophies of pain are presented. (USA)

103–106 Aus einer Serie grossformatiger Karten für ein Produkt gegen Schwindel. Jede Karte ist von einem anderen Künstler illustriert. Farbig. (USA)
107 Farbiges Titelblatt eines Prospektes für ein Präparat gegen Angstzustände. (ITA)
108, 109 Farbige Titelblätter aus einer Prospektserie für ein Schmerzmittel, die verschiedene Philosophien über den Schmerz präsentiert. (USA)

103–106 D'une série d'éléments de publicité directe pour un produit contre le vertige. Chaque élément présente l'interprétation d'un artiste particulier. (USA)
107 Couverture d'une brochure. Produit pour le traitement de l'anxiété. (ITA)
108, 109 D'une série de couvertures pour un sédatif, chacune illustrant un aspect des différentes philosophies concernant la douleur. (USA)

106

108

107

109

110

111

112

113

THE FIVE MINUTE HOUR

Geigy

Reflection on rejection in marriage

Peter A. Martin, M.D.
Adjunct Professor of Psychiatry
School of Medicine, Wayne State University, Detroit, Michigan
Clinical Professor of Psychiatry
University of Michigan Medical School, Ann Arbor, Michigan

The 5-Minute Hour is presented as a service to the psychiatric profession by Geigy Pharmaceuticals. The statements and opinions expressed in the text are those of the contributing authors and do not necessarily represent those of Geigy Pharmaceuticals.

© Copyright, 1973, Geigy Pharmaceuticals, Ardsley, New York

Things change with the passage of time, but yet, how little they change. Reflections on my clinical experiences with marital problems emphasize this. When I first started treating such problems, twenty-five years ago, as a young psychiatrist training to become a psychoanalyst, I accepted any case assigned or referred to me. Then, as now, the most highly trained therapists selected the most treatable (often the easiest) cases and the least trained therapists were assigned the most disturbed (often the hardest) cases. Residents in psychiatry then, as now, usually start with psychotics or borderline characters. Their teachers treat the psychoneurotics.

Many of the patients with whom I started my experience in psychotherapy presented severe marital problems which prevented progress in dyadic therapy and therefore were not considered good patients. Unless the mates were included in the treatment, the individual therapy foundered. Necessity forced the formulation of innovative techniques and mates were included in concurrent, consecutive, collaborative or conjoint therapies. These pioneering efforts may have been considered helpful by the involved patients but looked down upon as heretical by psychiatrists and psychoanalytic colleagues dedicated to dyadic psychotherapy. In the late 1940's, psychotherapy of marital problems was looked down upon as superficial or second-class therapy to be left for interested

clergy, social workers, and psychologists. These attitudes still persist so that the vast majority of training centers do not include teaching of marital therapy in core curriculum courses. These attitudes persist despite clinical experience and research studies which show that 60–75 percent of patients coming for psychoanalysis have marital problems.

I often get referrals of couples where one or both mates have been in lengthy psychotherapy, believe that they have been successful but now have a marital problem. Evaluation of the couple often reveals the attempts to hide the lack of intrapsychic change by highlighting the interpersonal conflict. Here, by working out the interpersonal conflict, we highlight the necessity to make the intrapsychic changes which had been successfully avoided in the individual therapies. When these changes have been accomplished, we then see marriages wherein the desired relationship between the man and the woman (in which the independence is equal, the dependence mutual, and the obligation reciprocal) is a joy to behold.

During these years there has been a change in clinical material. The greatest change has been in the area of sex. The usual presentation twenty-five years ago was that of a husband complaining about his wife's frigidity and a wife complaining that her husband was oversexed. The current presentation twenty-five years later is often that of a wife complaining that she came home from work, eager for

sex. He would complain that as soon as he opened the door to his home and before he got close enough for a kiss, his physically exhausted, "overworked" wife would say, "I have a headache." The message correctly read, said: "No sex tonight!"

Today, in contrast, we listen to the "overworked" husband complain of his wife's sexual demands and the wife complain of her husband's lack of sexual interest. Male patients bitterly say: "I come home after a long day at the office. I'm exhausted. There is my wife – fresh as a daisy. She has rested all day, is all dressed up and expecting me to take her out to dinner and dancing. Then I am supposed to bring her back to bed where I have to romance her and am expected to have intercourse with her." The wife reports that when her husband comes home, before she can run up to kiss him he says, "I have such a backache." The message, correctly read says: "No sex tonight!" The backache doesn't prevent 18 holes of golf on weekends but returns on the way home from the golf course.

Resistance to changing one's nature is especially observable with wives involved in that type of marriage called "The 'Love Sick' Wife and the 'Cold Sick' Husband." Here the wife, despite such symptoms as a psychotic break, depression, phobias, drug addiction, migraine or colitis, claims: 1) that she is not sick 2) that if her husband only loved her ('love sick'), she would be

114

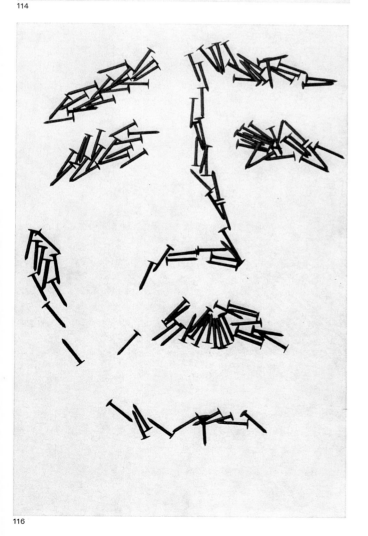

116

ARTIST / KÜNSTLER / ARTISTE:

110–113 Ziraldo Pinto
114, 115 Alan E. Cober
116 Van der Stockt

DESIGNER / GESTALTER / MAQUETTISTE:

116 May Néama

AGENCY / AGENTUR / AGENCE – STUDIO:

110–113 Merck-Div. Propaganda

115

110–112 Direct-mail cards for a *Merck* analgesic. The large colour illustrations allude to specific types of pain, such as sciatica, neuralgia and violent headaches. (BRA)
113 Page of a large folder sent as a birthday card to *Merck* clients and wishing them, among other things, long life. In colour on dark blue. (BRA)
114, 115 Opening page and double spread of a *Geigy* publication sent to psychiatrists and containing articles of interest to the profession. Colour illustrations. (USA)
116 Page of a folder about a *Roche* tranquillizer. Gold nails. (BEL)

110–112 Karten aus einer Direktwerbungsserie für ein Schmerzmittel gegen verschiedene Arten von Beschwerden, wie Ischias, Neuralgie und heftige Kopfschmerzen. Farbig. (BRA)
113 Seite aus einem grossformatigen Prospekt, als Geburtstagskarte an alle *Merck*-Kunden versandt, mit besten Wünschen – u. a. – für ein langes Leben. Farbig. (BRA)
114, 115 Titelblatt und Doppelseite einer *Geigy*-Publikation für Psychiater mit interessanten Artikeln aus ihrem Tätigkeitsgebiet. Mit Farbillustrationen. (USA)
116 Seite eines Prospektes über ein Beruhigungsmittel. Goldgelbe Nägel. (BEL)

110–112 Cartes de publicité directe pour un analgésique *Merck*. Les grandes illustrations en couleurs se réfèrent à la sciatique, aux névralgies et aux maux de tête violents. (BRA)
113 Page d'un dépliant grand format conçu comme carte de vœux par laquelle *Merck* souhaite à ses clients une longue vie en bonne santé. En couleurs sur fond bleu foncé. (BRA)
114, 115 Première page et page double d'une publication *Geigy* destinée aux psychiatres. Elle contient des articles traitant de sujets d'un intérêt professionnel. Illustrations en couleurs. (USA)
116 Page d'un dépliant pour un tranquillisant *Roche*. Clous dorés. (BEL)

Booklets / Prospekte / Prospectus

120

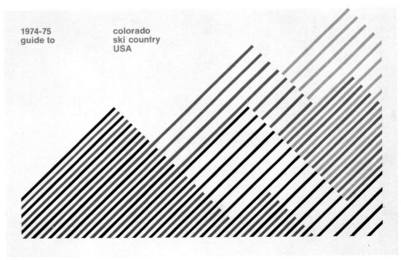

121

117–119 Covers of booklets comparing the *Roche* sleep-inducing drug *Mogadon* with the barbiturates. Red (for barbiturates), purple (for *Mogadon*) and white on black. (GBR)
120, 121 Two of six colour envelopes sent month by month to remind recipients to renew their subscriptions to *Ski* magazine. Mock-German idiom to suit the cuckoo clock. (USA)
122, 123 Cover (red/blue/yellow stripes) and double spread from a Colorado skiing guide. (USA)
124 Cover of a small booklet about a *Geigy* pharmaceutical against rheumatoid arthritis. (USA)
125 Cover of a catalogue of athletic equipment sent to dealers by Converse Rubber Corporation. Red and white, yellow lettering. (USA)
126 Programme cover symbolizing two centuries of skating for an ice show at Park Ridge. (USA)
127 Cover of a small booklet on how to thwart rapists, issued by the Denver authorities. Brown lettering, white sign on black. (USA)
128 Cover of a catalogue of sporting events issued by WBZ Television, Boston. (USA)

117–119 Umschläge von Broschüren über das Schlafmittel *Mogadon* im Vergleich mit Barbituraten. Rot für die Barbiturate, Violett für *Mogadon* und Weiss auf Schwarz. (GBR)
120, 121 Zwei von sechs Farbumschlägen, die den Adressaten jeden Monat daran erinnern, sein Abonnement für die Zeitschrift *Ski* zu erneuern. (USA)
122, 123 Titelblatt (rot-blau-gelbe Streifen) und Doppelseite aus einem Skiführer. (USA)
124 Titelblatt einer Broschüre über ein *Geigy*-Präparat gegen rheumatische Arthritis. (USA)
125 Titelblatt eines Händler-Werbekataloges für Sportausrüstung. Farbig. (USA)
126 Programmheft für eine Eisrevue: zwei Jahrhunderte Schlittschuhlaufen. (USA)
127 Titelblatt einer Broschüre über richtiges Verhalten bei Notzuchtversuchen. Braune Schrift, weisses Symbol auf Schwarz. (USA)
128 Titelblatt eines Kataloges über Sportereignisse, herausgegeben von einer Bostoner Fernsehgesellschaft. (USA)

117–119 Couvertures de brochures comparant le somnifère *Mogadon* de *Roche* aux barbiturates. Rouge (pour les barbiturates), violet (pour *Mogadon*) et blanc sur fond noir. (GBR)
120, 121 Deux enveloppes d'une série de six, envoyées chaque mois à tous ceux qui se sont abonnés au magazine *Ski* pour qu'ils n'oublient pas de renouveler leur abonnement. (USA)
122, 123 Couverture et page double d'un guide sur les stations d'hiver du Colorado. (USA)
124 Petite brochure pour un produit *Geigy* contre la polyarthrite chronique évolutive. (USA)
125 Couverture d'un catalogue pour des articles de sport; rouge et blanc, typo jaune. (USA)
126 Couverture du programme pour une présentation de patinage artistique, avec des illustrations qui devraient symboliser deux siècles de patinage.(USA)
127 Couverture d'une petite brochure sur les précautions à prendre au cas de viol; publication des autorités municipales de Denver. Typo brun, signe blanc sur fond noir. (USA)
128 Couverture d'un programme pour divers événements sportifs. Publié par une station TV. (USA)

122

123

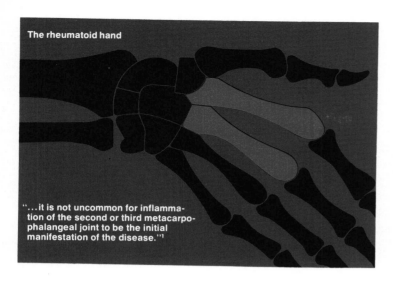

The rheumatoid hand

"...it is not uncommon for inflammation of the second or third metacarpo-phalangeal joint to be the initial manifestation of the disease."¹

1974 Converse Athletic Equipment

125

SECOND CENTURY

126

rape

127

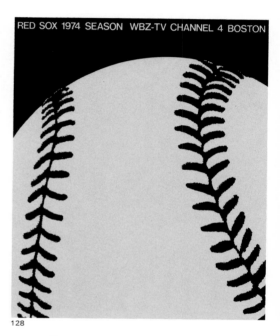

RED SOX 1974 SEASON WBZ-TV CHANNEL 4 BOSTON

128

ARTIST / KÜNSTLER / ARTISTE:

120, 121 Roy Schlemme
122, 123 John R. Rieben
124 Bob Paganucci
125 O'Shaughnessey
127 Connie Asher
128 George Canciani

DESIGNER / GESTALTER / MAQUETTISTE:

117–119 Mervyn Kurlansky
120 Rick Lawrence
121 Roy Schlemme
125 Robert Cipriani
126 Robert Qually

ART DIRECTOR / DIRECTEUR ARTISTIQUE:

117–119 Mervyn Kurlansky
120, 121 Bruce Laughlin
122, 123 John R. Rieben
124 Bob Paganucci
125 Robert Cipriani
126 Robert Qually
127 Connie Asher
128 Lou Bortone

AGENCY / AGENTUR / AGENCE – STUDIO:

117–119 Pentagram Design Partnership Ltd.
120, 121 Roy Schlemme
122, 123 Rieben & Craig
124 Geigy Pharmaceuticals
125 Gunn Associates
126 Stephens, Biondi, De Cicco Inc.
127 Channel 9 KBTV
128 WBZ-TV

Booklets / Prospekte / Prospectus

129

130

131

Bewahren Sie ihn vor der Gefahr
zu geringer körperlicher Bewegung.

Und geben Sie
Persantin forte

Regelmäßig spazierengehen soll er.

132

ARTIST / KÜNSTLER / ARTISTE:

129–132 Alexander Kamenz
133 Tony Bensted
134 Lorraine Fox

ART DIRECTOR:

129–132 Alexander Kamenz
133 Tony Bensted
134 Marty Minch

AGENCY / AGENTUR / AGENCE:

129–132 Scheibe, Hoymann &
        Schweers GmbH
133 Pfizer Group Studio
134 Kallir. Philips, Ross, Inc.

133

129–132 Illustrations from a series of folders, and complete inside spread of one of them, to promote *Persantin* for the treatment of coronary insufficiency. A heart-shaped perforation in the cover picks out the coronary patient in each picture. (GER)
133 Cover of a booklet about *Pfizer* research, also used for recruitment (slip with triangular tab). Blue, tan, pale grey, black. (GBR)
134 Cover of a case-history folder about the psychotropic drug *Haldol* as a treatment for agitation and depression. (USA)

129–132 Illustrationen und vollständige Innenseite von Prospekten über *Persantin* für die Behandlung von Koronarinsuffizienz. Ein herzförmiger Ausschnitt im Titelblatt jedes Prospektes zeigt den Herzpatienten auf dem Bild. Mehrfarbig. (GER)
133 Titelblatt einer Broschüre über die Forschung bei *Pfizer*, gleichzeitig für die Personalwerbung verwendet. Mehrfarbig. (GBR)
134 Titelblatt eines Krankheitsgeschichte-Prospektes für *Haldol*, ein Psychopharmakon gegen Erregung und Depression. Farbig. (USA)

129–132 Illustrations d'une série de dépliants et page double complète. Eléments publicitaires en faveur d'un produit pour le traitement de l'insuffisance coronaire. A travers chaque perforation en forme de cœur on voit un malade atteint d'une affection cardiaque. (GER)
133 Couverture d'une brochure consacrée aux recherches de *Pfizer*. Utilisée aussi pour le recrutement. Bleu, brun-roux, gris, noir. (GBR)
134 Couverture d'une brochure sous forme de dossier médical pour un produit psychotropique à effet sédatif et antidepresseur. (USA)

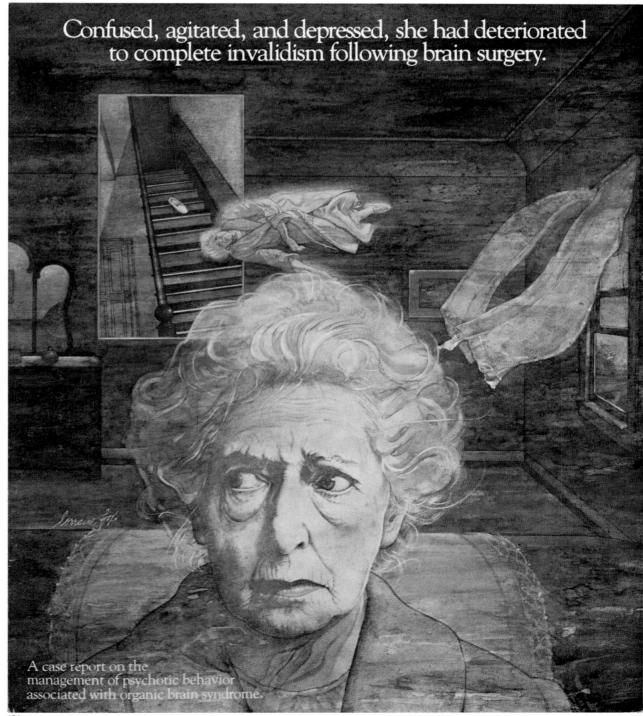

134

**Booklets
Prospekte
Prospectus**

135

136

ARTIST / KÜNSTLER:

135, 136 Tim Lewis
137, 138 Dan Glidden
139, 140 Kenneth MacKay
141 Mark & Nevosad
142 Robert Byrd

ART DIRECTOR:

135, 136 Jon Ferrari
137, 138 Jerry Herring
139, 140 Kenneth MacKay
141 Mark & Nevosad
142 Lew Ford/Jack Byrne

137

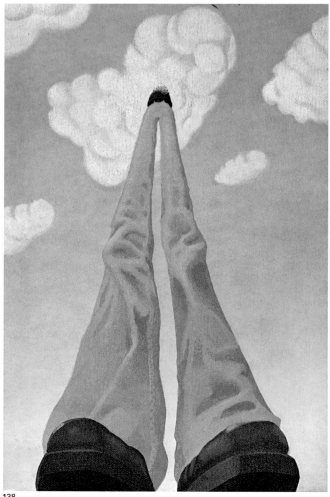

138

AGENCY / AGENTUR / AGENCE – STUDIO:

135, 136 Ferrari, Grayson & Co.
137, 138 Herring & Pirtle, Inc
139, 140 Xerox Communications
141 Hager Werbegesellschaft
142 Ford-Byrne & Associates

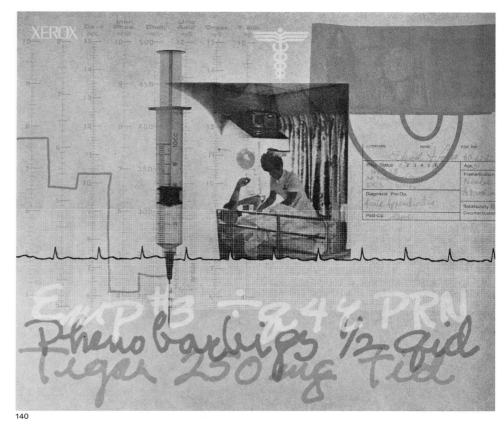

139

140

141

142

Booklets
Prospekte
Prospectus

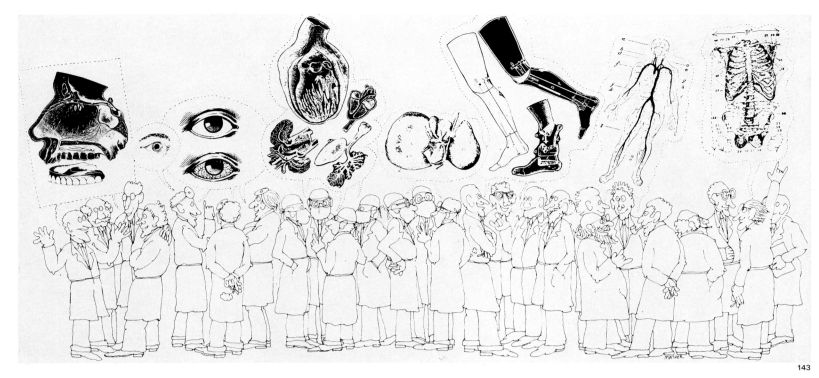

143

144

145

...and we'll tailor a wardrobe to suit you.

**Booklets
Prospekte
Prospectus**

The Bottom Line

146

A businessman contemplating an investment of his company's funds for any purpose considers the pros and cons of such an expenditure

Benefits received are analyzed in relationship to the funds required.

Questions are asked

☐ what does the company get for its money?
☐ what are the direct benefits?
☐ what are the services?
☐ what kind of return can be expected on the investment?
☐ does the company need it?
☐ can the same thing be obtained elsewhere for less money?

How does it add up on the bottom line?

An investment in annual dues (tax-deductible) in the Institute of Scrap Iron and

Steel prompts these same questions—is membership worth the money? What does the bottom line show?

More than 1,300 companies—active, allied and associate members of ISIS—have made that calculation and concluded it's a sound business investment.

They are realizing the benefits and services available through a national association which is able to do collectively what most member companies would find difficult or impossible to do by themselves.

Nearly 50 years ago, in 1928, the founders of the Institute of Scrap Iron and Steel recognized this concept of collective industry action—they realized that only by joining together—by pooling their talents and resources—could they develop a unified

voice for the industry and provide programs and services which would benefit the firms having the foresight to participate in such an undertaking.

That concept continues today. As the Institute grows in numbers, it also opens new horizons in services to its member companies. Although the Institute has numerous objectives, it has but one goal—service to its membership and the industry which they have built.

Institute of Scrap Iron and Steel, Inc.
1729 H. Street, N.W.
Washington, D.C. 20006
(202) 298-7660

The Bottom Line

147

Raychem **Thermofit®**

DR-25

148

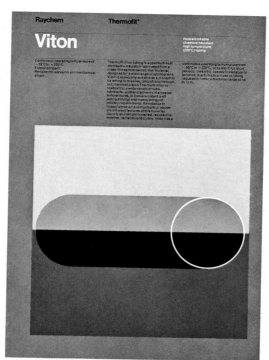

Raychem **Thermofit®**

Viton

149

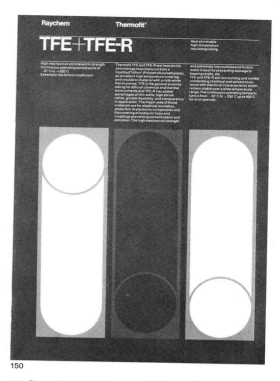

Raychem **Thermofit®**

TFE+TFE-R

150

143 Page from a folder about the School of Medicine Alumni Reunion at Tufts University. (USA)
144, 145 Cover and opening of a large motivation folder addressed to the *Westinghouse* industrial sales force and offering complete wardrobes as prizes to the best performers. Full colour. (USA)
146, 147 Cover and opening of a booklet about the services of the Institute of Scrap Iron and Steel, Inc. Cover lined in blue and red. (USA)
148–150 From a range of data sheets about various types of *Raychem* tubing. Flat colours. (GBR)
151 Invitation to visit the *Essochem* elastomers stand at an industrial fair in Munich. Die-cut cover, bright colours. (BEL)
152 Cover of a spirally bound booklet on the Dwight Building Company, a *Westinghouse* subsidiary. Design in blue, red and green. (USA)

143 Seite aus einem Prospekt über eine Zusammenkunft von Medizinern an der Tufts Universität. (USA)
144, 145 Titelblatt und Doppelseite eines grossformatigen Prospektes, der sich an die Reisevertreter von *Westinghouse* wendet und den Erfolgreichsten unter ihnen als Preis eine vollständige Garderobe in Aussicht stellt. Mehrfarbig. (USA)
146, 147 Titelblatt und Doppelseite aus einer Broschüre über die Dienste eines Institutes für die Verwertung von Schrott. Titelblatt blau und rot liniert. (USA)
148–150 Aus einer Reihe von Blättern mit Angaben über verschiedene *Raychem*-Röhren. Flach aufgetragene Farben. (GBR)
151 Einladung zum Besuch eines *Essochem*-Standes an einer Industriemesse in München. Bunter, gestanzter Umschlag. (BEL)
152 Titelblatt einer Broschüre mit Spiralheftung über die Dwight Building Company, eine Tochtergesellschaft von *Westinghouse*. In Blau, Rot und Grün. (USA)

143 Page d'un dépliant consacré à une réunion d'anciens étudiants en médecine de la Tufts University. (USA)
144, 145 Couverture et page initiale d'un dépliant grand format s'adressant aux représentants de *Westinghouse*. Pour les encourager on offre un choix de vêtements à ceux qui rapportent les commandes les plus importantes. En couleurs. (USA)
146, 147 Couverture et page initiale d'une brochure consacrée aux services rendus par l'Institute of Scrap Iron and Steel, Inc. Couverture lignée en bleu et rouge. (USA)
148–150 Exemples d'une série de feuilles publicitaires avec des données techniques concernant les différents genres de tubes *Raychem*. (GBR)
151 Invitation pour une visite du stand d'*Essochem* à la foire industrielle de Munich. Couverture à couleurs vives. (BEL)
152 Couverture d'une brochure à reliure à spirale consacrée à une filiale de *Westinghouse*. Bleu, rouge et vert. (USA)

151

The Dwight Building Company

152

ARTIST / KÜNSTLER / ARTISTE:

153 Mario Grasso
154 J. Seager
155 Just Reinhold
156–158 Elwyn Art Works

DESIGNER / GESTALTER / MAQUETTISTE:

154 Chris Keeble
156–158 Elwyn Mehlman

ART DIRECTOR / DIRECTEUR ARTISTIQUE:

155 Gerhard Marx
156–158 Bob Kwait

153 "Man is not a research laboratory..." Colour cover of a folder about a *Ciba-Geigy* product against rheumatism and arthritis. (SWI)
154 Hard cover of a booklet on tyres for veteran cars, issued by Vintage Tyre Supplies Ltd. Cars in shades of brown. (GBR)
155 Cover of a booklet about a *Schering* product used in making printed circuits. Black on silver and gold-green. (GER)
156–158 Double spreads in colour from a *B.F. Goodrich* sales motivation booklet. (USA)
159, 160 Two sides of a *Dictaphone* folder with a small bag of coffee powder attached, suggesting to bosses a talk over coffee about efficiency measures. (SWI)

153 «Der Mensch ist kein Versuchslaboratorium ...» Farbiges Titelblatt eines Prospektes für ein *Ciba-Geigy*-Produkt gegen Rheumatismus und Arthritis. (SWI)
154 Kartoneinband einer Farbbroschüre über Pneus für Automobil-Veteranen. (GBR)
155 Titelblatt einer Broschüre für ein *Schering*-Produkt, das in gedruckten Schaltungen Verwendung findet. Schwarz auf Silber und Goldgrün. (GER)
156–158 Farb-Doppelseiten aus einer Broschüre für Verkäufer von *B.F. Goodrich.* (USA)
159, 160 Zwei Seiten aus einem *Dictaphone*-Prospekt mit einem Säckchen Kaffeepulver und der Empfehlung, Rationalisierungsmassnahmen über einer Tasse Kaffee zu besprechen. (SWI)

153 Couverture d'un dépliant en faveur d'un produit *Ciba-Geigy* pour le traitement du rhumatisme et de l'arthrite. (SWI)
154 Couverture cartonnée d'une brochure pour des pneus spécialement conçus pour les vieilles voitures. Voitures en différentes teintes brunes. (GBR)
155 Couverture d'une brochure en faveur d'un produit *Schering* utilisé pour la fabrication de circuits imprimés. Noir sur fond argenté et vert doré. (GBR)
156–158 Pages doubles d'une brochure interne de *Goodrich.* En couleurs. (USA)
159, 160 Deux panneaux d'un dépliant avec un petit sachet de café y attaché. On y propose de discuter les démarches pour augmenter l'efficacité en buvant une tasse de café. (SWI)

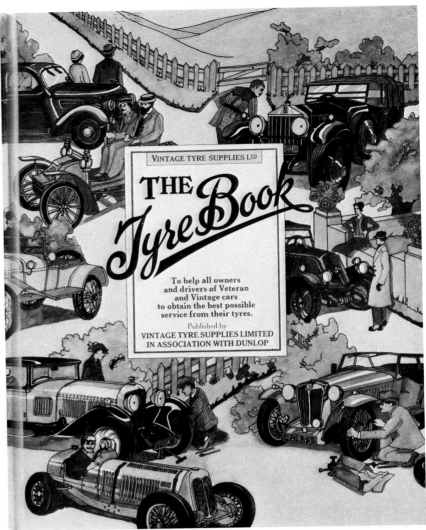

154

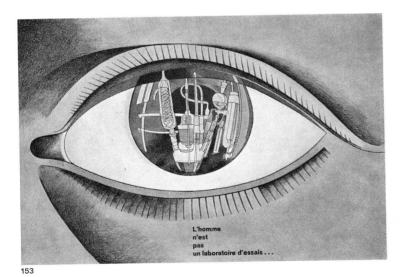

153

155

AGENCY / AGENTUR / AGENCE – STUDIO:

153 Ciba-Geigy, Zentrale Werbung
156–158 Griswold-Eshleman Co.

Big wheels, little wheels, we're rolling along together.

And we all have a role.
You BFG salesmen, for instance. You are your own best strategist. You've shown your ability
to skate rings around the competition by figuring out what
you want customers to do for you—and how to get them to do it for you.
BFG distributors? You're the experts. And you've rolled right over your
competitors by discovering the secrets of success.
You put the time and money needed to merchandise BFG products right.
You insist that salesmen make calls for every
product to every potential customer. You invest in training so
your people are experts, too. You stock a complete
inventory. And you put your money into service
facilities so you can do a superior job.
And we help you. We smooth the bumps out of
your path. So while we sign national
accounts, you service 'em. And we've helped things
roll along better with larger stocks,
fewer locations, centralized teletype, and
computerized order processing.
And from start to finish, old skate,
you're the key.

156

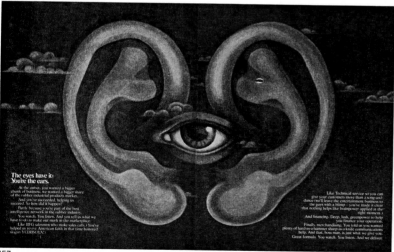

The eyes have it:
You're the ears.

157

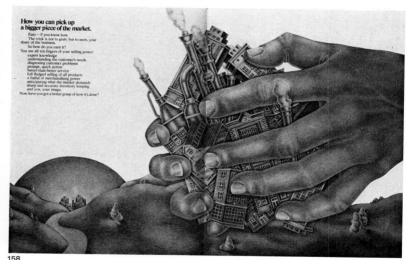

How you can pick up
a bigger piece of the market.

158

Eine Tasse guten Kaffees
hat schon manchen Chef
auf Ideen gebracht.

Zum Beispiel auf ein
neues Diktier-System.

159   160

Booklets / Prospekte / Prospectus

161 Die-stamped cover of a booklet on the *Intertech* architectural and engineering company. (USA)
162, 163 Card, with detail of artwork, advising AT & T salesmen to make appointments. (USA)
164 Panels of a concertina-type folder on an IBM communications control system. Red and blue type on orange. (USA)
165 Double spread from a booklet on *Thorn* discharge lamps. Diagram in colour. (GBR)
166 Spread from a booklet on an IBM system for broadcasting stations. Coloured figures. (USA)
167 Cover of an IBM folder about a course of study for employees. Two blues and white. (USA)
168 Back cover of a booklet about *Decca* record playing equipment. Pastel shades. (SAF)
169 Cover of a booklet about a *Xerox* learning programme for salesmen. Black on sepia. (USA)

161 Titelblatt einer Broschüre für ein Architektur- und Ingenieurunternehmen. (USA)
162, 163 Karte einer Telephon-Gesellschaft, mit Illustrationsausschnitt. Farbig. (USA)
164 Teile eines Leporello-Prospektes über ein IBM-Kommunikations-Kontrollsystem. Farbig. (USA)
165 Doppelseite aus einer Broschüre für *Thorn*-Fluoreszenzlampen. Diagramm in Farben. (GBR)
166 Doppelseite aus einer Broschüre über ein IBM-System für Sendestationen. Farbig. (USA)
167 Titelblatt eines IBM-Prospektes für einen Studiengang für Angestellte. Blau-weiss. (USA)
168 Rückseite einer Broschüre über *Decca* Plattenspieler-Geräte. Pastellfarben. (SAF)
169 Titelblatt einer Broschüre über ein *Xerox*-Lernprogramm für Reisevertreter. Schwarz auf Sepia. (USA)

161 Couverture d'une brochure pour une société d'architectes et d'ingénieurs. (USA)
162, 163 Avis pour les représentants d'AT & T de donner préavis aux clients. (USA)
164 Panneaux d'un dépliant en accordéon pour un système de contrôle électronique IBM. Typo rouge et bleu sur fond orange. (USA)
165 D'une brochure pour une marque de lampes fluorescentes. Diagramme en couleur. (GBR)
166 Page double d'une brochure en faveur d'un système IBM pour des stations émettrices. (USA)
167 Couverture d'un dépliant annonçant un cours pour employés. Deux bleus sur blanc. (USA)
168 4e page de couverture d'un prospectus pour divers appareils *Decca*. Teintes pastel. (USA)
169 Couverture d'une brochure sur un programme d'enseignement IBM pour représentants. (USA)

161

162

The Salesman's Call Ahead
It puts more selling time into your day

163

a better way

The growing complexity of modern data processing activities places increasing emphasis on the need for a better and more efficient way to get data from one place to another.

This latest version of CCAP/7 is a comprehensive communications control program that operates on the IBM System/7 computer. A high-speed processor, System/7 has a 400 nanosecond memory cycle, modular architecture, and readily expandable disk storage capability. These features, combined with the broad flexibility provided by the teleprocessing multiplexer under program control, make the System/7 particularly well suited to communications applications such as message switching, networking, front-end network control, data concentration, and data collection.

Version 2 expands the usefulness of CCAP/7... a usefulness that extends from standalone message switching applications controlling typewriter/keyboard terminals, to the more sophisticated data communications methods made available through the advanced display terminals of the IBM 3270 system.

Not only have all the important features of CCAP/7 Version 1 been retained by Version 2, but they've now been augmented by selective formatting, paging, and inquiry routing procedures. These new features, plus additional device support, make CCAP/7 Version 2 a most advanced communications control system.

A self-contained program, CCAP/7 Version 2 provides full network control without any need to rely on a "back-end" processor. However, it can communicate with other computers either by communications lines, or through a direct channel connection as dictated by your system requirements.

performance

Designed to provide top performance, CCAP/7 operates at over 2,000 characters per second on a sustained basis and also has the ability to handle short bursts at much greater data rates. The use of CCAP/7 resident display formats with IBM 3270 display terminals allows you to maximize transaction throughput by reducing the number of input characters needed, and by providing guidance information on transaction formats to your operators.

reliability

An area of primary importance in any comprehensive communications system, reliability is well served by CCAP/7 Version 2. That's because the program includes provisions for terminal and line error detection with retry, parity and redundancy checking, time and date stamping, and message sequence checking. It also queues messages for inoperative terminals. A key reliability feature is CCAP/7's checkpoint/restart capability with user-defined checkpoint intervals and alternate checkpoint records. This feature, coupled with a system monitored and controlled slowdown capability during low-buffer conditions, makes available a highly dependable system that can guard against overrun situations. CCAP/7 has been designed so that all transactions entered into the system can be delivered to the proper destinations in the intended way, and in a meaningful time frame.

164

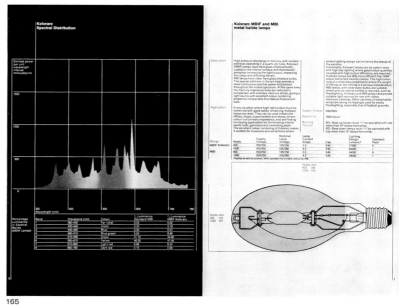

165

Avails and contract management

The System for Television and Radio gives you reports in this area that include: availability worksheet, availability summary, contract listing, contract exception listing, contract confirmation, conflict listing, and airing instructions listing.

These reports mean you can:
- Improve the control over commercial time.
- Cut the number of errors and makegoods.
- Pinpoint unsold time.
- Conduct spot analyses of commercial time sales.
- Reduce typing workloads at the station.

**3:02
3:01**

Daily log

The System for Television and Radio can give you a program format listing and a PSA/promo listing, or produce a legible daily log so you can:
- Improve broadcast efficiency through tighter scheduling.
- Get an early indication of potential problems.
- Have enough information flexibility and speed to make late changes.
- Keep track of changes by getting completely updated reports whenever you want them.

166

167

168

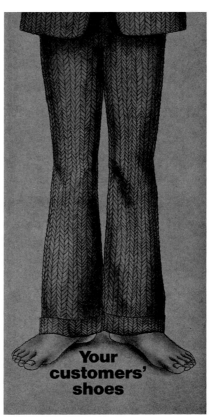

Your customers' shoes

169

**Booklets
Prospekte / Prospectus**

ARTIST / KÜNSTLER / ARTISTE:

170 Hans Stoller
171 Niels Vangsgaard/Imi Markos
173, 174 Bill Mayer/Richard Waldrop/Dale Verzaal

DESIGNER / GESTALTER / MAQUETTISTE:

172 Frank Rockwell
175, 176 Frank Deleno
177 Roslyn Eskind
178 Paul Ibou

170

171

Har du panntroll?

172

170 Cover of a booklet giving information about the Aluminium Company of Canada Ltd. Blue and green. (CAN)
171 "Have you got gremlins?" Four-page colour supplement addressed to boiler-owners by OK, an oil consumers' union, and drawing attention to the dangers of creeping corrosion in oil-fired boilers. (SWE)
172 Cover of a *Corning* booklet reviewing fifty years of glass-making at Central Falls. Brown stock. (USA)
173, 174 Cover and double spread from a brochure in scrapbook form reviewing the history of the Georgia Railroad Bank from 1833 to the present. (USA)
175, 176 Detail and complete cover of a booklet about *Westinghouse* thermocouples and leads. (USA)
177 Cover of a small booklet listing educational aids for school use sponsored by The Canadian Life Insurance Association. Orange arrows on anthracite. (CAN)
178 Panels of a concertina-type folder listing *Avia* fuels and lubricants. (BEL)

170 Titelblatt einer Broschüre, die über eine kanadische Aluminiumfirma, die Aluminium Company of Canada Ltd., informiert. Blau und grün. (CAN)
171 Vierseitige Farbbeilage einer Öl-Konsumentenvereinigung, die Kesselbesitzer auf die Gefahr schleichender Verrostung ihrer ölgefeuerten Kessel hinweist. (SWE)
172 Titelblatt einer *Corning*-Broschüre über «50 Jahre Glasfabrikation in Central Falls». Braunes Papier. (USA)
173, 174 Titelblatt und Doppelseite einer Broschüre, welche die Geschichte einer Bank (seit 1833) in Form eines Einklebealbums aufzeichnet. (USA)
175, 176 Ausschnitt und vollständige Titelseite einer Broschüre über *Westinghouse*-Thermoelemente. (USA)
177 Titelblatt einer kleinen Broschüre über Lehrmittel für den Schulgebrauch, gestiftet von einer Lebensversicherungsgesellschaft. Orange Pfeile auf Anthrazit. (CAN)
178 Ausschnitt aus einem Leporello-Prospekt für *Avia*-Brenn- und Schmierstoffe. (BEL)

170 Couverture d'une brochure contenant des informations sur l'Aluminium Co. du Canada. Bleu et vert. (CAN)
171 Supplément de quatre pages d'une union de consommateurs de mazout. Il s'adressent à ceux qui possèdent une chaudière au mazout pour les rendre attentifs aux dangers de la corrosion affectant les chaudières au mazout. (SWE)
172 Couverture d'une brochure présentant une vue d'ensemble de ce que la verrerie *Corning* a réalisé pendant les derniers cinquante ans, à Central Falls. Papier brun. (USA)
173, 174 Couverture et page double d'une brochure, sous forme d'un carnet de notes, sur l'histoire d'une banque. (USA)
175, 176 Détail et couverture complète d'une brochure pour des éléments thermo-électriques de *Westinghouse*. (USA)
177 Couverture d'une brochure au sujet des articles d'enseignement mis à la disposition des écoles par une compagnie d'assurance sur la vie. Flèches orange. (CAN)
178 Panneaux d'un dépliant en accordéon énumérant les différents carburants et lubrifiants d'*Avia*. (BEL)

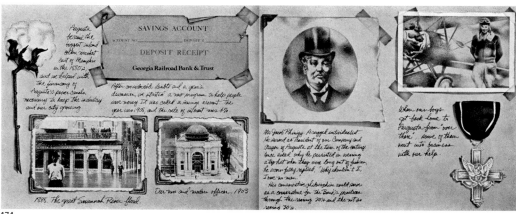

173

174

175

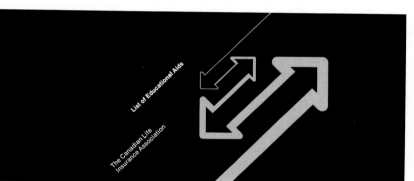

177

176

ART DIRECTOR / DIRECTEUR ARTISTIQUE:

170 Jacques Latreille
171 Niels Vangsgaard
172 Robert L. Ivers
173, 174 Arington Hendley
175, 176 Frank Deleno
177 Stuart Ash

AGENCY / AGENTUR / AGENCE – STUDIO:

170 Alcan Graphic Service
171 Plan Annonsbyra AB
172 Cornings Design Dept.
173, 174 Weltin Advertising Agency, Inc.
175, 176 Westinghouse Design Center
177 Gottschalk & Ash Ltd.

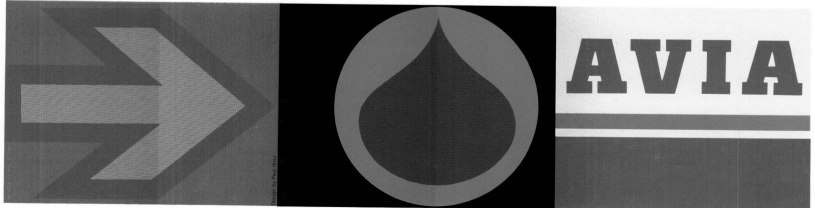

178

179

180

179–181 Pages from a booklet about the London Stock Exchange. Fig. 179 alludes to developments under Queen Elizabeth I and King Charles I, Fig. 180 to the present-day range of investments and Fig. 181 to the rise of the railways in the reign of Queen Victoria. (GBR)
182 Cover of a large *Esso* booklet telling the story of oil. Red ground. (ITA)
183 Cover of a large booklet about the "countless uses of electricity". Silver on black. (VEN)
184 Press information folder for CBS Television. Blue and black. (USA)
185 Cover (two blues, yellow and white) of a brochure about a new airport at Montreal. (CAN)
186, 187 Announcement (cover and opening spread) of a special NBC Television programme. (USA)

179–181 Seiten aus einer Broschüre über die Entwicklung des Londoner Stock Exchange. (GBR)
182 Umschlag einer grossen *Esso*-Broschüre über das Öl. Roter Grund. (ITA)
183 Umschlag einer umfangreichen Broschüre über die «unzähligen Nutzungsmöglichkeiten der Elektrizität». Silber auf Schwarz. (VEN)
184 Presse-Informationsmappe für das CBS-Fernsehen. Blau auf Schwarz. (USA)
185 Umschlag (zwei Blautöne, Gelb und Weiss) einer Broschüre über einen neuen kanadischen Flughafen. (CAN)
186, 187 Ankündigung (Umschlag und Doppelseite) eines speziellen NBC-TV-Programmes. (USA)

181

il petrolio

182

183

ARTIST / KÜNSTLER / ARTISTE:

179–181 Owen Wood
183 Jesus Emilio Franco
185 Fredy Jäggi/
       Peter Steiner (Design)
186, 187 Ner Beck

ART DIRECTOR / DIRECTEUR ARTISTIQUE

179–181 John Ben
183 Jesus Emilio Franco
184 Lou Dorfsman
185 Gottschalk + Ash, Ltd.
186, 187 Bob Greenwell

179–181 D'une brochure consacrée à la Bourse de Londres. Fig. 179 se réfère au développement sous l'empire d'Elizabeth I et Charles I; fig. 180 aux investissements de nos jours; fig. 181 à l'importance croissante des chemins de fer sous l'empire de la reine Victoria. (GBR)
182 Couverture d'une brochure grand format sur l'histoire de l'huile. Fond rouge. (ITA)
183 D'une brochure grand format sur «l'emploi diversifié de l'électricité». (VEN)
184 Dépliant d'information pour la presse sur les programmes TV de CBS. Bleu et noir. (USA)
185 Couverture (bleu, jaune, blanc) d'une brochure pour le nouveau aéroport de Montréal. (CAN)
186, 187 Publicité directe annonçant un programme spécial diffusé par NBC Television. (USA)

184

186   187

185

DESIGNER / GESTALTER / MAQUETTISTE:

184 Lou Dorfsman

AGENCY / AGENTUR / AGENCE – STUDIO:

179–181 Unit 5 Design Ltd.
182 Arnoldo Mondadori, Editore
183 El Cojo Ilustrado
184 CBS/Broadcast Group
185 Gottschalk + Ash Ltd.
186, 187 NBC TV Marketing Dept.

**Booklets
Prospekte
Prospectus**

188

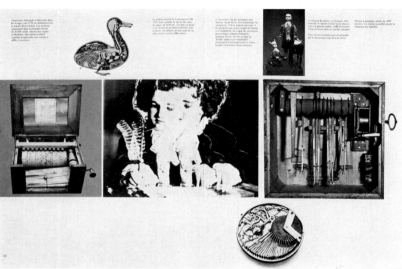

191

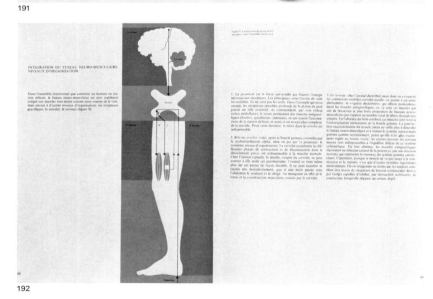

192

189

190

ARTIST / KÜNSTLER / ARTISTE:

188–190 Eugene Karun
191, 192 Monique Jacot
193, 194 Eckard Alker
195 Saul Mandel

DESIGNER / GESTALTER

191, 192 Peter Voigt
196, 197 Lou Dorfsman

ART DIRECTOR / DIRECTEUR ARTISTIQUE:

188–190 Richard Nelson
191, 192 Cyril Stauffenegger
193, 194 Eckard Alker
195 John Williams
196, 197 Lou Dorfsman

Booklets
Prospekte
Prospectus

Dynamit Nobel
CHEMIKALIEN

Grund- und Hilfsstoffe für die Kosmetik-Industrie

193

Personal Choice
Savings Plans.

195

188–190 Double spread (jewels in colour) and two transparent overlays from a Christmas booklet about *Neiman-Marcus* jewels. (USA)
191, 192 Double spreads (on history of clockwork and human nerves) from a *Micromégas* book about time and cybernetics. (SWI)
193 Cover in mauve and black of a catalogue of materials for the cosmetics industry. (GER)
194 Catalogue of chemicals supplied by Dynamit Nobel AG. Black and white on green. (GER)
195 Small folder about saving issued by the Bank of America. Blue figure, green belts. (USA)
196, 197 Double spread and drawing from a small CBS booklet about cable television. (USA)

188–190 Doppelseite (Edelsteine farbig) und zwei Klarsichtfolien aus der Weihnachtsbroschüre für *Neiman-Marcus*-Edelsteine. (USA)
191, 192 Zwei Doppelseiten (über die Geschichte des Uhrwerks und die menschlichen Nerven) aus einem *Micromégas*-Buch über Zeit und über Kybernetik. Mehrfarbig. (SWI)
193 Umschlag in Lila und Schwarz eines Kataloges über Stoffe für die kosmetische Industrie. (GER)
194 Katalog über die von der Dynamit Nobel AG hergestellten chemischen Stoffe. Schwarzweiss auf Grün. (GER)
195 Kleiner Prospekt über das Sparen, herausgegeben von einer amerikanischen Bank. Blaue Figur, grüne Ringe. (USA)
196, 197 Doppelseite und Zeichnung aus einer kleinen CBS-Broschüre über das Kabelfernsehen. (USA)

188–190 Page double (bijoux en couleurs) et deux feuilles transparentes figurant dans une brochure de Noël pour les bijoux de *Neiman-Marcus*. (USA)
191, 192 Pages doubles (l'histoire de l'horlogerie et les nerfs humains) de *Micromégas,* numéro consacré au temp et à la cybernétique. (SWI)
193 Couverture d'un catalogue pour des matières de base utilisés dans l'industrie cosmétique. En lilas et noir. (GER)
194 Catalogue présentant les matières chimiques fabriquées par Dynamit Nobel AG. Noir et blanc sur fond vert. (GER)
195 Petit dépliant que la Bank of America a publié au sujet de l'épargne. Figure en bleu, ceinturons verts. (USA)
196, 197 Page double et illustration tirées d'une petite brochure CBS sur la transmission télévisive par câbles. (USA)

Dynamit Nobel
CHEMIKALIEN

Verkaufsprogramm von A bis Z

194

196

AGENCY / AGENTUR / AGENCE – STUDIO:

188–190 Neiman-Marcus
191, 192 Stauffenegger Verlag
193, 194 Dr. Lorenz und Bogo KG
195 Grey Advertising Agency
196, 197 CBS/Broadcast Group

197

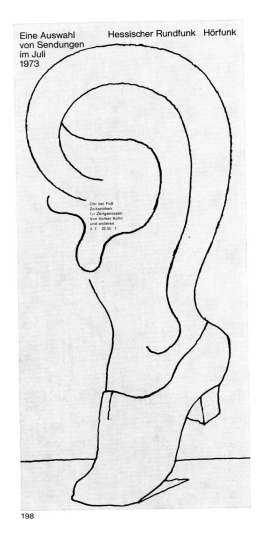

Eine Auswahl
von Sendungen
im Juli
1973

Hessischer Rundfunk   Hörfunk

Ohr bei Fuß
Zeitzeichen
für Zeitgenossen
Von Volker Kühn
und anderen
4.7. 22.30 1

198

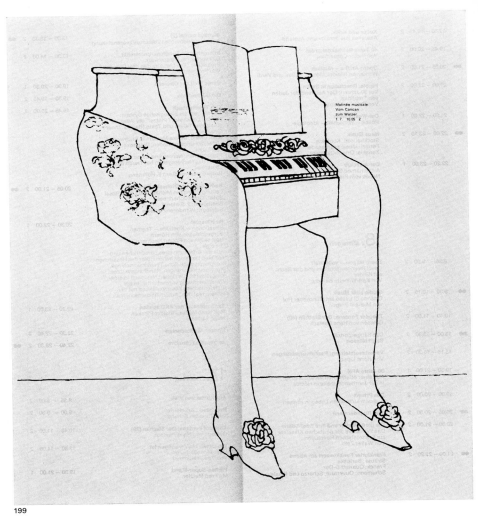

Matinée musicale
Vom Cancan
zum Walzer
1.7. 10.05 2

199

200

Le programme
de la télévision française
1974-1975

201

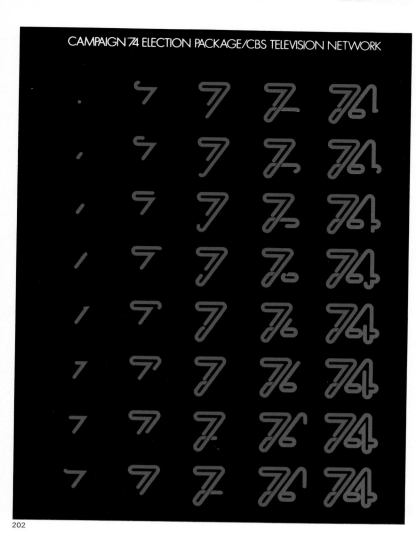

CAMPAIGN '74 ELECTION PACKAGE/CBS TELEVISION NETWORK

198, 199 Cover and spread from a monthly programme for the Hessian radio. The references are to hearing the signs of the times and to a matinée of dance music. Black and white. (GER)
200, 201 Double spread and cover of a large brochure listing the French autumn and winter television programmes of Radio-Canada. (CAN)
202 Cover of a spirally-bound booklet about CBS coverage of the 1974 elections. (USA)
203, 204 Covers of programmes of concerts to be broadcast by the Bavarian radio. Drawings in beige and brown shades. (GER)

198, 199 Umschlag und Doppelseite aus einem Monatsprogramm des Hessischen Rundfunks. Die Bemerkungen beziehen sich auf «die Zeichen der Zeit, die es zu hören gilt» und auf eine Tanz-musik-Matinée. Schwarzweiss. (GER)
200, 201 Doppelseite und Umschlag einer grossen Broschüre mit den französischen Herbst- und Winter-Fernsehprogrammen von Radio-Canada. (CAN)
202 Umschlag einer Broschüre mit Spiralheftung über CBS-Sendungen zu den Wahlen 1974. (USA)
203, 204 Umschläge von Konzertprogrammen des Bayrischen Rundfunks. (GER)

198, 199 Couverture et page double du programme mensuel de l'ORT de Hesse, se référant «aux signes des temps qu'il faut écouter» et à une émission matinale de musique de danse. (GER)
200, 201 Page double et couverture tirées d'une brochure grand format qui présente les pro-grammes en langue française diffusés en automne et en hiver par Radio Canada. (CAN)
202 Couverture d'une brochure à reliure à spirale contenant un aperçu sur l'ensemble des infor-mations diffusées par CBS lors des élections de l'année 1974. (USA)
203, 204 Couverture d'une série de programmes pour les concerts diffusés par la Radiodiffusion bavaroise. Illustrations en teintes beiges et brunes. (GER)

ARTIST / KÜNSTLER / ARTISTE:

198, 199 Günther Kieser
203, 204 Walter Tafelmaier

DESIGNER / GESTALTER / MAQUETTISTE:

200, 201 Ueli Dietiker

ART DIRECTOR / DIRECTEUR ARTISTIQUE:

198, 199 Günther Kieser
200, 201 Ueli Dietiker/Alain Leduc
202 Lou Dorfsman
203, 204 Walter Tafelmaier

AGENCY / AGENTUR / AGENCE – STUDIO:

198, 199 Günther Kieser
202 CBS/Broadcast Group

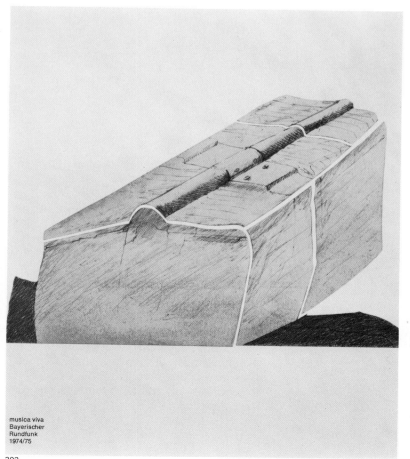

musica viva
Bayerischer
Rundfunk
1974/75

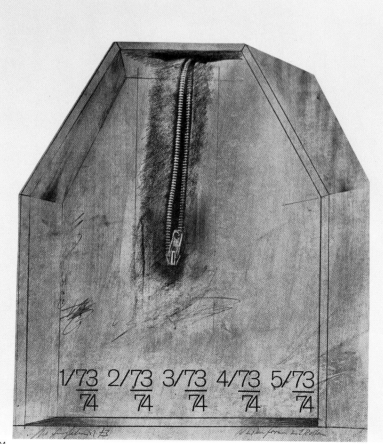

1/73 2/73 3/73 4/73 5/73
—— —— —— —— ——
74 74 74 74 74

205

A rollicking, fact-filled book about foods, fads, nutrition, diet, and health by the author of *The Foodbook*

JAMES TRAGER'S

The Bellybook

209

206

207

208

Le fumeur de pipe, un sage qui sait gagner puis savourer son plaisir. Dans la vie, les plaisirs de longue haleine refusent de se livrer spontanément. Avant de s'offrir à vous, ils exigent la conquête patiente. Le fumeur de pipe est un explorateur qui, à chaque étape de sa découverte, s'approche davantage de la pleine satisfaction.

Ce livret a deux objectifs: accompagner le néophyte au cours de son apprentissage et

Dr. Robert S. DeRopp's

THE NEW PROMETHEANS

210

squeeze it till the eagle grins

HOW TO SPEND,
SAVE AND ENJOY
YOUR MONEY

A SPECIAL
SELECTION

211

Booklets / Prospekte / Prospectus

205–207 Typical drawing and two spreads from a small booklet accompanying a twelve months' gift subscription to the *Reader's Digest*. (USA)
208 Page from a "Pipe-smoker's Breviary" issued by the Swiss Pipe Club. Black and white. (SWI)
209–211 Covers for books from a paperback series. Black and one colour. (USA)
212, 213 Cover and spread of a book in the form of a sandwich (cloth, foam plastic, board). (GBR)
214 Folder about a new paperback series. (NLD)

205–207 Typische Zeichnung und zwei Doppelseiten aus einer kleinen Begleit-Broschüre für *Reader's Digest*-Jahresgeschenk-Abonnemente. (USA)
208 Seite aus einem «Pfeifenraucher-Brevier» des Schweizer Pfeifenklubs. Schwarzweiss. (SWI)
209–211 Umschläge für Bücher aus einer Taschenbuchreihe. Eine Farbe mit Schwarz. (USA)
212, 213 Umschlag und Doppelseite eines Buches in Sandwich-Form (Tuch, Schaumstoff, Karton). (GBR)
214 Prospekt über eine neue Taschenbuchreihe. (NLD)

205–207 Illustration typique et deux pages doubles d'une petite brochure adressée à ceux qui reçoivent un abonnement-cadeau au *Reader s Digest*. (USA)
208 Page d'un «Bréviaire pour les fumeurs de pipes», publié par le Club suisse des fumeurs de pipes. (SWI)
209–211 Couvertures d'une série de livres de poche. Noir et une couleur. (USA)
212, 213 Couverture et page d'un livre sous forme de sandwich (tissu, caoutchouc mousse, carton). (GBR)
214 Dépliant annonçant une nouvelle série de livres de poche. (NLD)

212

213

ARTIST / KÜNSTLER / ARTISTE:

205–207 Peter Cross
208 Serge Tcherdyne
209–211 Stanislaw Zagorski
212, 213 Vanessa Strong/Andy Ewan
214 Erik De Meyer

ART DIRECTOR / DIRECTEUR ARTISTIQUE:

205–207 Louis Portuesi
208 Serge Tcherdyne
209–211 John Channell
212, 213 Vanessa Strong/Andy Ewan
214 Erik De Meyer

AGENCY / AGENTUR / AGENCE – STUDIO:

205–207 Habbas, Inc.
208 Florian Martin
209–211 Group One Creative Graphics, Inc.
212, 213 Mayflower Cottage
214 Graphic Group U.C.

de nederlandsche boekhandel · patmos · opdebeek   herfst '74

214

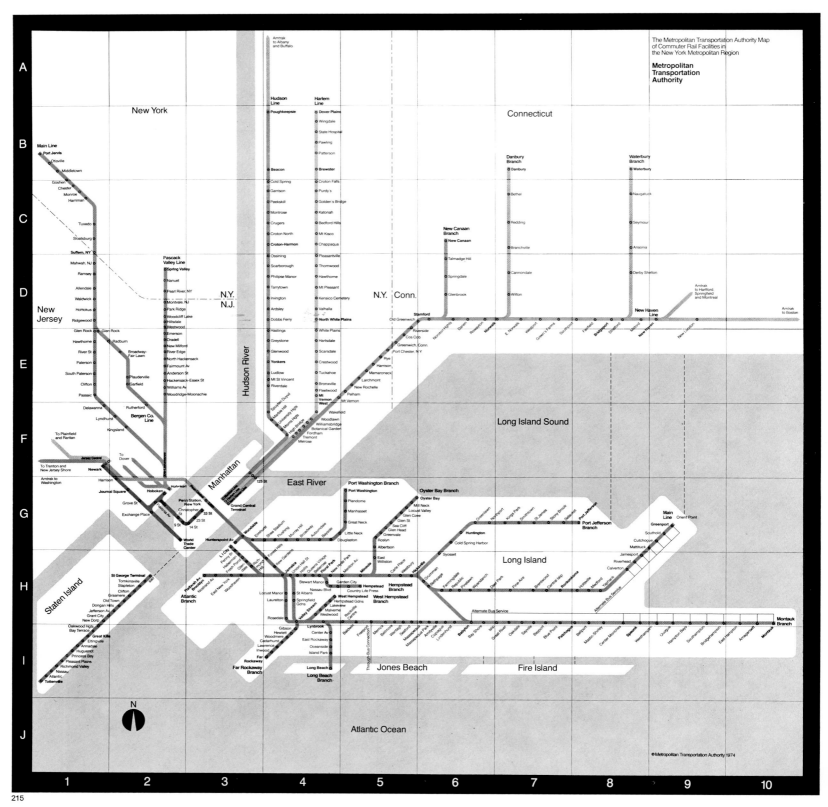

215

ARTIST / KÜNSTLER / ARTISTE:

215 Joan Charysyn
216 Manoru Shimokochi
217 Salvatore Adduci
218 F. Kneubühler
219 Walter Tafelmaier/Helmut Bauer (Photo)
220 Josef R. Olbinski

ART DIRECTOR / DIRECTEUR ARTISTIQUE:

215 Joan Charysyn
216 Art Doodman/Nancy von Lauderback
217 Salvatore Adduci
218 F. Mast

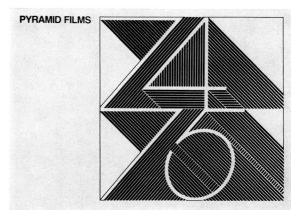

216

Booklets / Prospekte / Prospectus

215 Commuter rail guide for the New York area, issued by the Metropolitan Transportation Authority. Rail lines in various colours. (USA)
216 Catalogue of the products of Pyramid Films for 1974/75. (USA)
217 Cover of a series of *Eurunion* brochures on sound transmission problems. Red head. (SPA)
218 Cover of a *Sulzer* booklet on district heating. Red and orange shades on blue. (SWI)
219 Cover of a booklet on Munich's new mail station. Plastic band in bright colours. (The German word for "junction" has the literal meaning of "knot-point".) (GER)
220 Programme cover for an International Song Festival in Sopot. Red apple on green. (POL)

215 Guide pour le service de navette dans la région newyorkaise. Publication de la Metropolitan Transportation Authority. Lignes de chemins de fer en différentes couleurs. (USA)
216 Catalogue présentant le programme de Pyramid Films pour 1974/75. (USA)
217 Couverture figurant dans une série de brochures traitant des problèmes de la transmission du son. Tête rouge. (SPA)
218 D'une brochure pour un système de chauffage régionale. Rouge et orange sur bleu. (SWI)
219 D'une brochure sur le nouveau bâtiment des PTT à Munich. Bande en couleurs vives. (GER)
220 Programme pour un festival international de la chanson. Pomme rouge sur fond vert. (POL)

215 Führer für Bahnpendler im Gebiet von New York, herausgegeben von den städtischen Verkehrsbehörden. Bahnlinien mehrfarbig. (USA)
216 Produkt-Katalog der *Pyramid*-Filme für 1974/75. (USA)
217 Umschlag einer Serie von *Eurunion*-Broschüren über Ton-Übertragungs-Probleme. (SPA)
218 Umschlag einer *Sulzer*-Broschüre über Fernheizung. Rot, orange, blau. (SWI)
219 Umschlag einer Broschüre über Münchens neuen Postbahnhof. (GER)
220 Programm-Umschlag für ein in Sopot veranstaltetes internationales Song-Festival. Roter Apfel auf grünem Hintergrund. (POL)

AGENCY / AGENTUR / AGENCE – STUDIO:

215 Studio Joan Charysyn
216 Saul Bass & Associates
217 Asterisco
218 Werbeabteilung Sulzer

217
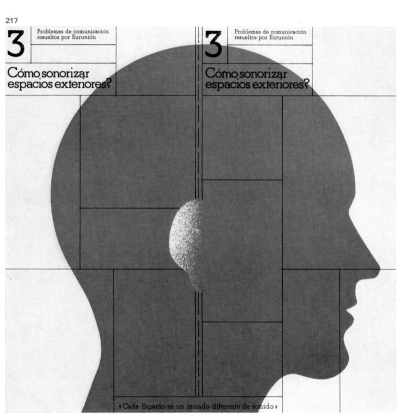

218

219

220

221

222

223

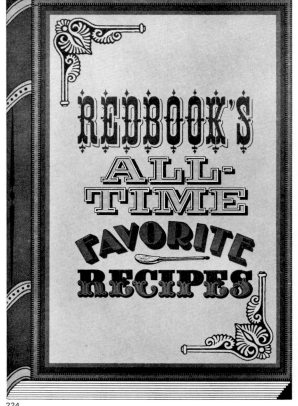

224

ART DIRECTOR / DIRECTEUR ARTISTIQUE:

221, 222 Torbjörn Lenskog
223, 224 Valerie Kleckner
225 Andrew Kner
226 Olaf Leu
227 David M. Seager

AGENCY / AGENTUR / AGENCE – STUDIO:

221, 222 Lenskog & Co. AB
223, 224 Redbook Promotion
227 Sanders & Noe, Inc.

226

225

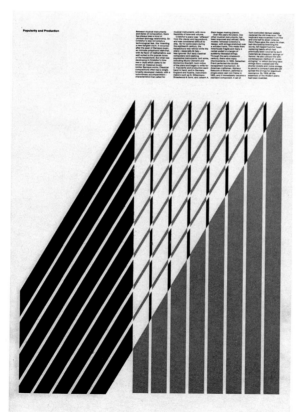

227

221, 222 Detail of the illustration and complete sheet demonstrating a new typesetting system of Typografen AB, with a text by Mark Twain. (SWE)
223, 224 Double spread and cover of a *Redbook* booklet of favourite recipes. In colour on thin board. (USA)
225 Panel of a folder promoting *The New York Times* as a vehicle of resort and travel advertising. Yellow sun, blue sky. (USA)
226 Inside of a folder for the *Zanders* art paper *Chromolux*. (In German *Luchs* is a ynx and *Zander* a pike-perch.) Full colour. (GER)
227 From a large self-promotion folder issued by Stephenson Lithograph Inc., printers. The text is about the piano. Design red and blue. (USA)

221, 222 Illustrationsausschnitt und vollständiges Blatt über ein neues typographisches System. Mit einem Text von Mark Twain. (SWE)
223, 224 Doppelseite und Umschlag einer *Redbook*-Broschüre mit populären Rezepten. Farbig auf dünnem Karton. (USA)
225 Ausschnitt aus einem Prospekt der *New York Times* als Werbemedium für Touristik und Reisen. Gelbe Sonne, blauer Himmel. (USA)
226 Innenseite eines Prospektes für das Kunstdruckpapier *Chromolux* von *Zanders*. Mehrfarbig. (GER)
227 Aus einer grossen Eigenwerbungs-Broschüre der Stephenson Lithograph Inc. mit einem Text über das Klavier. In Rot und Blau. (USA)

221, 222 Détail de l'illustration et feuille complète présentant un nouveau système de composition, avec un texte de Mark Twain. (SWE)
223, 224 Page double et couverture d'une brochure *Redbook* contenant une série de recettes. Polychrome sur carton. (USA)
225 Panneau d'un dépliant promotionnel présentant la *New York Times* en tant que moyen de publicité idéal pour les vacances et les voyages. (USA)
226 Intérieur d'un dépliant pour les papiers couchés *Chromolux* de *Zanders*. Le mot allemand *Luchs* = lynx, *Zander* = sandre.) En couleur. (GER)
227 D'un dépliant autopromotionnel, grand format, publié par une imprimerie. Le texte se réfère au piano. Dessin en rouge et bleu. (USA)

Booklets / Prospekte / Prospectus

228–230 Two full-colour panels and complete side of a self-promotion folder from a series for California Printing. They offer replicas of medals, here of the Blue Max won by von Richthofen (Fig. 228) as a pilot in the First World War, and of the Brilliant Star of Zanzibar won by Rear Admiral Harry Holdsworth Rawson (Fig. 230). (USA)
231 Cover of an index of articles published in *Fortune* in 1973. White on silver-grey. (USA)
232 Folder for loose reprints from *Fortune*. Blind-embossed name. (USA)
233 Poster-type mailer from a series for the Container Corporation of America. (USA)
234 Page from a booklet about the products of a packaging factory. (SWI)
235 Cover for a casebook of design projects issued by the National Endowment for the Arts. (USA)
236 CCA folder on a new carton-opening system. Blue and red elements rise as it is opened. (USA)

228–230 Zwei mehrfarbige Ausschnitte und vollständige Seite einer Eigenwerbungs-Broschüre. Angeboten werden Kopien von Medaillen. Hier der «Blaue Max», vom Piloten von Richthofen im Ersten Weltkrieg gewonnen (Abb. 228), sowie der «Brilliant Star of Zanzibar», gewonnen von Rear-Admiral Harry Holdsworth Rawson (Abb. 230). (USA)
231 Umschlag eines Inhaltsverzeichnisses von 1973 veröffentlichten *Fortune*-Artikeln. (USA)
232 Mappe für lose Nachdrucke aus *Fortune*. Name in Blindprägung. (USA)
233 Poster aus einer Serie der Container Corporation of America. (USA)
234 Seite aus einer Broschüre über die Produkte der Kartonnagefabrik Haass AG. Muttenz. (SWI)
235 Umschlag der Broschüre eines amerikanischen Kunstinstitutes über Design-Projekte. (USA)
236 Prospekt über ein neues Schachtel-Öffnungs-System. (USA)

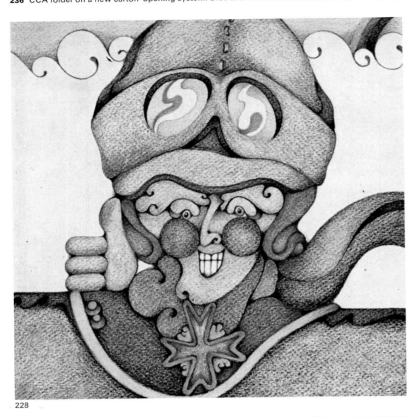

228

230

229

THE FORTUNE INDEX 1973

231

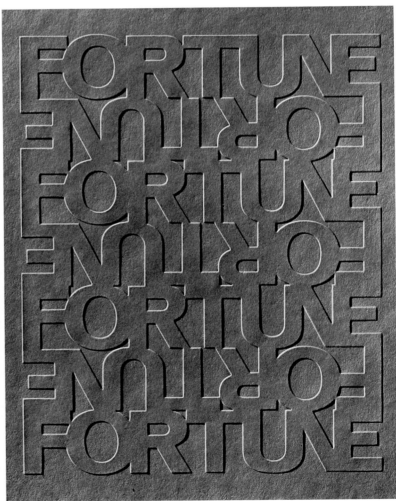

232

Booklets
Prospekte
Prospectus

228–230 Deux panneaux polychromes et page complète d'un dépliant autopromotionnel d'une imprimerie qui offre des répliques de médailles: en fig. 228 celle du «Max Bleu» que le pilote von Richthofen a reçue pendant la Première Guerre Mondiale et en fig. 230 celle de «L'étoile brillante de Zanzibar» gagnée par le contre-amiral Harry Holdsworth Rawson. (USA)
231 Couverture d'un index des articles publiés dans le magazine *Fortune* en 1973. (USA)
232 Dépliant contenant une liste des tirés à part du magazine *Fortune.* Gaufrage à sec. (USA)
233 Elément de publicité directe sous forme d'affiche. D'une nouvelle série pour CCA. (USA)
234 Page d'une brochure présentant les articles d'une entreprise de conditionnement. (SWI)
235 Couverture d'un recueil de projets de design d'une institution pour les arts. (USA)
236 Dépliant CCA au sujet d'un nouveau système pour ouvrir les cartons. (USA)

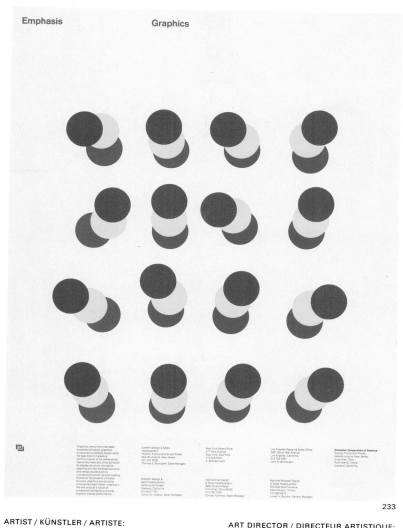

233

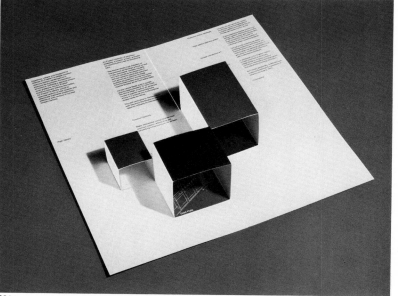

234

ARTIST / KÜNSTLER / ARTISTE:

228, 229 Mark Matsuno
230 Lars Melander
231 Richard Walukanis
232 Gilbert Lesser
233, 236 Bill Bonnell III
234 Maya Stange ASG
235 Peter Bradford

ART DIRECTOR / DIRECTEUR ARTISTIQUE:

228–230 Jack Jannes
231 Richard Walukanis
232 Gilbert Lesser
233, 236 Bill Bonnell III
235 Richard S. Wurman

AGENCY / AGENTUR / AGENCE – STUDIO:

228–230 Danzer-Fitzgerald-Sample, Inc.
233, 236 Container Corp. of America

235

236

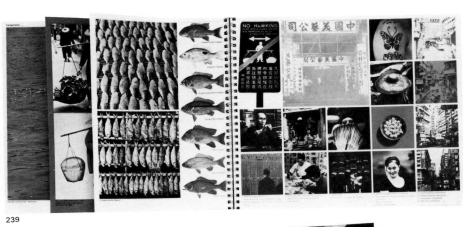

239

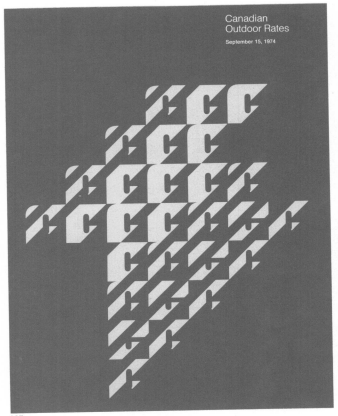

Canadian
Outdoor Rates

September 15, 1974

237

240

241

Freedom of the Press

238

ARTIST / KÜNSTLER / ARTISTE:

238 Art Goodman
239, 240 James Miho
241 Lee Kwok Wing
242, 243 Paul Giovanopoulos
244 Elwyn Art Works

DESIGNER / GESTALTER / MAQUETTISTE:

237 Fritz Gottschalk/Stuart Ash/Tiit Telmet
242, 243 Allen Weinberg
244 Elwyn Mehlman

ART DIRECTOR / DIRECTEUR ARTISTIQUE:

237 Gottschalk & Ash Ltd.
238 Bruce Dobson
239–241 Eduard Russell, Jr.
242, 243 Andrew Kner
244 Bob Kwait

242

FOOD FOR THOUGHT

243

237 Cover of a brochure issued by the Outdoor Advertising Association of Canada and indicating poster-hanging rates for the various locations. (CAN)
238 Cover of a programme for the American Civil Liberties Union, here for freedom of the press. (USA)
239–241 Double spreads and cover of an issue of *Imagination*, a self-promotion publication of Champion Papers. This issue is about Hong Kong. Spirally bound with pages of varying width, full-colour printing. (USA)
242, 243 Disposable paper apron as self-promotion for *The New York Times*, and detail of one of the lines of lettering on it. Printed in two reds. (USA)
244 Cover of a large self-promotion brochure for *Industry Week*, which professes to supply managers with the essential information, without their having to wade through all the published literature. Full colour. (USA)

237 Umschlag einer Broschüre einer kanadischen Plakataushang-Firma mit Tarifangaben über Plakataushänge im Freien an verschiedenen Orten. (CAN)
238 Umschlag eines Programmes der amerikanischen «Union für bürgerliche Freiheit». Hier für Pressefreiheit. (USA)
239–241 Doppelseiten und Umschlag einer Ausgabe von *Imagination*, Eigenwerbungs-Publikation eines Papierherstellers. Diese Nummer befasst sich mit Hong-Kong. Spiralgeheftet, mit Seiten verschiedener Breite. Mehrfarbig. (USA)
242, 243 Wegwerf-Papierschürze als Eigenwerbung der Zeitung *The New York Times*, mit Detail einer Druckzeile. In zwei verschiedenen Rottönen gedruckt. (USA)
244 Umschlag einer grossen Eigenwerbungsbroschüre für *Industry Week*, die sich rühmt, Managern alle wichtigen Informationen zu liefern, ohne dass sie die ganze entsprechende Literatur durchackern müssen. Mehrfarbig. (USA)

237 Couverture d'une brochure mise en circulation par une association pour la publicité extérieure, avec indication des prix pour l'affichage en différents endroits. (CAN)
238 Couverture d'un programme pour une organisation américaine pour la protection des droits civiques, ici se référant à la liberté de la presse. (USA)
239–241 Pages doubles et couverture d'un numéro d'*Imagination*, publication autopromotionnelle d'une papeterie. Ce numéro est consacré à Hong-Kong. Reliure à spirale avec des pages de grandeur différente. En couleurs. (USA)
242, 243 Tablier en papier en tant qu'élément de publicité autopromotionnel de la *New York Times*, et une ligne imprimée. Rouge. (USA)
244 Couverture d'une brochure grand format pour l'autopromotion d'*Industry Week* qui prétend donner aux managers toutes les informations importantes sans qu'ils ont à parcourir toutes les publications relatives. Polychrome. (USA)

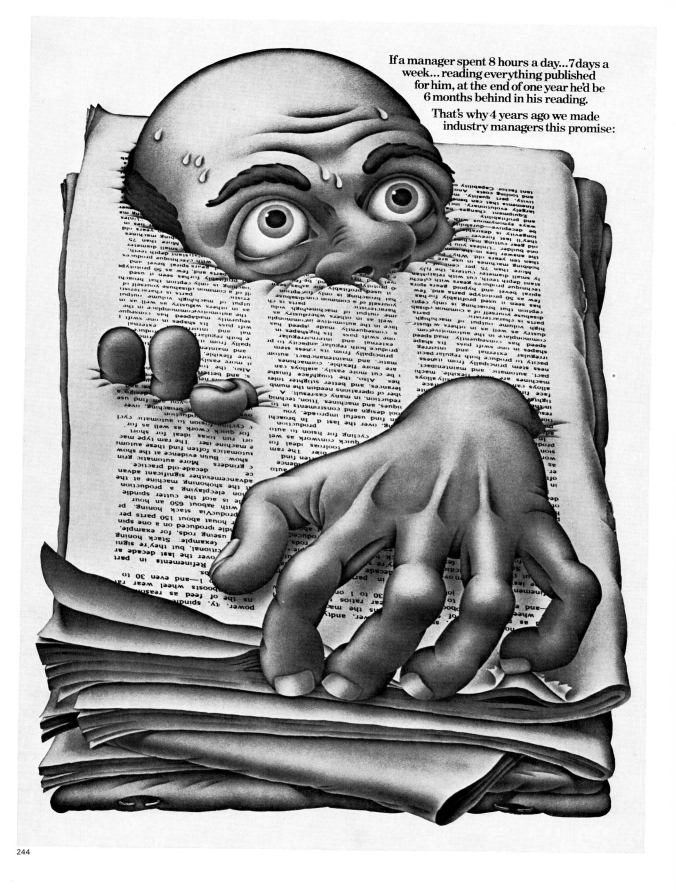

244

AGENCY / AGENTUR / AGENCE – STUDIO:

237 Gottschalk & Ash Ltd.
238 Saul Bass & Associates
239–241 Miho, Inc.
244 Griswold Eshleman

Booklets / Prospekte / Prospectus

245

246

Booklets / Prospekte / Prospectus

ARTIST / KÜNSTLER / ARTISTE:

245 Rainbow Grinder
246, 247 Norman Green
248, 249 Alan E. Cober
250, 251 István Bányai
252 Ted Andresakes

DESIGNER / GESTALTER / MAQUETTISTE:

245 Arnold Kushner
246, 247 Allen Weinberg
252 Peter Schaefer
253 Karl Lierl

ART DIRECTOR / DIRECTEUR ARTISTIQUE:

245–249, 252 Andrew Kner
250, 251 László Weber
253 Karl Lierl

AGENCY / AGENTUR / AGENCE – STUDIO:

250, 251 Hungexpo Werbeagentur
253 DPG, Inc.

247

245 Cover of a self-promotion booklet issued by *The New York Times*. (USA)
246, 247 Complete space promotion mailer addressed by *The New York Times* to department stores, and detail of the illustration (in blue, red and black). The monthly mailers list the events of the months and give a weather forecast. This one is for June, and the illustration refers to Graduation Day. (USA)
248, 249 Illustrations in colour from a space promotion brochure presenting *The New York Times* as "the national newspaper of the élite". (USA)
250, 251 Cover and page, both in colour, from a brochure about the *Hungexpo* advertising agency. Fig. 251 refers to the maze of newspapers and magazines. (HUN)
252 Space promotion mailer for *The New York Times* referring to readers with an income from stocks and bonds. (USA)
253 Spread on the subject of photocomposition from a brochure of the Frederic Ryder Company. Black and white. (USA)

245 Umschlag einer Werbebroschüre der *New York Times*. (USA)
246, 247 Werbeaussand an Warenhäuser für Inseratenraum in der *New York Times* und Ausschnitt der Illustration (blau, rot, schwarz). Diese monatlichen Aussände zählen die Ereignisse des Monats auf und enthalten eine Wettervorhersage. Dieser ist für den Monat Juni, und die Illustration bezieht sich auf den «Graduation Day». (USA)
248, 249 Farbillustrationen aus einer an Inserenten gerichteten Broschüre, in der die *New York Times* als «Nationalzeitung der Elite» vorgestellt wird. (USA)
250, 251 Umschlag und Seite, beide farbig, aus einer Broschüre über die *Hungexpo*-Werbeagentur. Abb. 251 bezieht sich auf den Wirrwarr von Zeitungen und Zeitschriften. (HUN)
252 Werbeaussand für Inseratenraum in der *New York Times*, über Leser mit Einkommen aus Aktien und Obligationen. Teppich und Sessel (teilweise) grün. (USA)
253 Doppelseite über Photosatz aus einer Broschüre der Frederic Ryder Company. Schwarzweiss. (USA)

245 Couverture d'une brochure pour la *New York Times*. (USA)
246, 247 Elément de publicité directe de la *New York Times* (adressé aux grands magasins) et détail de l'illustration (en bleu, rouge et noir). Ces publications mensuelles reprennent les événements du mois et donnent une prévision du temps. Numéro de juin avec illustration se référant au «Graduation Day». (USA)
248, 249 Illustrations en couleur figurant dans une brochure promotionnelle qui présente la *New York Times* en tant que journal national lu par l'élite. (USA)
250, 251 Couverture et page polychromes tirées d'une brochure pour une agence de publicité. La fig. 251 se réfère au grand nombre de journaux et de magazines publiés. (HUN)
252 Publicité directe pour la promotion de la *New York Times*, avec référence aux lecteurs gagnant leur argent grâce aux actions et obligations qu'ils possèdent. Tapis et siège (partiellement) en vert. (USA)
253 Page double traitant de la photo-composition. Elément de la brochure publicitaire d'une imprimerie. Noir et blanc. (USA)

248

249

250

251

252

253

ORDERING DISPLAY SIZES—There are two primary methods of getting large display types in film: 1 The "Typositor" machine on which an operator optically positions letters to form words on strips of film or photographic paper. This method can produce type from 18 point to almost 2 inches high (and larger via camera) with every nuance of spacing you may require. The operator has exact control of the spacing of each individual letter. If additional refinements are necessary, further spacing adjustments can be done by hand-stripping. 2 Set the type with an enlarger font on a machine keyboard, and then enlarge photographically ("scale up") to the desired size. The first method provides the best spacing, but it is comparable to the handsetting of foundry type, and thus relatively slow and expensive (it is charged for by the word). It is excellent where you have a few display lines—and where you don't require justification, which is not practical by this method. Therefore, where you have lengthy copy all specified to the same cap height, or require lines to be flush left and right, use the keyboard method. It is faster, costs less, and gives excellent results. Of course, it has always been possible to "scale up" in metal typography. The difference is that in film the original keyboard composition can be set tighter-than-normal, so that the enlarged type has the proper spacing for the larger size and the image will be sharper.

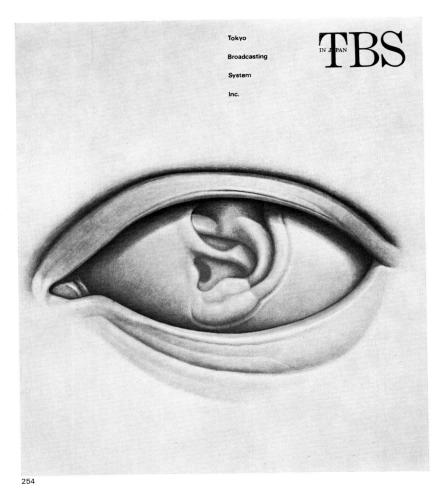

254

256

255

254 Cover (subdued colours) of a booklet about the Tokyo Broadcasting System. (JPN)
255 Drawing from a self-promotion booklet on flying saucers for The Weller Institute. (USA)
256 Page symbolizing the replacement of trees from an issue of the *Weyerhaeuser* publication *Innovations in Paper,* this time devoted to trees. Full colour. (USA)
257, 258 Double spread and detail of the colour illustration from an issue of *Innovations in Paper* about annual reports—here recommending precisely defined aims. (USA)
259 Blind-embossed announcement of an exhibition of cycles and motorcycles from Italy. (GBR)
260 Cover of a roster of the Art Directors Club of Boston. Glossy on mat black. (USA)

254 Umschlag (gedämpfte Töne) einer Broschüre über das Tokioter Radio. (JPN)
255 Zeichnung aus einer Eigenwerbungs-Broschüre über fliegende Untertassen, für das Weller-Institut, eine Werbeagentur. (USA)
256 Seite aus der *Weyerhaeuser*-Publikation *Innovations in Paper.* Farbig. (USA)
257, 258 Doppelseite und Ausschnitt der Farbillustration aus einer Ausgabe von *Innovations in Paper* über Jahresrapporte – hier mit einer Empfehlung für klar formulierte Ziele. (USA)
259 Ankündigung in Blindprägung einer Ausstellung von in Italien hergestellten Fahr- und Motorrädern. (GBR)
260 Umschlag eines Mitgliederverzeichnisses des Art Directors Club, Boston. (USA)

254 Couverture (couleurs atténuées) d'une brochure pour la radiodiffusion de Tokyo. (JPN)
255 Illustration d'une brochure autopromotionnelle consacrée aux soucoupes volantes. Publicité du Weller Institute. (USA)
256 Page avec illustration symbolisant le remplacement d'arbres. D'une publication *Weyerhaeuser (Innovations in Paper),* cette fois-ci consacrée aux arbres. En couleurs. (USA)
257, 258 Double page et détail de l'illustration polychrome tirés d'un numéro d'*Innovations in Paper* consacré aux rapports annuels – proposant ici de préciser les objets. (USA)
259 Publicité (gaufrage à sec) pour une exposition de bicyclettes et motos italiennes. (GBR)
260 Couverture d'une publication du Club des directeurs artistiques de Boston. (USA)

257

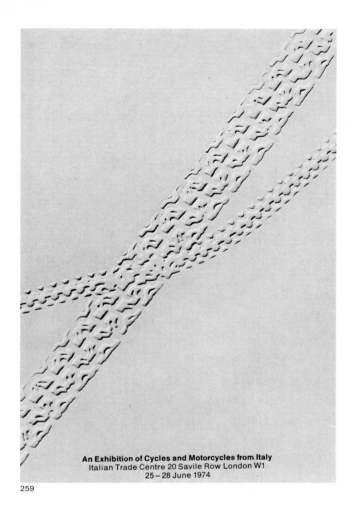

An Exhibition of Cycles and Motorcycles from Italy
Italian Trade Centre 20 Savile Row London W1
25 – 28 June 1974

259

ART
DIRECTORS
CLUB
OF BOSTON
ROSTER
1974

260

258

ARTIST / KÜNSTLER / ARTISTE:

254   Haruo Takino
255   Don Weller
256   Vicki Vebell
257, 258   Jean-Michel Folon

DESIGNER / GESTALTER:

256   Peter Sasgen/Elmer Pizzi
257, 258   Mandala
259   Brian Tattersfield
260   Robert Capriani/Linda Behar

ART DIRECTOR:

254   Sadao Sugaya
255   Don Weller
256–258   Elmer Pizzi
259   Marcelo Minale
260   Robert Capriani/Linda Behar

AGENCY / AGENTUR / AGENCE:

254   Sugaya Design Office Ltd.
255   The Weller Institute
256–258   Gray + Rogers, Inc.
259   Minale Tattersfield Provinciali Ltd.
260   Gunn Associates

261

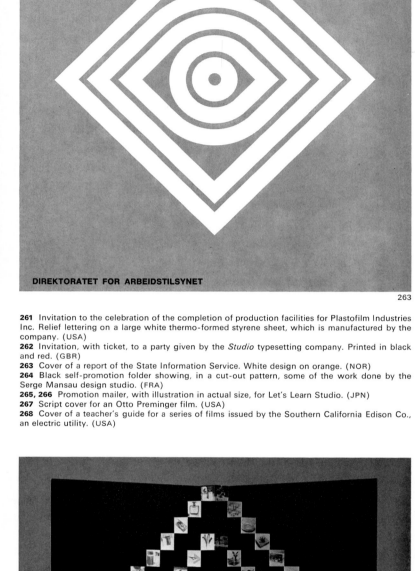

DIREKTORATET FOR ARBEIDSTILSYNET

263

ARTIST / KÜNSTLER / ARTISTE:

262 Arthur Robins
265, 266 Akiko Minura
267 Art Doodman
268 Don Weller

261 Invitation to the celebration of the completion of production facilities for Plastofilm Industries Inc. Relief lettering on a large white thermo-formed styrene sheet, which is manufactured by the company. (USA)
262 Invitation, with ticket, to a party given by the *Studio* typesetting company. Printed in black and red. (GBR)
263 Cover of a report of the State Information Service. White design on orange. (NOR)
264 Black self-promotion folder showing, in a cut-out pattern, some of the work done by the Serge Mansau design studio. (FRA)
265, 266 Promotion mailer, with illustration in actual size, for Let's Learn Studio. (JPN)
267 Script cover for an Otto Preminger film. (USA)
268 Cover of a teacher's guide for a series of films issued by the Southern California Edison Co., an electric utility. (USA)

262

264

265

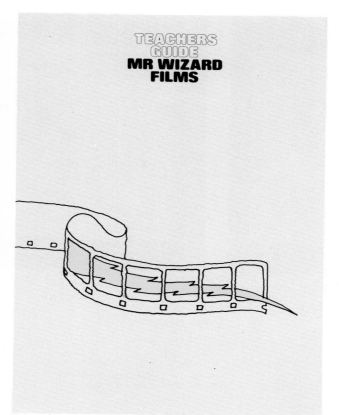

267

268

261 Einladung zur Feier anlässlich der Inbetriebnahme einer Produktionsanlage für eine amerikanische Plastikfirma. Reliefschrift auf weissem warmgeformtem Styrol, das von der Firma hergestellt wird. (USA)
262 Einladung, mit einem Billet, zu einer Party einer Setzerei. Schwarz/rot. (GBR)
263 Umschlag eines Berichtes eines staatlichen Informationsdienstes. Weiss auf Orange. (NOR)
264 Schwarzer Eigenwerbungs-Prospekt in Schattenbild-Manier, einige Arbeiten des graphischen Ateliers Serge Mansau zeigend. (FRA)
265, 266 Versandprospekt mit Illustration 1:1 für das Let's Learn Studio. (JPN)
267 Umschlag für das Drehbuch eines Otto-Preminger-Films. (USA)
268 Umschlag einer Einführung für Lehrer zu einer Reihe von Schulfilmen, die von einem Elektrizitätsunternehmen hergestellt wurden. (USA)

261 Invitation pour la fête d'inauguration de nouvelles installations de production pour matières plastiques. Typo gaufré sur une feuille grand format en styrène modelé à chaud – un produit de cette compagnie. (USA)
262 Invitation avec carte d'entrée pour un party organisé par un atelier de composition. Impression en noir et rouge. (GBR)
263 Couverture du rapport d'un service d'information. Blanc, orange. (NOR)
264 Dépliant autopromotionnel en noir présentant en forme de silhouettes quelques créations d'un studio publicitaire. (FRA)
265, 266 Publicité directe d'un studio pour l'enseignement permanent. (JPN)
267 Couverture d'un script pour un film d'Otto Preminger. (USA)
268 Couverture d'un guide de films. Publication d'une usine d'électricité adressée aux professeurs. (USA)

266

DESIGNER / GESTALTER:

261 James V. Neill
262 Christopher Keeble
263 Paul Brand
264 Serge Mansau Design
268 Dan Hanrahan

ART DIRECTOR:

261 James V. Neill
262 Christopher Keeble
263 Paul Brand
265, 266 Hayao Izuhara
267 Saul Bass/Art Goodman
268 Don Weller

AGENCY / AGENTUR / AGENCE:

261 Source, Inc.
262 Christopher Keeble
263 Statens Informasjonstien-
    este Oslo Dep.
264 Serge Mansau Design
265, 266 Let's Learn Studio
267 Saul Bass & Associates
268 The Weller Institute

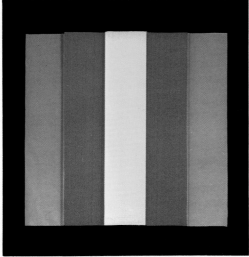

269

270

ARTIST / KÜNSTLER / ARTISTE:

272 Eva Salamoun
273 André Amstutz
274, 275 Günther Murr
276 Tom Carnase

DESIGNER / GESTALTER / MAQUETTISTE:

269, 270 Linda Powell
271 Herb Lubalin

ART DIRECTOR / DIRECTEUR ARTISTIQUE:

271 Herb Lubalin
273 Alan Goldsmith
274, 275 Günther Murr
276 Alan Peckolick

AGENCY / AGENTUR / AGENCE – STUDIO:

269, 270 Design Center Western Michigan University
271, 276 Lubalin, Smith, Carnase

271

J. Břízová /M. Klimentová/ Nové domácí kuchařka III. díl/ 1972   J. Břízová /M. Klimentová/ Nové domácí kuchařka IV. díl/1972   J. Břízová /M. Klimentová/ Nové domácí kuchařka IV. díl/1972   James Krüss / Můj pradědeček a já / 1973

272

CENTRES D'EXCURSIONS DANS LE
SUD-EST DE
L'ANGLETERRE

BTA
Publication 1974

273

KITSCH. Der manipulierte Geschmack

274

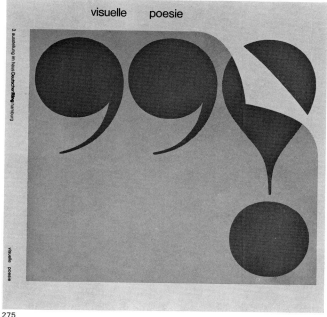

visuelle poesie

275

269, 270 Folding programme, shown closed and open, of the Michigan Inter-Arts Conference 1974. (USA)
271 Invitation to an exhibition of 20 years (= one tenth of a bicentennial) of work by Herb Lubalin. (USA)
272 Panels of a black-and-white folder-catalogue for an exhibition of work by the artist. (CSR)
273 Cover design in full colour for a tourist information booklet on South-East England, from a series. (GBR)
274, 275 Colour covers of catalogues for exhibitions staged by a life assurance company. The first is on kitsch, the second on visual poetry. Fig. 275: silver on deep orange, black title. (GER)
276 Design for a personal Christmas card for Alan Peckolick. (USA)

269, 270 Falzprogramm, offen und geschlossen gezeigt, einer Kunstkonferenz in Michigan. (USA)
271 Einladung zu einer Ausstellung, in der Herb Lubalin seine Arbeiten der letzten 20 Jahre zeigt. (USA)
272 Ausschnitte eines schwarzweissen Falzkataloges für eine Ausstellung der Arbeiten des Künstlers. (CSR)
273 Mehrfarbige Umschlagillustration einer Touristenbroschüre über Südost-England. Aus einer Serie. (GBR)
274, 275 Farbumschläge von Katalogen für Ausstellungen, die von einer Lebensversicherungsgesellschaft organisiert wurden. Abb.: 275: Silber auf dunklem Orange, schwarzer Titel. (GER)
276 Stilisierte Zahl für eine persönliche Weihnachtskarte von Alan Peckolick. (USA)

269, 270 Programme, montré fermé et ouvert, pour une conférence sur les arts. (USA)
271 Pour une retrospective de l'œuvre graphique de Herb Lubalin des 20 dernières années. (USA)
272 Panneaux d'un dépliant en noir et blanc pour une exposition des œuvres de l'artiste. (CSR)
273 Illustration de couverture d'une série pour la promotion touristique du sud-est de l'Angleterre. (GBR)
274, 275 Couvertures polychromes de catalogues d'expositions organisées par une compagnie d'assurance. La première se réfère au kitsch, la seconde à la poésie visuelle. Fig. 275: argent sur fond orange foncé. (GER)
276 Détail d'une carte de vœux d'Alan Peckolick. (USA)

Booklets / Prospekte / Prospectus

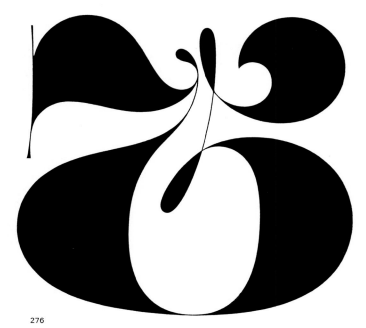

276

277

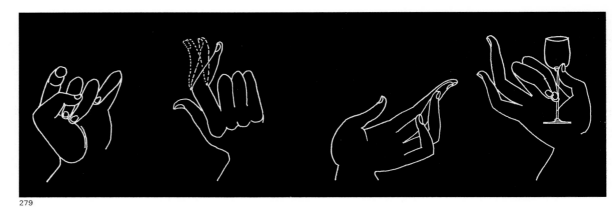

279

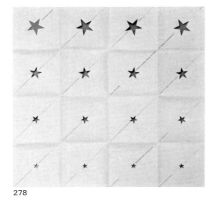

278

280

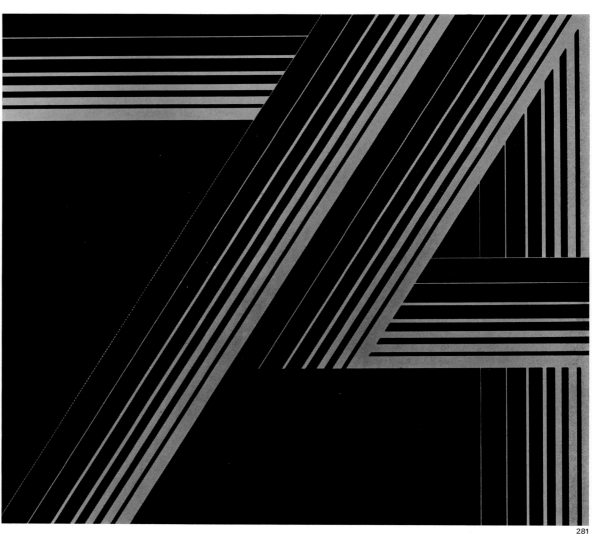

281

282

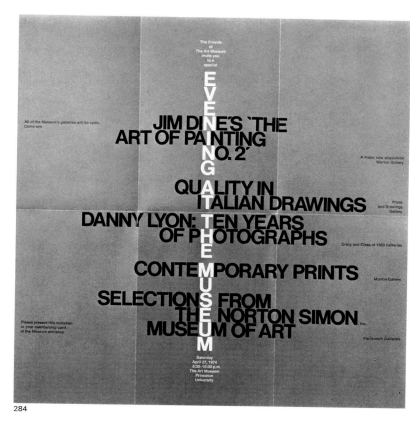

284

283

285

286

277, 278 Programme of exhibitions mounted by the Swain School of Design, shown closed and open. Each exhibition announcement appears in colour on one of the squares. (USA)
279 Invitation in sign language to the preview of an exhibition of paintings and graphics in the Luisa Muller Gallery, Brussels. (BEL)
280 Mailer announcing tours to printing and processing plants organized by the American Institute of Graphic Arts to provide "nuts-and-bolts" information. Silver and black. (USA)
281 Cover in black and silver of a booklet about galleries and exhibitions issued by the Ministry of Cultural Affairs in Quebec. (CAN)
282 Invitation to an exhibition of the work of Celestino Piatti. Pale mauve owl. (SWI)
283 Invitation to an exhibition of work by a Constructivist in Zurich. Yellow ground. (SWI)
284 Invitation of the Princeton Art Museum to various exhibitions. Two greens, white. (USA)
285 Invitation to an exhibition (Magic of Paper) in the Zurich Museum of Applied Art. (SWI)
286 Invitation to an exhibition of book bindings and paper objects by Kurt Londenberg. (GER)

277, 278 Programm von Ausstellungen, organisiert von der Swain School of Design, offen und geschlossen gezeigt. Jede Ausstellung erscheint in Farbe in einem der Quadrate. (BEL)
279 Einladung in Zeichensprache zur Vernissage einer Ausstellung von Gemälden und Graphik in der Luisa Muller Galerie, Brüssel. (BEL)
280 Werbeaussand zur Ankündigung von Fahrten zu Druckereien und graphischen Anstalten, organisiert vom American Institute of Graphic Arts. Silber auf Schwarz. (USA)
281 Umschlag in Schwarz und Silber einer Broschüre über Galerien und Ausstellungen, herausgegeben vom Kulturministerium in Quebec. (CAN)
282 Einladung zu einer Ausstellung der Werke von Celestino Piatti. Eule lila. (SWI)
283 Einladung zu einer Ausstellung der Werke eines Konstruktivisten in Zürich. (SWI)
284 Einladung des Kunstmuseums von Princeton zu verschiedenen Ausstellungen. (USA)
285 Einladung zu einer Ausstellung (*Magie des Papiers*) im Kunstgewerbemuseum Zürich. (SWI)
286 Einladung zu einer Ausstellung von Einbänden und Papier-Objekten von Kurt Londenberg. (GER)

277, 278 Programme (fermé et ouvert) pour des expositions présentées par la Swain School of Design. Chaque exposition est annoncée en couleurs dans l'un des carrés. (USA)
279 Invitation au vernissage d'une exposition d'œuvres peintes et graphiques dans la Galerie Louisa Muller à Bruxelles. (BEL)
280 Publicité directe pour des visites d'imprimeries et d'ateliers de lithographies, organisées par l'American Institute of Graphic Arts. Argent et noir. (USA)
281 Couverture (noir et argent) d'une brochure contenant une liste des galeries et expositions à Québec. Publication du Ministère des affaires culturelles du Québec. (CAN)
282 Invitation pour une exposition de Celestino Piatti. Hibou en lilas pâle. (SWI)
283 Invitation pour une exposition des œuvres d'un constructiviste, à Zurich. Jaune. (SWI)
284 Invitation pour différentes expositions d'un musée. Deux verts et blanc. (USA)
285 Pour une exposition (Magie du papier) au Musée des arts appliqués de Zurich. (SWI)
286 Pour une exposition d'objets en papier et de reliures conçus par Kurt Londenberg. (GER)

Booklets / Prospekte / Prospectus

287

288

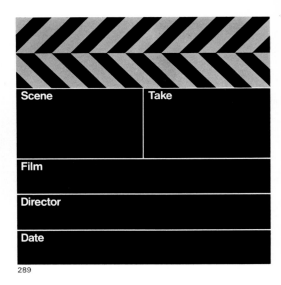

289

290

291

ARTIST / KÜNSTLER / ARTISTE:

287, 288 Kristian Roth
289 Bob Ross
290, 291 Werner Jeker
292 John Dolby

ART DIRECTOR / DIRECTEUR ARTISTIQUE:

287, 288 Kristian Roth
289 Bob Ross
290, 291 Freddy Huguenin

AGENCY / AGENTUR / AGENCE – STUDIO:

289 Ross Design
290, 291 Atelier Huguenin
292 BBDM, Inc.

287, 288 Two sides of an invitation to an exhibition of Frankfurt graphics of the 70's in the Kommunale Galerie in Frankfurt. Blue and black. (GER)
289 Back cover in black and orange of a call for entries for a film award of the Society for Encouragement of Contemporary Art. (USA)
290, 291 Artwork and complete call for entries for a *Kodak Ektapan* photographic competition. (SWI)
292 Cover in actual size of a folder inviting recipients to call at the booth of the Amoco Chemicals Corporation at the Paint Show in Atlanta. (USA)

Booklets / Prospekte / Prospectus

292

287, 288 Zwei Seiten einer Einladung zu einer Ausstellung von Frankfurter Graphik der 70er Jahre in der Kommunale Galerie, Frankfurt. Blau und Schwarz. (GER)
289 Vierte Umschlagseite in Schwarz und Orange einer Einladung zur Unterbreitung von Arbeiten für den Filmwettbewerb einer Kunstvereinigung. (USA)
290, 291 Detail und vollständige Einladung zur Unterbreitung von Arbeiten für einen *Kodak-Ektapan*-Photowettbewerb. (SWI)
292 Umschlag im Format 1:1 einer Broschüre, die zum Besuch des Standes der Amoco Chemicals Corp. an der Anstrichfarben-Ausstellung in Atlanta einlädt. (USA)

287, 288 Recto et verso d'une invitation pour une exposition d'art graphique des années 70 dans la Kommunale Galerie à Francfort. Bleu et noir. (GER)
289 Verso d'une invitation pour une compétition cinématographique organisée par une société pour l'encouragement des arts contemporains. Noir et orange. (USA)
290, 291 Illustration et invitation complète pour une compétition de photographie, organisée par *Kodak*. (USA)
292 Invitation (recto en grandeur originale) d'une entreprise de l'industrie chimique pour une visite du stand à l'exposition des colorants à Atlanta. (USA)

293

294

293 Detail in actual size of a Christmas card for the *Studio* type-setting company. (GBR)
294 Christmas card which the Post Office sends to children who write to Father Christmas. (GBR)
295 Christmas card for Scad Promotions. "Music" red/green. (USA)
296 Large New Year's greeting sent to customers by a photoengraver. Full colour. (SWI)
297, 298 New Year's greeting cards for *Fiat* tractors and trucks, which are shown in the form of colourful confections. (ITA)

293 Ausschnitt im Massstab 1:1 einer Weihnachtskarte für eine Setzerei. (GBR)
294 Weihnachtskarte, welche die englische Post an alle Kinder versendet, die an den Weihnachtsmann schreiben. (GBR)
295 Weihnachtskarte der «Scad Promotions». Rot und Grün. (USA)
296 Grosse Weihnachtskarte einer Klischieranstalt. Mehrfarbig. (SWI)
297, 298 Neujahrskarten von *Fiat*. Traktoren und Lastwagen werden in Form von bunten Confiseriewaren dargestellt. (ITA)

293 Détail (grandeur originale) d'une carte de vœux, adressée aux clients d'un atelier de composition. (GBR)
294 Carte de vœux de Noël que les PTT envoient aux enfants qui adressent une lettre au Père Noël. (GBR)
295 Carte de vœux d'une agence publicitaire. Rouge/vert. (USA)
296 Carte de vœux d'un photolithographe. Polychrome. (SWI)
297, 298 Cartes de vœux de la section des tracteurs et camions de *Fiat*. Représentations en forme de pâtisserie en couleurs vives. (ITA)

AGENCY / AGENTUR:

293 Christopher Keeble
295 Ancona/Gianakos, Inc.
296 Studio A. Crivelli
297, 298 Armin Vogt Partner

ARTIST / KÜNSTLER:

293 Arthur Robins
294 André Amstutz
295 Stephen Ancona
296 Adriano Crivelli
297, 298 Armin Vogt

ART DIRECTOR:

293 Christopher Keeble
294 Norman Farrah
295 Stan Anton/Cal Donly
296 Adriano Crivelli
297, 298 Armin Vogt

295

296

297

298

Booklets
Prospekte
Prospectus

ARTIST / KÜNSTLER / ARTISTE:

299 Hubert Hilscher
300, 301 Peter Adam
302 Pete Traynor
303 Loriot
304, 305 Lois Ehlert

ART DIRECTOR / DIRECTEUR ARTISTIQUE:

299 Hubert Hilscher
300, 301 Stuart Ash
302 Pete Traynor
304, 305 Ray Dennis

AGENCY / AGENTUR / AGENCE – STUDIO:

300, 301 Gottschalk & Ash Ltd.
302 Ashton-Worthington, Inc.
304, 305 E. F. Schmidt Company

299

300

301

302

Booklets / Prospekte / Prospectus

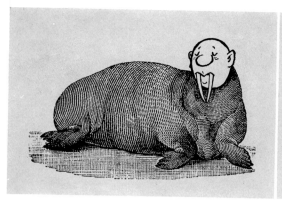

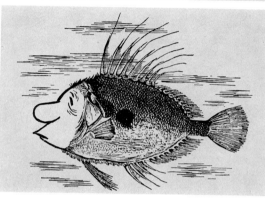

303

Price 35c

MILWAUKEE COUNTY ZOO FOR CHILDREN

304

GOAT TOWERS

Our adult goats love to climb up
to the platform, sun themselves,
and get a good look at
the entire Children's Zoo.
You can get the same view,
by climbing up to
The Lookout Tower.

305

299 Large polychrome New Year's card from the Polish art review *Projekt*. (POL)
300, 301 Cover and double spread from a booklet about Elliot Lake Centre, a new type of educational community. Two greens, blue and lilac. (CAN)
302 Postcard (in colour) enclosed with an annual report of the Institute of Scrap Iron and Steel, Inc., in the form of a tape cassette. The card shows ugly scrap disposal (left) and the landscape as it should look (right). (USA)
303 Concertina-type card from *Diogenes*, publishers, illustrating a few New Year's resolutions: to watch one's weight; to eat more fruit; to develop a thick skin; not to neglect things of the intellect; to keep cool; to speak one's mind to the boss. Black and white. (SWI)
304, 305 Cover and double spread (goats) from a booklet about the Milwaukee County Zoo, which has a special section for children. Animals in bright colours. (USA)

299 Grosse, mehrfarbige Neujahrskarte der polnischen Kunstzeitschrift *Projekt*. (POL)
300, 301 Umschlag und Doppelseite einer Broschüre über Elliott Lake Centre, eine neue Art von Lern-Schulgemeinschaft. Verschiedene Grüntöne, Blau und Lila. (CAN)
302 Postkarte (farbig) als Beilage zum Jahresbericht einer Schrottverwertungs-Organisation in Form einerTonbandkassette. Die Karte zeigt (links) hässliche Umweltverschmutzung und (rechts) die Landschaft, wie sie aussehen sollte. (USA)
303 Karte in Leporello-Form des *Diogenes*-Verlages mit guten Neujahrsvorsätzen: auf sein Gewicht zu achten; mehr Früchte zu essen; eine dicke Haut zu entwickeln; Intellektuelles nicht zu vernachlässigen; kühl zu bleiben; dem Chef seine Meinung zu sagen. Schwarzweiss. (SWI)
304, 305 Umschlag und Doppelseite aus einer Broschüre über den Milwaukee County Zoo, der über eine spezielle «Kinderzoo-Abteilung» verfügt. Tiere in lebhaften Farben. (USA)

299 Carte de vœux grand format (en couleur) de la revue d'art polonais, *Projekt*. (POL)
300, 301 Couverture et page double d'une brochure pour un nouveau centre d'enseignement, fonctionnant d'après le principe d'une communauté éducative. Vert, bleu et lilas. (CAN)
302 Carte postale polychrome jointe au rapport annuel d'une aciérie. Elle se réfère à la pollution de l'environnement (à gauche) et aux belles régions d'autrefois (à droite). (USA)
303 Carte en accordéon de la maison d'édition *Diogenes* avec allusions à quelques résolutions à prendre lors du Nouvel An; soient: de contrôler son poids, de manger plus de fruits, de développer une peau dure, de ne pas négliger tout ce qui concerne l'intellecte, de garder son sang-froid et d'avoir son franc parler avec le chef. Noir et blanc. (SWI)
304, 305 Couverture et page double d'une brochure sur le jardin zoologique de Milwaukee County, dont une région est réservée aux enfants. Animaux en couleurs vives. (USA)

308

306

309

311

307

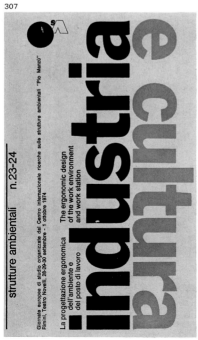

310

312

ARTIST / KÜNSTLER / ARTISTE:

306 Hans Schleger & Associates
307 Gerhard Forster
309 Paul Schuster
310 Stan Malcolm
311 Herb Lubalin
315 Stephen Osborn

DESIGNER / GESTALTER / MAQUETTISTE:

303 Bruce Naftel
310 John Milligan
312 Herman & Lees Assoc.
313 Jean Robert
314 Michael Baviera

ART DIRECTOR:

306 Hans Schleger
307 Gerardo Filiberto Dasi
309 Paul Schuster
310 John Milligan
311 Herb Lubalin
312 John W. Lees
313 Colin Forbes
314 Michael Baviera
315 Stephen Osborn

AGENCY / AGENTUR / AGENCE – STUDIO:

306 Hans Schleger & Assoc.
307 Centro internazionale ricerche sulle strutture ambientali
308 Western Michigan University, Design Center
309 Paul Schuster
311 Lubalin, Smith, Carnase
312 Herman & Lees Assoc.
313 Pentagram Design Partnership Ltd.
314 M. & M. Baviera
315 Stephen Osborn & Assoc., Inc.

313

315

314

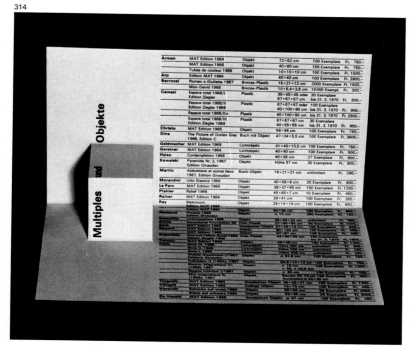

306 Preliminary programme folder for the 1975 Edinburgh Festival. Blue and black. (GBR)
307 Cover (black and red on yellow) for the proceedings of a conference on ergonomics. (ITA)
308 Announcement of an exhibition mounted by the Swain School of Design. (USA)
309 Programme of flower shows and concerts in the Palmengarten, Frankfurt. Red ground. (GER)
310 Booklet cover for Young Audiences of Massachusetts (music for children). Blue clef. (USA)
311 Announcement of the opening of a new studio by a photographer. Green and ochre. (USA)
312 Cover of a booklet about the human relations centre *Cumbres*. (USA)
313 Pamphlet holder produced by PAC Limited for the UN in World Population Year 1974. (GBR)
314 Catalogue of an exhibition of multiples and objects in the Galerie Renée Ziegler, Zürich. (SWI)
315 Cover of a booklet about the Stanford Alumni Association. Full colour. (USA)

306 Vorprogramm-Prospekt für das Edinburgh-Festival 1975. Blau und schwarz. (GBR)
307 Umschlag (Schwarz und Rot auf Gelb) für Berichte über eine Konferenz. (ITA)
308 Ankündigung einer Ausstellung der Swain School of Design. (USA)
309 Programm einer Blumenschau und Konzerten im Palmengarten, Frankfurt. (GER)
310 Umschlag einer Broschüre über Musik für Kinder. Blauer Notenschlüssel. (USA)
311 Ankündigung der Eröffnung eines neuen Photostudios. Grün und Ocker. (USA)
312 Umschlag einer Broschüre über das «Zentrum für menschliche Beziehungen *Cumbres*». (USA)
313 Prospekthalter der PAC Ltd. für die UN im Weltbevölkerungsjahr 1974. (GBR)
314 Katalog einer Ausstellung von Multiples und Objekten in der Galerie R. Ziegler, Zürich. (SWI)
315 Umschlag einer Broschüre über eine Altherren-Vereinigung. Farbig. (USA)

306 Programme préliminaire pour le festival d'Edinbourg 1975. Bleu et noir. (GBR)
307 Couverture des travaux d'une conférence sur l'ergonomie. En couleurs. (ITA)
308 Publicité pour une exposition présentée par la Swain School of Design. (USA)
309 Programme pour une exposition de fleurs et pour des concerts à Francfort. (GER)
310 Couverture d'une brochure au sujet de concerts pour enfants. Clef bleue. (USA)
311 Elément de publicité pour annoncer l'ouverture d'un nouveau studio de photographie. (USA)
312 Couverture d'une brochure pour un centre de relations humaines. (USA)
313 Porte-prospectus de PAC fabriqué pour l'ONU (Année de la population mondiale). (GBR)
314 Catalogue pour une exposition de multiples et d'objets dans une galerie de Zurich. (SWI)
315 Couverture d'une brochure pour une association d'anciens étudiants de Stanford. (USA)

316

Strategic Planning

318

ARTIST / KÜNSTLER / ARTISTE:

316 Robert Miles Runyan and Assoc.
317 Seymour Chwast
318, 319 William D. Peebles
320 Gilbert Lesser
321 Nancy C. Pokross
322, 323 Bradford Herzog
324, 325 Atelier Ade

DESIGNER / GESTALTER / MAQUETTISTE:

317 Mo Leibowitz

ART DIRECTOR / DIRECTEUR ARTISTIQUE:

318, 319 Stephen D. Chapman
320 Gilbert Lesser
321 Nancy C. Pokross
322, 323 Harold Pattek
324, 325 Albrecht Ade

AGENCY / AGENTUR / AGENCE – STUDIO:

318, 319 Westinghouse Design Center
320 Gilbert Lesser Design
321 M.I.T. Office of Publications
322, 323 Harold Pattek Design

**Booklets
Prospekte
Prospectus**

317

322

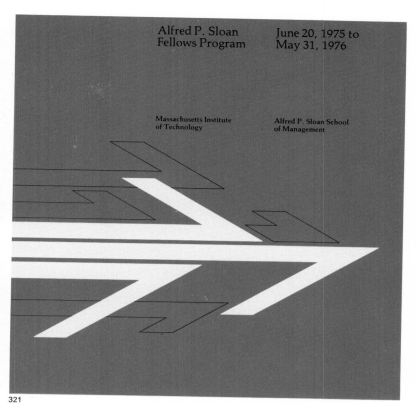

319

Alfred P. Sloan
Fellows Program

June 20, 1975 to
May 31, 1976

Massachusetts Institute
of Technology

Alfred P. Sloan School
of Management

321

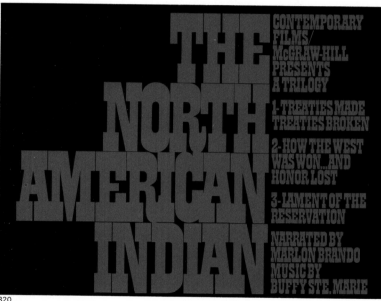

320

316 Covers of catalogues of BFA educational films. Grey-brown and red. (USA)
317 Woodcut (Earl Scruggs) for a broadside on blue-grass music designed by Mo Leibowitz. (USA)
318, 319 Cover of a programme for an engineering and manufacturing symposium, and detail of the design element symbolizing strategic planning. (USA)
320 Promotion brochure on a film trilogy about the North American Indian. (USA)
321 Cover of a booklet about a management study course at the MIT. (USA)
322, 323 Cover and spread from a quarterly brochure issued by Simmons College, Boston. (USA)
324, 325 Cover and double spread from the catalogue of a careers exhibition in Düsseldorf. (GER)

316 Umschlag von Katalogen für BFA-Lehr-Schulfilme. Graubraun und rot. (USA)
317 Holzschnitt (Earl Scruggs) für ein Flugblatt von Mo Leibowitz über Country-Musik. (USA)
318, 319 Umschlag eines Programmes für ein Ingenieur- und Produktions-Symposium und Detail der Graphik, die strategisches Planen symbolisiert. (USA)
320 Werbebroschüre für eine Filmtrilogie über den nordamerikanischen Indianer. (USA)
321 Umschlag einer Broschüre über Management-Studienkurse. (USA)
322, 323 Umschlag und Doppelseite aus der Broschüre einer Bostoner Hochschule. (USA)
324, 325 Umschlag und Doppelseite aus dem Katalog einer Ausstellung in Düsseldorf über berufliche Möglichkeiten. (GER)

316 Couverture d'un catalogue pour des films éducatifs. Brun gris et rouge. (USA)
317 Feuille imprimée pour une présentation de musique texane conçue par Mo Leibowitz. Gravure sur bois (Earl Scruggs). (USA)
318, 319 Couverture d'un programme pour un colloque sur le génie civil et la production industrielle et détail de l'illustration se référant aux projets stratégiques. (USA)
320 Brochure pour une trilogie cinématographique sur les indiens de l'Amérique du Nord. (USA)
321 Couverture d'une brochure pour un cours d'étude de management au MIT. (USA)
322, 323 Couverture et page double d'une brochure trimestrielle du Simmons College. (USA)
324, 325 Couverture et page d'un catalogue pour une exposition sur les professions. (GER)

324   325

323

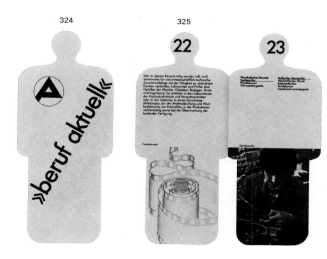

326

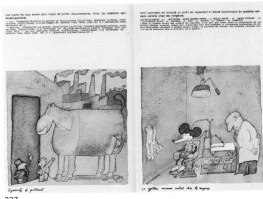

327

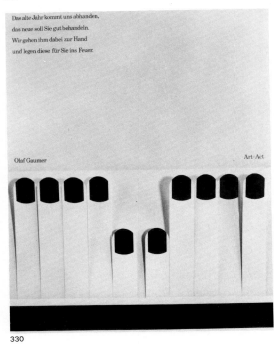

Das alte Jahr kommt uns abhanden,
das neue soll Sie gut behandeln.
Wir gehen ihm dabei zur Hand
und legen diese für Sie ins Feuer.

Olaf Gaumer   Art·Act

330

331

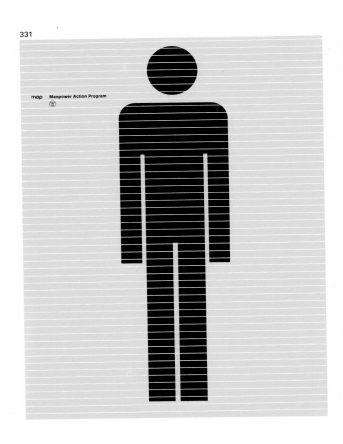

map Manpower Action Program

332

328

329

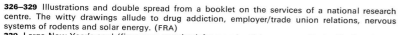

326–329 Illustrations and double spread from a booklet on the services of a national research centre. The witty drawings allude to drug addiction, employer/trade union relations, nervous systems of rodents and solar energy. (FRA)
330 Large New Year's card (fingers as matches) for an advertising agency. Red nails. (GER)
331 Cover of a *Westinghouse* booklet on a programme of personnel evaluation. (USA)
332 Point-of-sale showcard for *Calanda* beer from the Grisons, where the ibex still lives. (SWI)
333 Cover of an MIT booklet on nuclear engineering studies. Red on black on blue. (USA)
334 Panel of a folder with tips and information issued by a dry-cleaning firm. Green frog. (GER)

326–329 Illustration und Doppelseite aus einer Broschüre über die Dienste eines nationalen Forschungszentrums. Die witzigen Zeichnungen beziehen sich auf Drogensucht, Beziehungen Arbeitgeber/Gewerkschaften, das Nervensystem der Nager, die Sonnenenergie. (FRA)
330 Grosse Neujahrskarte (Finger als Zündhölzer) einer Werbeagentur. Rote Nägel. (GER)

331 Umschlag einer *Westinghouse*-Broschüre über ein Personal-Beurteilungs-Programm. (USA)
332 Ladensteller für *Calanda*-Bier aus Graubünden, wo der Steinbock noch lebt. (SWI)
333 Umschlag einer MIT-Broschüre über Studienkurse in Kernspaltungstechnologie. (USA)
334 Ausschnitt aus einem Prospekt der chemischen Reinigungsanstalt *Röver*. (GER)

326–329 Illustration et page double d'une brochure du Centre National de la Recherche Scientifique. Les illustrations piquantes se réfèrent à l'abus des drogues, aux relations employé/syndicat, au système nerveux des rongeurs et à l'énergie solaire. (FRA)
330 Grande carte de vœux (doigts-alumettes) d'une agence publicitaire. Ongles rouges. (GER)
331 Couverture d'une brochure sur les critères de qualification des employés. (USA)
332 Pancarte pour la bière *Calanda* des Grisons, où il existe encore des bouquetins. (SWI)
333 Couverture d'une brochure MIT sur les études dans le domaine du génie atomique. (USA)
334 D'un dépliant d'information, publié par un établissement de nettoyage à sec. (GER)

333

Nuclear Engineering at MIT

334

Umsatz nach dem Barometer

Saisonale Abhängigkeit der Chemischreinigung

Auch der bisherige Geschäftsverlauf dieses Jahres hat bewiesen, daß die Chemischreinigung wie kaum eine andere Branche vom Wetter abhängig ist. Regnet es z. B. kurz vor Ostern, warten die Mitarbeiterinnen und Mitarbeiter in den Röver-Filialen und Ladenbetrieben vergeblich auf den sonst gewohnten Ansturm. Denn die Frühlingskleidung bleibt im Schrank.
Zu den Problemen, die der Wettergott den Chemischreinigern stellt, kommt ein weiteres hinzu: Erst ein Teil der Verbraucher – wenn auch ein stetig wachsender – hat erkannt, daß Chemischreinigung nichts anderes bedeutet als eine regelmäßige Pflege, wie sie jeder Wäsche und Kleidung zusteht. Wer legt schon benutzte Bettwäsche ungewaschen in den Schrank zurück, ganz zu schweigen von einem getragenen Hemd. Für jede Hausfrau ist es selbstverständlich, daß das, was von den Familienmitgliedern in den Wäschebeutel gesteckt wird, erst wäscht und bügelt, bevor es wieder in der Truhe oder im Kleiderschrank verschwindet. Abgesehen davon, daß dieses Verfahren weitaus praktischer ist, weil man den Überblick über die Kleidungsstücke behält, die man wieder tragen kann, entspricht es den normalen Anforderungen an die Hygiene.
Doch Kleidung, die zu ihrer Pflege der Chemischreinigung bedarf, wird allzuoft weitaus liebloser behandelt. Der Wintermantel verschwindet bei der ersten Frühlingssonne im Schrank, weil er nicht mehr gebraucht wird. Im nächsten Spätherbst wird man dann weitersehen.
Jetzt, nachdem die Urlaubszeit zu Ende geht, und die Sommerbekleidung aus dem Verkehr gezogen ist, stellt sich die gleiche Gewissensfrage: Gereinigt oder ungereinigt in den Schrank?
Für die Reinigung sprechen neben der Forderung nach zeitgemäßer Hygiene viele praktische Gründe. So ist erwiesen, daß Kleidung, die regelmäßig gereinigt wird, eine längere Lebensdauer hat. Denn Staub- und Schmutzpartikel, die sich im Stoff festsetzen, schädigen auf Dauer das Gewebe.
Außerdem sind Flecken grundsätzlich dann am leichtesten zu entfernen, wenn sie so frühzeitig wie möglich vom Detachur-Fachmann behandelt werden. Und schließlich, im nächsten Frühjahr wird die Chemischreinigung sowieso fällig. Ob zu höheren oder niedrigeren Preisen, das kann sich jeder angesichts der anhaltenden allgemeinen Preisentwicklung ausmalen.
Bisher müssen sich die Chemischreiniger in der Bundesrepublik – anders als in den USA – alljährlich auf die saisonalen Spitzen einstellen. Eine grundlegende Änderung des Verbraucherverhaltens würde für sie bedeuten, daß ihre Kapazitäten weitaus besser ausgelastet wären – und dies käme wiederum dem Verbraucher zugute.

**Booklets
Prospekte
Prospectus**

335

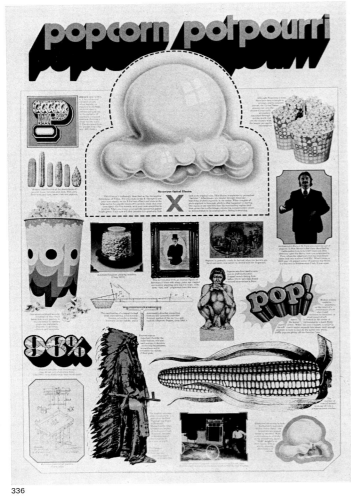

336

338

337

ARTIST / KÜNSTLER / ARTISTE:

335 Fritz Gottschalk
336 Al Navarre Jr./Robert Packo (Photo)
337 Gad Ullman
338–340 Milton Glaser
341 John Nowland

DESIGNER / GESTALTER / MAQUETTISTE:

342 Galerie Art in Progress

ART DIRECTOR / DIRECTEUR ARTISTIQUE:

336 Al Navarre Jr.
337 Gad Ullman
338–340 David Ashton
341 John Nowland

AGENCY / AGENTUR / AGENCE – STUDIO:

335 Gottschalk + Ash Ltd.
338–340 Ashton-Worthington
341 John Nowland, Graphic Design

340

335 Concertina-type folder about a subscription campaign of the Ecole Polytechnique de Montréal. (CAN)
336 Point-of-sale card for the Lily Division of Owens-Illinois with interesting facts about popcorn. (USA)
337 Cover of a small brochure addressed to Soviet immigrants in Israel. Red and black on green. (ISR)
338–340 Two pages and a double spread in black and umber from a booklet about a women's educational centre at Barnard College, New York. (USA)
341 One side of the official opening programme of the Adelaide Festival Centre. Bright colours. (AUL)
342 Invitation to the preview of an exhibition of works and projects by Christo. The black perforated cover can be torn off to reveal an orange card. (SWI)

335 Leporello-Prospekt über eine Sammlung für die Ecole Polytechnique de Montréal. (CAN)
336 Ladensteller eines Popcorn-Fabrikanten mit interessanten Tatsachen über Popcorn. (USA)
337 Umschlag einer kleinen Broschüre für sowjetische Einwanderer in Israel. Rot, Schwarz auf Grün. (ISR)
338–340 Zwei Seiten und eine Doppelseite in Schwarz und Umbra aus einer Broschüre über ein Ausbildungszentrum für Frauen am Barnard College, New York. (USA)
341 Seite des offiziellen Eröffnungsprogrammes für eine Festhalle in Adelaide. Bunte Farben. (AUL)
342 Einladung zur Vernissage einer Ausstellung von Werken und Projekten des Künstlers Christo. Das Deckblatt in Schwarz kann weggerissen werden; darunter befindet sich eine orange Karte. (SWI)

335 Dépliant en accordéon d'une campagne publicitaire pour l'Ecole Polytechnique de Montréal. (CAN)
336 Carte publicitaire d'une entreprise américaine avec des faits concernant le popcorn. (USA)
337 Couverture d'une petite brochure adressée aux immigrants soviétiques s'établissant en Israël. (ISR)
338–340 Deux pages et page double d'une brochure au sujet d'un centre d'études pour femmes. Noir et terre d'ombre. (USA)
341 Page du programme pour l'inauguration officielle de l'Adelaide Festival Centre. Couleurs vives. (AUL)
342 Invitation au vernissage d'une exposition des œuvres et projets de Christo. Une carte orange apparaît si on enlève la couverture noire perforée. (SWI)

339

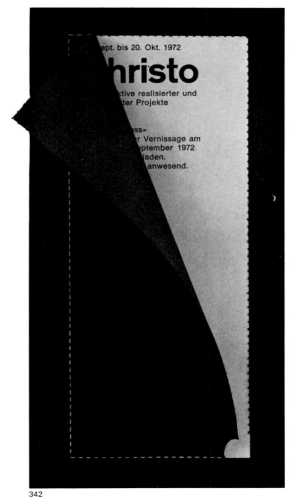

342

341

3

Magazine Covers
Trade Magazines
Magazine Illustrations
Newspaper Illustrations
Annual Reports
House Organs
Book Covers

Zeitschriften-Umschläge
Fachzeitschriften
Zeitschriften-Illustrationen
Zeitungs-Illustrationen
Jahresberichte
Hauszeitschriften
Buchumschläge

Couvertures de périodiques
Revues professionnelles
Illustrations de périodiques
Illustrations de journaux
Rapports annuels
Journaux d'entreprises
Couvertures de livres

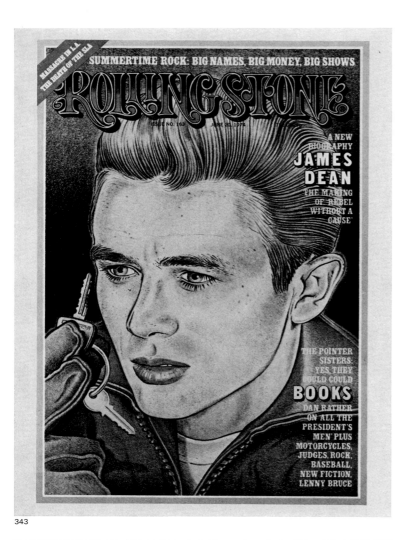

343

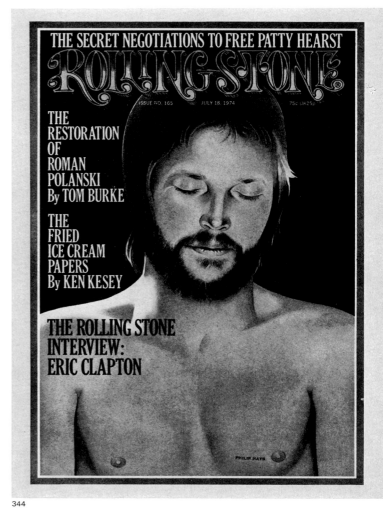

344

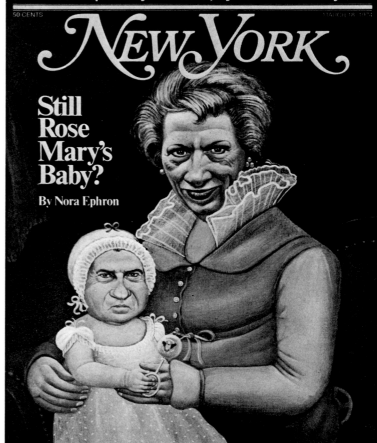

345

346

ARTIST / KÜNSTLER / ARTISTE:

343 John Van Hamersveld
344 Philip Hays
345 Wendell Minor
346 Richard Hess
347 Seymour Chwast

DESIGNER / GESTALTER / MAQUETTISTE:

343 Mike Salisbury
344 Lloyd Ziff
346, 347 Milton Glaser

343, 344 Covers of the magazine *Rolling Stone* featuring James Dean and the rock star Eric Clapton. Full colour. (USA)
345 Cover of *cue*, an entertainment guide to the New York area. Three-dimensional painted figure (USA)
346, 347 Covers of *New York* magazine. The issues contain features on Richard Nixon's backers and on fall events—here interpreted as The Fall. Full colour. (USA)

343, 344 Titelblätter der Zeitschrift *Rolling Stone* mit Jeames Dean und dem Rock-Star Eric Clapton. Mehrfarbig. (USA)
345 Titelblatt von *cue*, einem Unterhaltungs-führer für New York. Dreidimensionale, gemalte Figur. (USA)
346, 347 Titelblätter der Zeitschrift *New York.* Die Ausgaben enthalten Artikel über Nixon-Anhänger und Herbstereignisse (Wortspiel um den Ausdruck «fall»: «Herbst» oder «Fall»). (USA)

343, 344 Couvertures du magazine *Rolling Stone* contenant des articles sur James Dean et Eric Clapton, l'un des stars de la musique rock. En couleurs. (USA)
345 Couverture de *cue*, un guide des spectacles et divertissements pour la région new-yorkaise. Figure tridimensionnelle. (USA)
346, 347 Couvertures du magazine *New York* se référant à des articles sur les partisans de Richard Nixon et sur les événements de l'automne. Jeu de mots sur la signification du mot anglais «fall», qui veut dire «automne», aussi bien que «chute». (USA)

ART DIRECTOR / DIRECTEUR ARTISTIQUE:

343, 344 Mike Salisbury
345 Kent Salisbury
346, 347 Walter Bernard/Milton Glaser

AGENCY / AGENTUR / AGENCE – STUDIO:

345 Salisbury Assoc.

PUBLISHER / VERLEGER / EDITEUR:

343, 344 Straight Arrow Publishers, Inc.
345 Cue Magazine
346, 347 The New Yorker Magazine

347

348–350 Covers of the satirical weekly *Szpilki* (Pins). Fig. 348, yellow ground; Fig. 349, blue eyes, pink face. (POL)
351 Complete cover of *Ameryka*, the magazine of the American Information Agency for the Eastern countries (here for Poland). The subject is housing—the reality and future developments. Full colour. (USA)
352 Cover of an issue of *Ameryka* devoted to the business world. (USA)
353 Cover of *The New Yorker*, with a study in reflections. Full colour, blue title. (USA)

348–350 Titelblätter der satirischen Wochenzeitschrift *Szpilki* (Die Stecknadeln). Abb. 348, gelber Hintergrund; Abb. 349, blaue Augen, rosa Gesicht. (POL)
351 Vollständiges Titelblatt von *Ameryka*, der amerikanischen Zeitschrift für die Ostblockländer (hier für Polen). Das Thema heisst «Wohnen» – die Gegenwart und künftige Entwicklungen. Mehrfarbig. (USA)
352 Titelblatt einer Ausgabe von *Ameryka*, die der Handelswelt gewidmet war. (USA)
353 Titelblatt von *The New Yorker* mit einer Studie über Rückspiegelungen. Mehrfarbig. (USA)

348–350 Couvertures de l'hebdomadaire satirique *Szpilki* (Aiguilles). Fig. 348: illustration sur fond jaune; fig. 349: yeux bleus, visage rose. (POL)
351 Couverture complète d'*Ameryka*, une revue américaine destinée aux pays de l'Europe orientale (reproduite ici est l'édition pour la Pologne). L'article correspondant est consacré aux problèmes du logement – la situation actuelle et les démarches à prendre. (USA)
352 Couverture d'un numéro d'*Ameryka* consacré aux affaires. (USA)
353 Couverture du magazine *The New Yorker* avec une étude sur les réflexions. (USA)

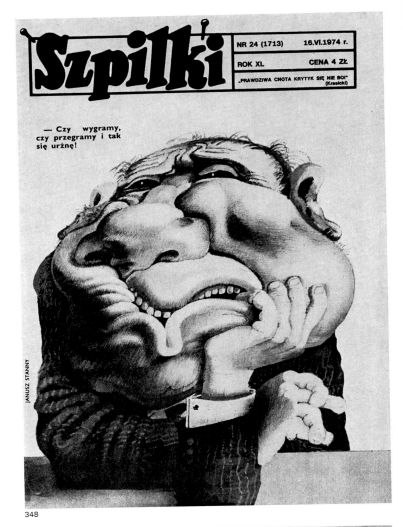

348

351

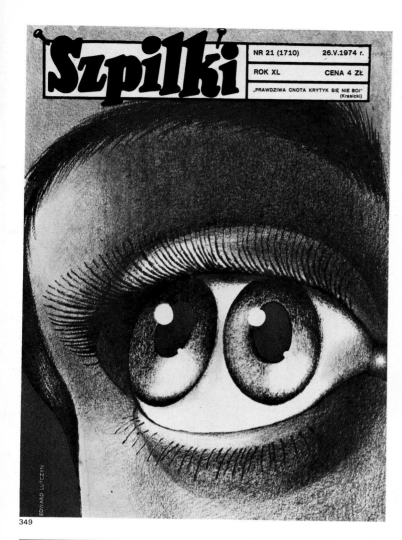

349

350

352

353

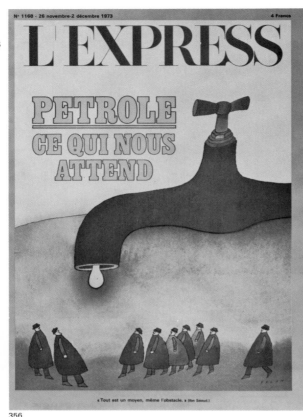

354

356

357

354–359 Covers of the weekly magazine *L'Express*. They refer to Wilson's risky policy, to oil, the Debré system, the "end of private life" and the "second turn". Full colour. (FRA)
360, 361 Covers of the satirical weekly *Nebelspalter*. The caption of Fig. 360 says that "the modern tourist is too lazy to look at things. The camera does it for him. Till such time as the index finger loses the strength to press the button..." Full colour. (SWI)

355

358

359

ARTIST / KÜNSTLER / ARTISTE:

354, 355 Tim
356, 358 Jean Michel Folon
357 Manuel Biedermanas/
Jacques Haillot (Photo)
359 Sempé
360 Barth
361 Heinz Stieger

DESIGNER / GESTALTER / MAQUETTISTE:

354–357 Bernard Durin
359 Jean Cubaud

ART DIRECTOR / DIRECTEUR ARTISTIQUE:

354–359 Georges Lacroix

PUBLISHER / VERLEGER / EDITEUR:

354–359 Express-Union
360, 361 Nebelspalter

354–359 Umschläge der Wochenzeitschrift *L'Express*. Sie beziehen sich auf Wilsons risikofreudige Politik, Öl, das System Debré, das «Ende des Privatlebens» und «die zweite Tour». Mehrfarbig. (FRA)
360, 361 Umschläge der satirischen Wochenzeitschrift *Nebelspalter*. Der moderne Tourist ist zum Schauen zu faul geworden (Abb. 360). Die Kamera tut es für ihn. Bis zu dem Tag, da auch dem Zeigfinger die Kraft zum Abdrücken ausgeht ... Farbig. (SWI)

354–359 Couvertures de l'hebdomadaire *L'Express* avec références à la politique aléatoire de Wilson, à l'huile, au système Debré, à la «fin de la vie privée» et au «second tour». En couleur. (FRA)
360, 361 Couvertures du magazine satiraire *Nebelspalter*. Fig. 360: «le touriste moderne est trop paresseux pour regarder les curiosités; c'est sa caméra qui le fait à son tour, jusqu'au moment où son index n'a plus la force de presser le déclencheur.» En couleur. (SWI)

360

361

362

363

362, 363 Covers of a magazine entitled "Collection of Stories" published by Nihon-sha. Full colour. (JPN)
364 Cover of an issue of *Chicago Tribune Magazine* with a feature on businesswomen. (USA)
365 Cover of *Scholastic Scope*. The issue contains an article on Mark Twain. (USA)
366 Cover of a test magazine published by a consumers' association. This issue deals with noise nuisance. Red and black. (BEL)
367, 368 Covers of the magazine *Poland*. The titles are "Tandem" (a tandem with a bottle of champagne on the carrier is shown on the back cover) and "Composition" (black and mauve on green ground). (POL)

362, 363 Umschläge einer Zeitschrift mit dem Titel «Geschichtensammlung», herausgegeben von Nihon-sha. Mehrfarbig. (JPN)
364 Umschlag einer Ausgabe von *Chicago Tribune Magazine*, die einen Artikel über Geschäftsfrauen enthält. (USA)
365 Umschlag von *Scholastic Scope*. Ausgabe mit einem Artikel über Mark Twain. (USA)
366 Umschlag einer Test-Zeitschrift, herausgegeben von einer Konsumentenvereinigung. Die Ausgabe handelt von Belästigung durch Lärm. Rot und schwarz. (BEL)
367, 368 Umschläge der Zeitschrift *Poland*. Die Titel heissen «Tandem» (die vierte Umschlagseite zeigt ein Tandem mit einer Flasche Champagner auf dem Gepäckträger) und «Komposition» (Schwarz und Lila auf Grün). (POL)

362, 363 Couvertures d'une revue intitulée «Collection d'histoires». Publication de la maison d'édition Nihon-sha. En couleur. (JPN)
364 Couverture d'un numéro du magazine hebdomadaire du *Chicago Tribune*, contenant un article sur les femmes d'affaires. (USA)
365 Couverture d'un numéro de *Scholastic Scope*, avec un article sur Mark Twain. (USA)
366 Couverture d'un numéro d'une revue publiée par une association de consommateurs. Ce numéro est consacré au bruit et ses influences sur la vie de l'homme. Rouge et noir. (BEL)
367, 368 Couvertures du magazine *Poland*. Ces deux numéros sont intitulés «Tandem» (un tandem avec une bouteille de champagne sur le porte-bagages est reproduit à la 4e page de couverture) et «Composition» (noir et mauve sur fond vert). (POL)

364

ARTIST / KÜNSTLER / ARTISTE:

362, 363 Tadanori Yokoo
364 Chuck Slack
365 Frank Bozzo
366 Benoit De Pierpont
367 Andrzej Krajewski
368 Henryk Tomaszewski

ART DIRECTOR / DIRECTEUR ARTISTIQUE:

362, 363 Tadanori Yokoo
364 Jack Lund
365 Vicki Romaine
366 Lemineur
368 Lech Zahorski

PUBLISHER / VERLEGER / EDITEUR

362, 363 Hanashi-No-Tokushu
364 The Chicago Tribune
365 Scholastic Publishing Co.
366 Association des Consommateurs
367, 368 Polonia Verlag

365

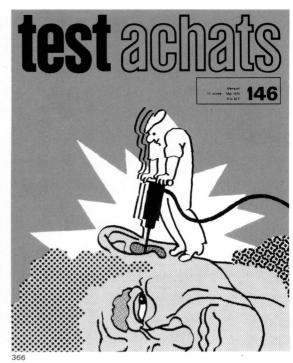

366

367

368

Magazine Covers
Zeitschriften-Umschläge
Couvertures de périodiques

369

370

374

Trade Magazines
Fachzeitschriften
Revues professionnelles

ARTIST / KÜNSTLER / ARTISTE:

369, 370 Christoph Blumrich
371 Frank Bozzo
372 Heinrich Fleischhacker
373 Walter Grieder
374 Gert Wunderlich
375 Donald M. Hedin
376 William S. Shields/Shig Ikeda (Photo)
377 Gervasio Gallardo

DESIGNER / GESTALTER / MAQUETTISTE:

375–377 Tom Lennon

ART DIRECTOR / DIRECTEUR ARTISTIQUE:

369–371 James Farrell
373 Walter Grieder
374 Gert Wunderlich
375–377 Ira Silberlicht

PUBLISHER / VERLEGER / EDITEUR:

369–371 Wine Journal, Inc.
372 Schweiz. Typographenbund
373 Verlag CVA
374 Verlag Die Wirtschaft
375–377 Emergency Medicine

369, 370 Artwork and complete cover of *wine now*, a magazine intended "to bring wine and people together". (USA)
371 A further cover of *wine now* magazine. Full colour. (USA)
372 Cover of TM/SGM/RSI, the organ of the Swiss Federation of Typographers. The issue contains a feature on communication by signs. Black and white. (SWI)
373 Cover of *Manège,* a monthly about the world of the circus. Red and white. (SWI)
374 Cover of *Neue Werbung,* a magazine of advertising. Black on silver, white title. (GDR)
375–377 Covers of *Emergency Medicine.* The subjects are wound sutures, sexual problems (three-dimensional figure on brown ground) and asthma (blue ground). (USA)

369, 370 Illustration und vollständiger Umschlag von *wine now,* einer Zeitschrift über Wein. Mehrfarbig. (USA)
371 Ein weiterer Umschlag der Zeitschrift *wine now.* (USA)
372 Umschlag von TM/SGM/RSI, dem Organ des Schweizerischen Typographenbundes. Die Ausgabe enthält einen Artikel über Verständigung durch Zeichen. Schwarzweiss. (SWI)
373 Umschlag von *Manège,* einer Monatsschrift über die Zirkuswelt. Rot und weiss. (SWI)
374 Umschlag von *Neue Werbung,* einer Zeitschrift über Werbung. Schwarz auf Silber, weisser Titel. (GDR)
375–377 Umschläge von *Emergency Medicine.* Die Themen heissen Wundnähte, sexuelle Probleme (dreidimensionale Figur) und Asthma (blauer Grund). (USA)

369, 370 Illustration et couverture complète de *wine now,* un magazine destiné «à réunir le vin et les hommes». (USA)
371 Une autre couverture du magazine *wine now.* (USA)
372 Couverture du magazine de la Fédération Suisse des Typographes. L'article correspondant est consacré à la communication par signes. Noir et blanc. (SWI)
373 Couverture de *Manège,* un magazine mensuel consacré au cirque. Rouge et blanc. (SWI)
374 Couverture de *Neue Werbung,* une revue de publicité. Noir sur argent, titre blanc. (GDR)
375–377 Couvertures d'*Emergency Medicine* avec des articles sur la suture de plaies, les problèmes sexuels (figure tridimensionnelle sur fond brun) et l'asthme (fond bleu). (USA)

371

372

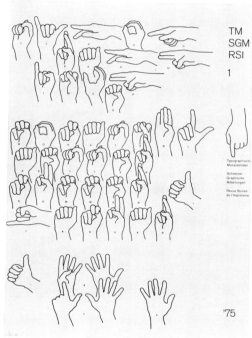

373

375

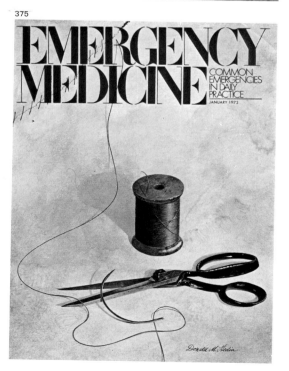

376

377

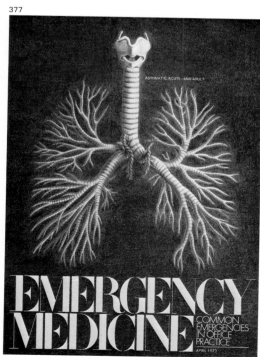

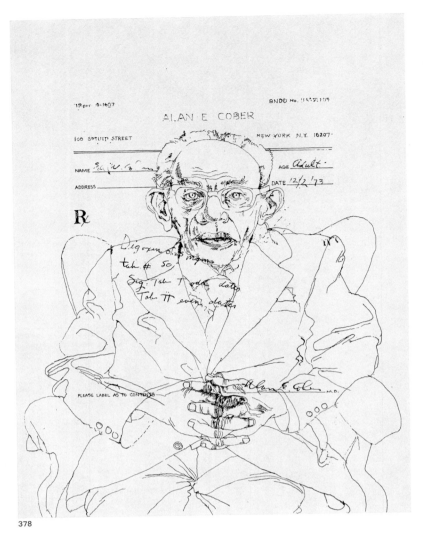

378

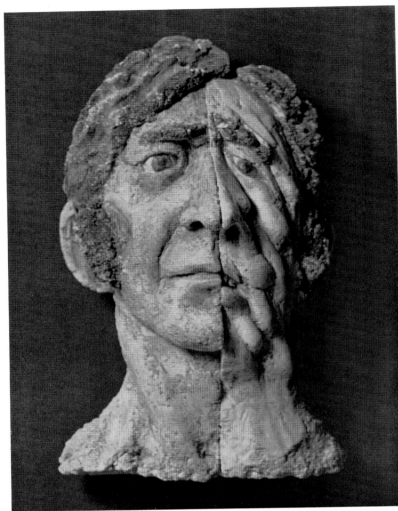

379

382

378–384 Pages and double spreads from the magazine *Emergency Medicine*. Fig. 378: pen drawing illustrating an article on drug prescription for the aged; Fig. 379: full-colour plastic model, on the choice of medicine or surgery for treating Bell's palsy (shown on right side of head); Fig. 380: painting, on dying children; Fig. 381: pen drawing, on the dangers of dog and cat bites; Fig. 382: drawing, on food dangers on holiday; Fig. 383: flat colours, on myocardial infarction; Fig. 384: flat colours, introducing a glossary of important questions for doctors in several languages. (USA)

378–384 Seiten und Doppelseiten aus der Zeitschrift *Emergency Medicine*. Abb. 378: Federzeichnung, einen Artikel über Rezeptverschreibung für Betagte illustrierend; Abb. 379: mehrfarbiges Plastik-Modell, über die Wahl zwischen medikamentöser Behandlung und Chirurgie in Fällen von einseitiger Gesichtslähmung (rechte Seite des Kopfes); Abb. 380: Gemälde, über sterbende Kinder; Abb. 381: Federzeichnung, über die Gefahren von Hunde- und Katzenbissen; Abb. 382: Zeichnung, über Nahrungsmittelgefahren in den Ferien; Abb. 383: flächige Farben, Herzinfarkt; Abb. 384: flächige Farben, Einführung eines Verzeichnisses von wichtigen Fragen für Ärzte in mehreren Sprachen.(USA)

378–384 Pages et pages doubles du magazine *Emergency Medicine*. Fig. 378: dessin à la plume illustrant un article sur les médicaments donnés aux gens âgés; fig. 379: le procédé – opération ou médicaments – à choisir pour traiter la paralysie de Bell (indiquée du côté droit de la tête), modèle en plastique, polychrome; fig. 380: les enfants mourants, peinture; fig. 381: les dangers de morsures de chiens et de chats, dessin à la plume; fig. 382: les dangers de la cuisine inaccoutumée en vacances, dessin; fig. 383: l'infarctus du myocarde, couleurs à plat; fig. 384: page initiale d'un lexique en différentes langues, destiné aux médecins. (USA)

Trade Magazines
Fachzeitschriften
Revues professionnelles

380

381

383

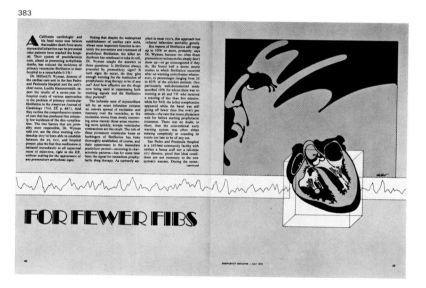

384

ARTIST / KÜNSTLER / ARTISTE:

378 Alan E. Cober
379 William S. Shields/Shig Ikeda (Photo)
380 Ed Soyka
381 William S. Shields
382 Geoffrey Moss
383 Don Weller
384 Dan Culhane

DESIGNER / GESTALTER / MAQUETTISTE:

378–384 Tom Lennon

ART DIRECTOR / DIRECTEUR ARTISTIQUE:

378–384 Ira Silberlicht

PUBLISHER / VERLEGER / EDITEUR:

378–384 Emergency Medicine

385–390 Umschläge und Illustrations-Ausschnitte (Abb. 389 in ungefährer Original-grösse) aus der medizinischen Zeitschrift *Modern Medicine*. Abb. 385: illustriert stressbedingte Leiden, schwarzumrandete Figur in rotem Wasser; Abb. 386: über die Ménière'sche Krankheit, die Schwindel und Ohrendröhnen verursacht, Figur auf Seil und Wirbel farbig; Abb. 387: über die Beurteilung der Gesundheit von Ungeborenen. farbige Holzkonstruktion; Abb. 388: über das Schmerzproblem, mehrfarbig; Abb. 389/390: über Instrumente als «Verlängerung» der Hände und Augen des Arztes, Holzkonstruktionen in verschiedenen Farben. (USA)

385–390 Covers and details of the artwork (Fig. 389 in roughly actual size) for the medical magazine *Modern Medicine*. Fig. 385: illustrating stress-related disease, black-line figure in red water; Fig. 386: on Ménière's disease, which causes dizziness and ringing in the ears, with figure on tightrope and maelstrom in colour; Fig. 387: on assessing the unborn, coloured wooden construction; Fig. 388, on the problem of pain, full colour; Figs. 389/390: on extending the physician's eyes and hands, coloured wooden constructions. (USA)

385–390 Couvertures et détails des illustrations (fig. 389 approx. en grandeur nature) du magazine médical *Modern Medicine*. Fig. 385: les affections causées par le stress, figure noir-blanc dans l'eau rouge; fig. 386: maladie de Ménière, qui cause des affections vertigineuses ou des bruissements d'oreille, figure sur la corde tendue et tourbillon polychromes; fig. 387: l'estimation prénatale de la santé, construction en bois, polychrome; fig. 388: le problème de la douleur, en couleur; figs. 389/390: l'extension de la sphère d'action et d'influence du médecin ,construction en bois. (USA)

385

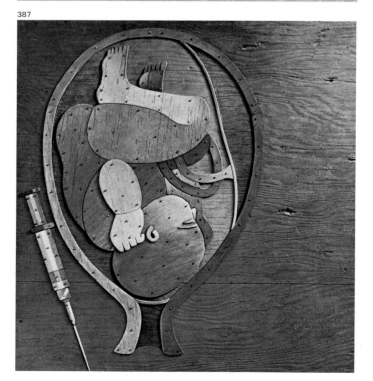

386

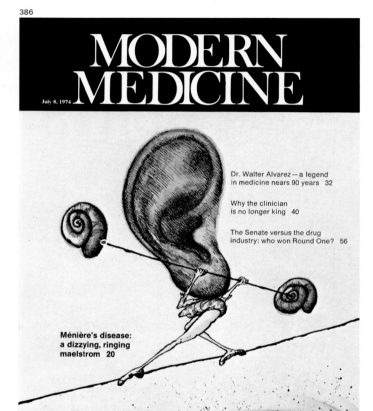

387

388

ARTIST / KÜNSTLER / ARTISTE:

385 Robert Osborn
386 Ronald Searle
387, 389, 390 Vin Giuliani
388 Gilbert Stone

DESIGNER / GESTALTER / MAQUETTISTE:

389, 390 George Miles Ryan

ART DIRECTOR / DIRECTEUR ARTISTIQUE:

385–390 Phillip Dykstra

PUBLISHER / VERLEGER / EDITEUR:

385–390 Modern Medicine Publications, Inc.

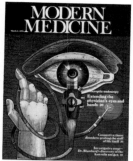

390

389

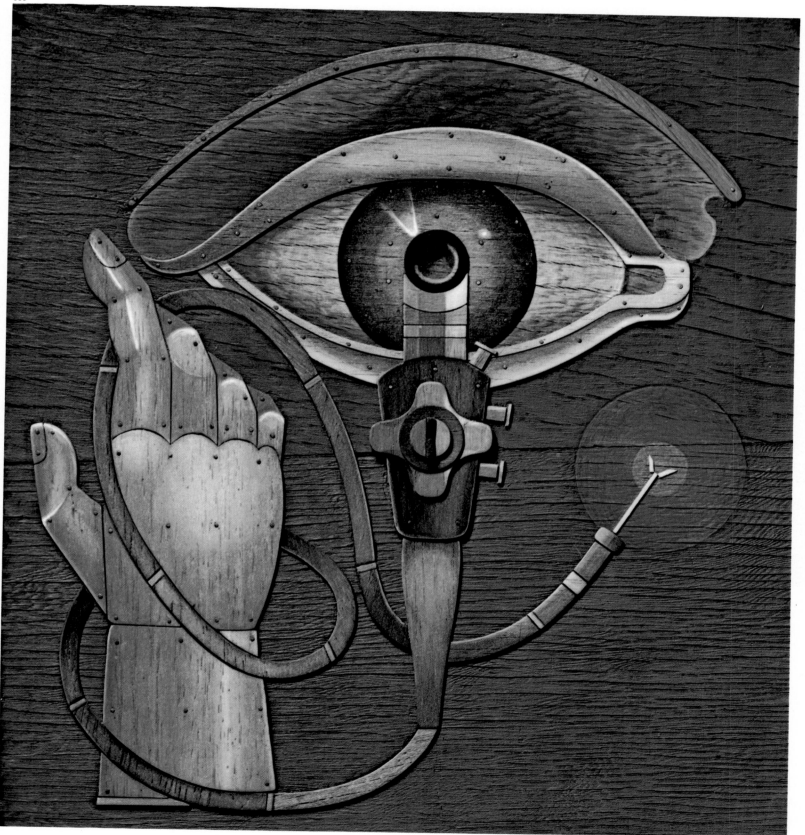

391

ARTIST / KÜNSTLER / ARTISTE:

391, 392 Haruo Miyauchi
393 Terry Lamb
394 Georges Lemoine
395 Frédérique Court
396 Don Ivan Punchatz

ART DIRECTOR / DIRECTEUR ARTISTIQUE:

391, 392 Hiroshi Ohchi
393–395 Daniel Sinay
396 Rod Kamitsuka

AGENCY / AGENTUR / AGENCE – STUDIO:

393–395 Hollenstein Création
396 Sketch Pad Studio

PUBLISHER / VERLEGER / EDITEUR:

391, 392 Seibundo-Shinkosha Publishing Co.
393–395 Centre d'étude et de promotion
de la lecture
396 Psychology Today Magazine

391, 392 Detail and cover of the graphic design magazine *Idea*. (JPN)
393–395 Pages in full colour from the magazine *Psychologie,* illustrating the inheritance of talents (Fig. 393); the psychology of actors (Fig. 394); and an interview with Emma Santos (Fig. 395). (FRA)
396 Full-page illustration, from *Psychology Today,* accompanying a feature on Stanley Milgrim, a social scientist concerned with the psychology of "the familiar stranger". Full colour. (USA)

391, 392 Illustrations-Ausschnitt und vollständiger Umschlag der Zeitschrift für Design und Graphik *Idea.* (JPN)
393–395 Mehrfarbige Seiten aus der Zeitschrift *Psychologie* über die Vererbung von Talenten (Abb. 393), die Psychologie von Schauspielern (Abb. 394) und ein Interview mit Emma Santos (Abb. 395). (FRA)
396 Ganzseitige Illustration aus *Psychology Today* zu einem Artikel über den «wohlbekannten Unbekannten». Farbig. (USA)

391, 392 Détail de l'illustration et couverture complète d'*Idea,* une revue d'art graphique. (JPN)
393–395 Pages polychromes du magazine *Psychologie* avec des illustrations se référant aux talents héréditaires (fig. 393), à la psychologie des acteurs (fig. 394) et à un interview avec Emma Santos (fig. 395). (FRA)
396 Illustration pleine page de *Psychology Today* pour un article sur le problème de «l'inconnu connu». En couleur. (USA)

Trade Magazines
Fachzeitschriften
Revues professionnelles

392

393

394

395

396

397

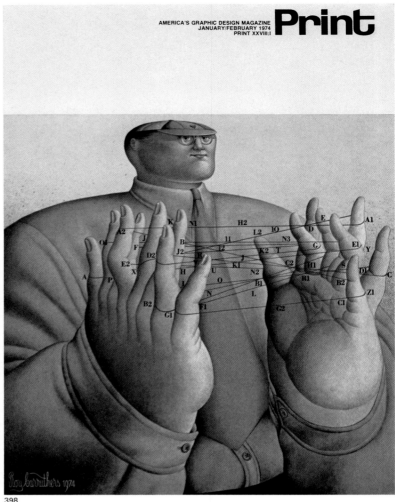

398

399

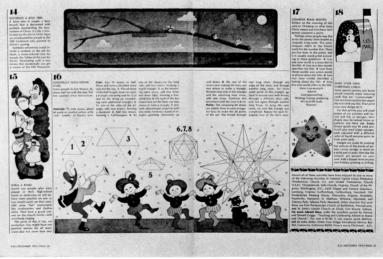

400

ARTIST / KÜNSTLER / ARTISTE:

397 Roman Cieslewicz
398 Roy Carruthers
399, 400 John O'Leary/Lou Brooks/Bea Widener
401, 402 Dennis Pollard
403, 404 Lee O. Warfield III

ART DIRECTOR / DIRECTEUR ARTISTIQUE:

398 Andrew Kner
399, 400 Raymond Waites
401–404 Phil Jordan

AGENCY / AGENTUR / AGENCE – STUDIO:

401–404 Beveridge & Associates, Inc.

PUBLISHER / VERLEGER / EDITEUR:

397 Wydawnictwo Artystyzno-Graficzne
398 R.C. Publications, Inc.
399, 400 A.D. Publications
401–404 Construction Specifications Institute

Trade Magazines
Fachzeitschriften
Revues professionnelles

401

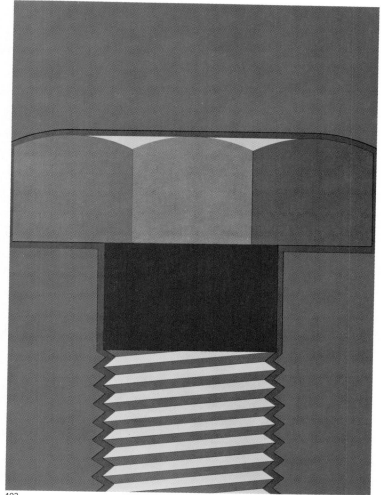

402

403

397 Cover of the art and design magazine *Projekt*. Black hand with red, yellow and green rings on blue background. (POL)
398 Cover of the graphic design magazine *Print*. Figure in green and buff shades. (USA)
399, 400 Double spreads from a feature in A. D. magazine about various ways of preparing for Christmas in the home. (USA)
401–404 Three colour pages, with a corresponding double spread, from *The Construction Specifier*, organ of the Construction Specifications Institute. The accompanying articles deal with lead waterproofing for a plaza, galvanized steel for construction products and steel reinforcing bars for road bridges. (USA)

397 Umschlag der Zeitschrift für Kunst und Design *Projekt*. Schwarze Hand mit roten, gelben und grünen Ringen auf blauem Grund. (POL)
398 Umschlag der Zeitschrift für graphisches Design *Print*. Figuren farbig. (USA)
399, 400 Doppelseiten aus einem Artikel im Magazin A. D. über verschiedene Möglichkeiten der Weihnachtsvorbereitungen im Hause. (USA)
401–404 Drei Farbseiten, mit einer entsprechenden Doppelseite, aus *The Construction Specifier*, Organ eines technischen Institutes. Die begleitenden Artikel handeln von Wasserabdichtungen aus Blei für eine Terrasse, von galvanisiertem Stahl für Bauprodukte und von Eisenverstärkungen für Strassenbrücken. (USA)

397 Couverture de *Projekt*, une revue d'art graphique. Main noire avec des bagues rouges, jaunes et vertes sur fond bleu. (POL)
398 Couverture du magazine de design *Print*. Figure en teintes vertes et chamois. (USA)
399, 400 Pages doubles d'un article paru dans le magazine A. D. sur les différentes manières de préparer la fête de Noël à la maison. (USA)
401–404 Trois pages polychromes avec double page correspondante figurant dans le journal d'entreprise d'un institut spécialisé dans la construction. Les articles sont consacrés aux revêtements de plomb imperméables, à l'acier galvanisé utilisé pour la fabrication de produits de construction et aux barres d'acier pour la construction de ponts. (USA)

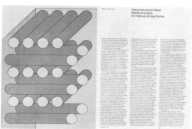

404

405

406

ARTIST / KÜNSTLER / ARTISTE:

405, 406 Terry Lamb
407 Christian Piper
408 David Wilcox
409, 410 Jacqueline Chwast

DESIGNER / GESTALTER / MAQUETTISTE:

405–407 Lloyd Ziff
408 Paula Hollander

ART DIRECTOR / DIRECTEUR ARTISTIQUE:

405–407 Mike Salisbury
408 Al Braverman
409, 410 Raymond Waites

PUBLISHER / VERLEGER / EDITEUR:

405–407 Straight Arrow Publishers, Inc.
408 Mac-Fadden Bartell
409, 410 A.D. Publications

Magazine Illustrations
Zeitschriften-Illustrationen
Illustrations de périodiques

405, 406 Full-page illustration and corresponding spread from a feature on the "retirement capital" of St. Petersburg, Florida, in *Rolling Stone*. (USA)
407 Full-page illustration in full colour from *Rolling Stone* magazine. The subject is increasing violence, often racially triggered, in US high schools. (USA)
408 Double spread from *Sport*, with the opening of a novel about professional football. (USA)
409, 410 Consecutive double spreads from A.D. magazine with suggestions as to what to do on a rainy day. Illustrations in colour. (USA)

405, 406 Farbillustration und entsprechende Doppelseite aus einem Artikel über die «Rentner-metropole» von St. Petersburg, Florida, in *Rolling Stone*. (USA)
407 Ganzseitige, mehrfarbige Illustration aus der Zeitschrift *Rolling Stone*. Das Thema heisst zunehmende Gewalttätigkeit, oft durch Rassenunterschiede entfacht, an amerikanischen Mittel-schulen. (USA)
408 Doppelseite aus *Sport* mit dem Beginn eines Romans über Profi-Fussball. (USA)
409, 410 Aufeinanderfolgende Doppelseiten aus dem Magazin A.D. mit Beschäftigungs-Vor-schlägen für einen regnerischen Tag. Farbillustrationen. (USA)

405, 406 Illustration sur page entière et page double correspondante d'un article de *Rolling Stone* sur St. Petersburg, Florida, «la capitale de la retraite». (USA)
407 Illustration pleine page du magazine *Rolling Stone*. L'article correspondant est consacré à la violence et la brutalité, souvent déclenchées pour des raisons raciales, qui règnent actuelle-ment dans les lycées américains. (USA)
408 Page double de *Sport* introduisant un récit sur le football professionnel. (USA)
409, 410 Doubles pages consécutives du magazine A.D. contenant des suggestions de passe-temps pour les jours de pluie. Illustrations en couleur. (USA)

408

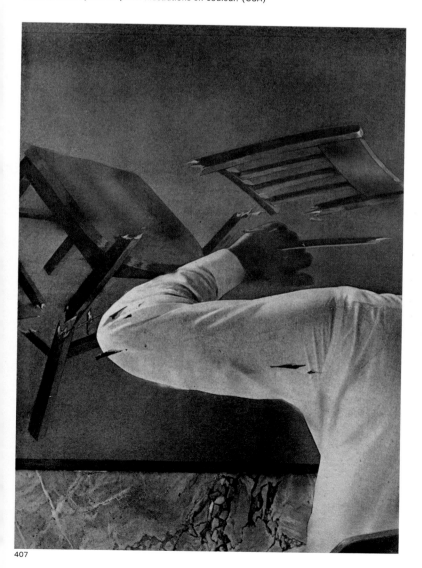

407

409

410

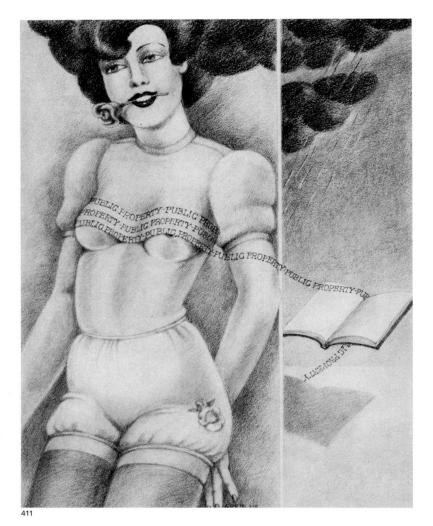

411

412

414

415

Magazine Illustrations
Zeitschriften-Illustrationen
Illustrations de périodiques

ARTIST / KÜNSTLER / ARTISTE:

411, 412 Grete Lis
413 Erhard Göttlicher
414, 415 Josse Goffin
416 Werner Jeker
417 Michael Trevithick

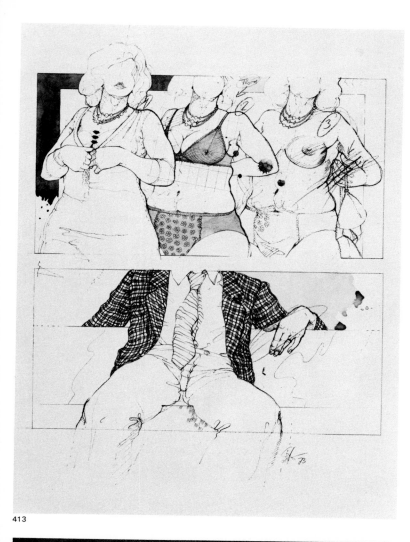

413

ART DIRECTOR / DIRECTEUR ARTISTIQUE:

411–415 David Hillman
417 Richard Weigand

PUBLISHER / VERLEGER / EDITEUR:

411–415 IPC Magazines Ltd.
416 AG für Radiopublikationen AGRAP
417 Esquire

411, 412 Pencil drawings illustrating short stories in the women's magazine *Nova*. Full page, black and white. (GBR)
413 Drawing illustrating a short story in *Nova*. Black and white. (GBR)
414, 415 Black-and-white illustrations of the signs of Leo and Scorpio from an astrology section in *Nova* magazine. (GBR)
416 Illustration from *TV-Radio-Zeitung* referring to the radio play *War of the Worlds* with which Orson Welles caused a panic in America in 1938. Full colour, full page. (SWI)
417 Full-page illustration from the men's magazine *Esquire*. (USA)

411, 412 Bleistiftzeichnungen als Illustrationen zu Kurzgeschichten in der Frauenzeitschrift *Nova*. Ganzseitig, schwarzweiss. (GBR)
413 Zeichnung als Illustration einer Kurzgeschichte in *Nova*. Schwarzweiss. (GBR)
414, 415 Schwarzweiss-Illustrationen der Tierkreiszeichen Löwe und Skorpion aus einer Astrologierubrik der Zeitschrift *Nova*. (GBR)
416 Illustration aus der *TV-Radio-Zeitung*, die sich auf das Radio-Hörspiel *War of the Worlds* bezieht, mit dem Orson Welles 1938 in Amerika eine Panik auslöste. (SWI)
417 Ganzseitige Illustration aus der Männerzeitschrift *Esquire*. (USA)

411, 412 Dessin à la plume illustrant divers essais parus dans la revue pour femmes *Nova*. Pages entières en noir et blanc. (GBR)
413 Dessin illustrant une nouvelle qui a paru dans *Nova*. Noir et blanc. (GBR)
414, 415 Illustrations en noir et blanc se référant aux signes du Zodiaque (lion et scorpion). D'un article sur l'astrologie paru dans *Nova*. (GBR)
416 Illustration du programme hebdomadaire des émissions radiophoniques et télévisées, ici se référant à une pièce radiophonique (La Guerre des mondes) d'Orson Welles, qui a affolé la foule de l'Amérique de l'année 1938. Polychrome. (USA)
417 Illustration pleine page du magazine masculin *Esquire*. (USA)

416

417

418

418, 421 Illustrations from an article on Hubert Grooteclaes in *Avenue*. The designs are obtained from photographs with the use of mirrors and colouring techniques. (NLD)
419, 420 Full-page illustrations from an astrological article on the Sign of the Fishes in the magazine *Avenue*. Pale reddish greys, with the fish only in bright colours. (NLD)
422 Full-colour cover of an issue of *Avenue* containing an article on the secret life of plants, which can "feel, think, calculate and listen". (NLD)
423 Double spread from a fashion feature in *Avenue*. One figure in black and white, the other in green shades. (NLD)

418, 421 Illustrationen aus einem Artikel über Hubert Grooteclaes in *Avenue*. Die Illustrationen entstanden aus Photographien unter Verwendung von Spiegeln und Farbtechniken. (NLD)
419, 420 Ganzseitige Illustrationen aus einem astrologischen Artikel über das Tierkreiszeichen der Fische in der Zeitschrift *Avenue*. Bleiche Grautöne, Fische farbig. (NLD)
422 Ganzseitiger Umschlag einer Ausgabe von *Avenue* mit einem Artikel über das geheime Leben der Pflanzen, die «fühlen, denken, rechnen und horchen». (NLD)
423 Doppelseite aus einem Modeartikel in *Avenue*. Eine Figur in Schwarzweiss, die andere in Grüntönen. (NLD)

418, 421 Illustrations d'un article sur Hubert Grooteklaes, paru dans *Avenue*. Design réalisé par une combinaison de coloration et de prises de vues avec miroirs. (NLD)
419, 420 Illustrations consacrées au signe du poisson extraites d'un article sur l'astrologie paru dans le magazine *Avenue*. Gris rougeâtre, poissons en couleurs vives. (NLD)
422 Couverture polychrome d'un numéro d'*Avenue* contenant un article sur la vie secrète des plantes, qui sont capables «de sentir, de penser, de calculer et d'écouter». (NLD)
423 Double page d'un supplément de mode paru dans *Avenue*. L'une des figures est en noir et blanc, l'autre en teintes vertes. (NLD)

421

Magazine Illustrations
Zeitschriften-Illustrationen
Illustrations de périodiques

419

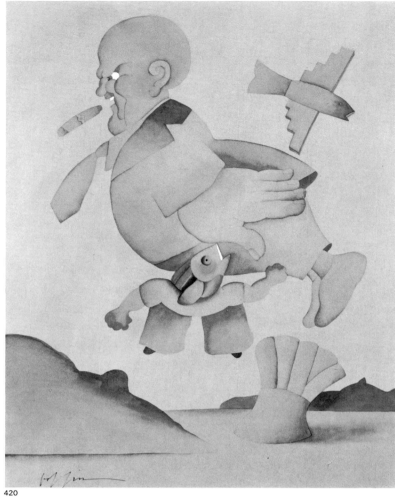

420

422

423

ARTIST / KÜNSTLER / ARTISTE:

418, 421 Hubert Grooteclaes
419, 420 Josse Goffin
422 Erno Tromp
423 Milou Hermus

ART DIRECTOR / DIRECTEUR ARTISTIQUE:

418–423 Dick de Moei

PUBLISHER / VERLEGER / EDITEUR:

418–423 De Geillustreerde Pers, B.V.

424

ARTIST / KÜNSTLER / ARTISTE:

424–427 Caroline Browne
428 Terry Pastar
429 James McMullan

ART DIRECTOR / DIRECTEUR ARTISTIQUE:

424–428 Dick de Moei
429 Henry Wolf

AGENCY / AGENTUR / AGENCE – STUDIO:

424–427 Art Connection
428 Andrew Archer Assoc.

PUBLISHER / VERLEGER / EDITEUR:

424–428 De Geïllustreerde Pers, B.V.
429 Children's Television Workshop

424–427 Detail of a painting and complete colour pages from an issue of the magazine *Avenue* devoted to travel and holidays. Figs. 424/425: villages in the hills; Fig. 426: skiing in the mountains; Fig. 427: the safari. All illustrations in pastel shades. (NLD)
428 Full-page illustration introducing an astrological section in *Avenue* examining the relations of the Bull (Taurus) with the other signs. (NLD)
429 Full-page illustration from the children's magazine *Sesame Street*. "S for shoe" is one letter of an "artist's alphabet". Blue and white shoe. (USA)

424–427 Ausschnitt aus einem Bild und vollständige Farbseiten aus einer Ausgabe der Zeitschrift *Avenue,* die Reisen und Ferien gewidmet war. Abb. 424/425: hochgelegene Dörfer; Abb. 426: Skifahren in den Bergen; Abb. 427: Safari. Alles in Pastelltönen. (NLD)
428 Ganzseitige Illustration als Einführung eines astrologischen Beitrages in *Avenue* über den Stier und seine Beziehung zu den andern Tierkreiszeichen. (NLD)
429 Ganzseitige Illustration aus der Kinderzeitschrift *Sesame Street*. «S wie Schuh» aus einem Künstleralphabet. Blau-weisser Schuh. (USA)

424–427 Détail d'une peinture et pages complètes, tirés d'un numéro du magazine *Avenue* qui était consacré aux voyages et aux vacances. Figs. 424/425: village de montagne; fig. 426: station d'hiver; fig. 427: le safari. Toutes les illustrations en teintes pastel. (NLD)
428 Illustration sur page entière introduisant un article sur l'astrologie, paru dans *Avenue*. On y examine les relations du taureau par rapport aux autres signes du Zodiaque. (NLD)
429 Illustration pleine page figurant dans le magazine pour enfants *Sesame Street*. «S pour soulier» fait partie de l'alphabet d'un artiste. Soulier bleu et blanc. (USA)

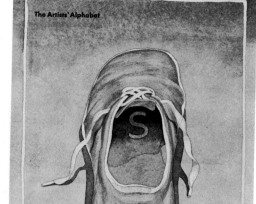

425

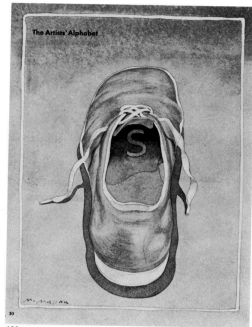

426

427

428

429

The Artists' Alphabet

ART DIRECTOR / DIRECTEUR ARTISTIQUE:

431, 432, 434, 435 Dick de Moei
433 Leendert Van Pelt

PUBLISHER / VERLEGER / EDITEUR:

430 Comité de Sauvegarde des berges de la Seine
431, 432, 434, 435 De Geillustreerde Pers, B.V.
433 Europese Gemeenschap

430 Magazine illustration in actual size in connection with a campaign to save Paris from the private car. (FRA)
431, 432 Illustrations from a feature in *Avenue* on the hermetic nature of modern science. Monochrome. (NLD)
433 Cartoon from the magazine *Europese Gemeenschap* on the subject of the Comecon. Black with pink. (NLD)
434, 435 Illustration and double spread from an astrological feature in *Avenue* on the Scorpion as a staff member. Dark blue figure, blue walls, girl in yellow dress. (NLD)

430

430 Zeitschriftenillustration in Originalgrösse im Zusammenhang mit einer Kampagne, die Paris vor dem Privatauto retten möchte. (FRA)
431, 432 Illustrationen aus einem Artikel in *Avenue* über die Unzugänglichkeit der modernen Wissenschaft. Monochrom. (NLD)
433 Karikatur aus der Zeitschrift *Europese Gemeenschap* über das Thema Comecon. Schwarz mit Rosa. (NLD)
434, 435 Illustration und Doppelseite aus einem astrologischen Artikel in *Avenue* über den Skorpion als Mitarbeiter. Dunkelblaue Figur, blaue Wände, gelbes Kleid. (NLD)

430 Illustration grandeur nature figurant dans une campagne contre la circulation de voitures privées dans la ville de Paris. (FRA)
431, 432 Illustrations tirées d'un article du magazine *Avenue*. Il se réfère au caractère hermétique des sciences modernes. Monochrome. (NLD)
433 Caricature du magazine *Europese Gemeenschap* pour un article sur le Comécon. (NLD)
434, 435 Illustration et page double d'un article sur l'astrologie, paru dans le magazine *Avenue*. Il est consacré aux traits caractéristiques du scorpion en tant que membre du personnel. Figure en bleu foncé, parois bleues, fille en robe jaune. (NLD)

431

432

434

433

435

ARTIST / KÜNSTLER / ARTISTE:

430 Rosado Puig
431, 432, 434, 435 Roger Wolfs
433 Ton Hoogendoorn

Magazine Illustrations

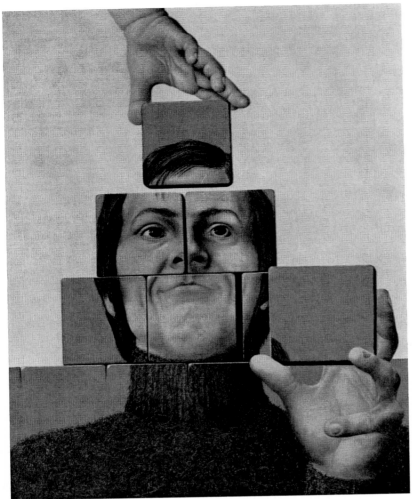

436

Magazine Illustrations
Zeitschriften-Illustrationen
Illustrations de périodiques

ARTIST / KÜNSTLER / ARTISTE:

436 John Holmes
437, 438 Roger Wolfs
439 Ute Osterwalder

ART DIRECTOR / DIRECTEUR ARTISTIQUE:

436 Michael Rand
437 J. Anthierens
438 Dick de Moei
439 Markus Osterwalder

AGENCY / AGENTUR / AGENCE – STUDIO:

439 Osterwalder's Office

PUBLISHER / VERLEGER / EDITEUR:

436 The Sunday Times Magazine
437 Dupuis Editions Belgique
438 De Geillustreerde Pers, B.V.
439 Zeit-Verlag/Gerd Bucerius

436 Full-page illustration from a series of articles in *The Sunday Times Magazine* on pre-school education, here on the role of the father. Full colour. (GBR)
437 Illustration from an article on bachelors. Blue-green shades. (BEL)
438 Illustration from an article on impotence in *Avenue*. Full colour. (NLD)
439 Illustration from *Zeit-Magazin*. Full colour. (GER)

436 Ganzseitige Illustration aus einer Serie von Artikeln im *Sunday Times Magazine* über Vorschul-Erziehung, hier in bezug auf die Rolle des Vaters. Mehrfarbig. (GBR)
437 Illustration aus einem Artikel über Junggesellen. Blaugrüne Töne. (BEL)
438 Illustration aus einem Artikel über die Impotenz in *Avenue*. Mehrfarbig. (NLD)
439 Illustration aus dem *Zeit-Magazin*. In Farben. (GER)

436 Illustration pleine page accompagnant une série d'articles parus dans le supplément hebdomadaire du *Sunday Times*. Ils orientent sur l'enseignement préparatoire, ici en particulier sur le rôle du père. Polychrome. (GBR)
437 Illustration d'un article sur les célibataires dans le magazine Bonne soirée. (BEL)
438 Illustration d'un article sur l'impotence, paru dans *Avenue*. (NLD)
439 Illustration du magazine hebdomadaire du journal *Die Zeit*. En couleur. (GER)

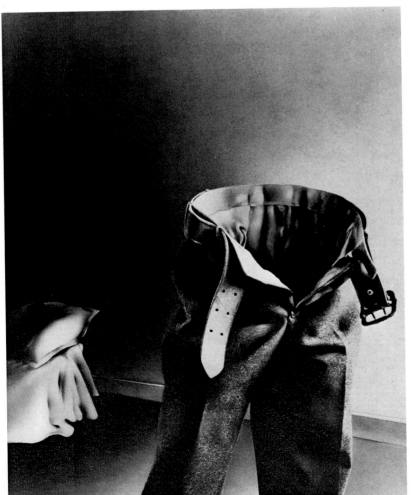

437

438

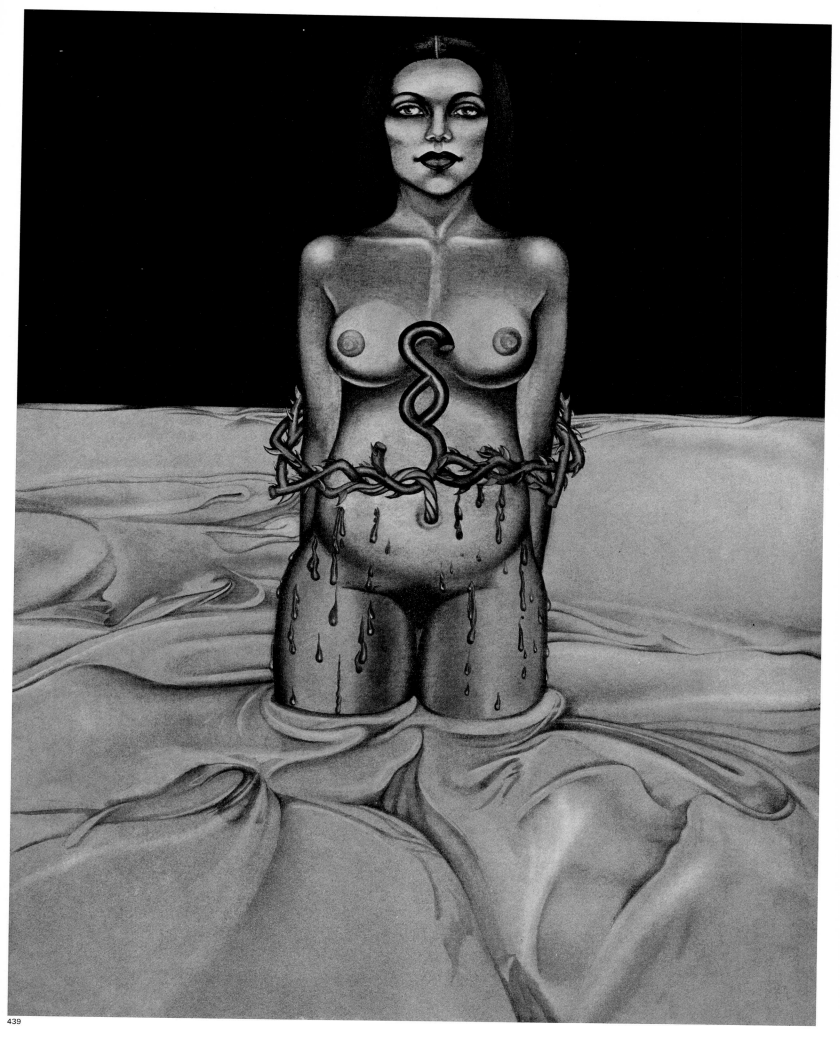

ARTIST / KÜNSTLER / ARTISTE:

440 Dickran Palulian
441 John Alcorn
442 Alan Magee
443, 444 Roy Carruthers

ART DIRECTOR / DIRECTEUR ARTISTIQUE:

440–444 Joe Brooks

PUBLISHER / VERLEGER / EDITEUR:

440–444 Penthouse

443

The Short Yappy Wife of Francis Macomber

Francis Macomber was very wealthy and very tall and he was going to be wealthier although probably no taller.

By Dan Greenburg

156 PENTHOUSE

It was now lunchtime and they were all sitting in the shade of the dining tent, pretending that nothing had happened. Half an hour before, Francis Macomber had been carried into camp in triumph on the shoulders of the native boys, along with the glossy 3⅜-by-4¼ color Polaroid of the lion.

"Well, you've got your lion," said Robert Wilson the white hunter, looking at him with his flat cold subma-chine-gunner's eyes, "and a damned fine one he is too."

"He is a good lion, isn't he?" said Francis Macomber. His wife looked at him as though she had never seen him before. She had, of course, seen him before, although you would not have known it to look at her, not at that particular moment; not, that is, unless you had actually seen her see him before.

Francis Macomber was very tall and very handsome in a particularly American boy-man way, if you liked that sort of handsomeness. He was wearing a brand-new safari jacket, new safari trousers, safari boots, safari socks, and safari undershorts. He was a man who kept himself very fit. He was an expert skier, flier, scuba diver, shot-putter, spelunker, motorcyclist, juggler, sword-swallower, and lotto player. He had a black belt in judo, karate, and origami, and he had just shown himself very

157

440

441

442

144

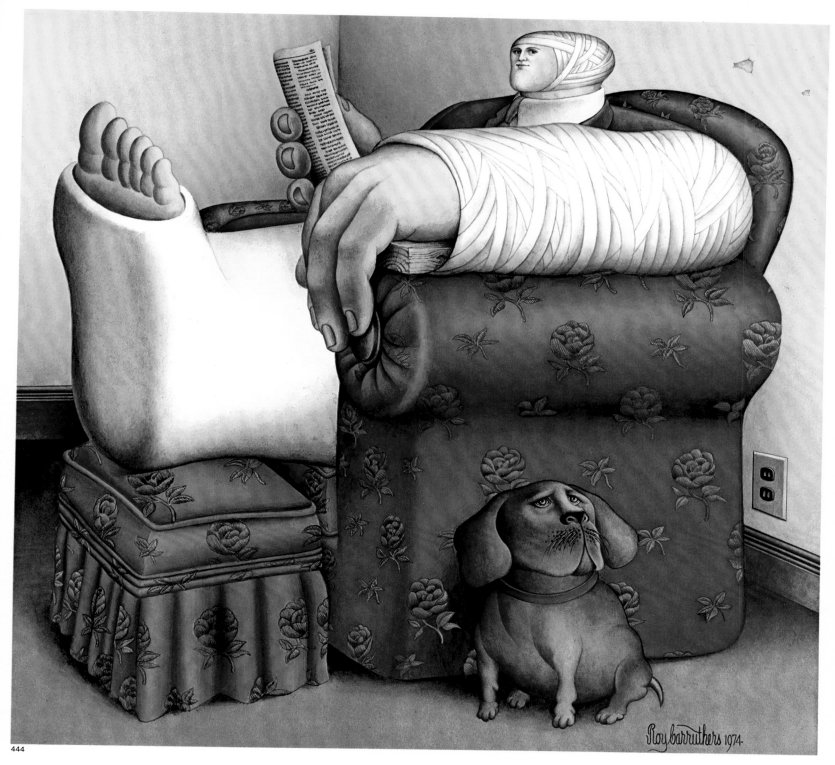

444

440 Double spread with full-colour illustration opening a short story about a safari in *Penthouse* magazine. (USA)
441 Opening spread of a fiction feature in *Penthouse*. Polychrome. (USA)
442 Opening spread of a story in *Penthouse* magazine about a rock 'n' roll disc jockey. Yellow title and print, deep purple ground. (USA)
443, 444 Complete double spread and detail of the artwork from *Penthouse* magazine. Opening of a feature on stunt men. (USA)

440 Doppelseite mit Farbillustration im Magazin *Penthouse* als Eröffnung einer Kurzgeschichte über eine Safari. (USA)
441 Einleitende Doppelseite einer Erzählung in *Penthouse*. In Farben. (USA)
442 Einleitende Doppelseite einer Erzählung im Magazin *Penthouse* über einen Rock'n'Roll-Disc-Jockey. Gelber Titel, gelbe Schrift, Grund dunkelviolett. (USA)
443, 444 Vollständige Doppelseite und Illustrationsausschnitt aus dem Magazin *Penthouse* zur Einleitung eines Artikels über Stuntmen und ihren harten, oft überaus gefährlichen Beruf. Mehrfarbig. (USA)

440 Page double avec illustration en couleur introduisant un récit sur un safari. Article paru dans le magazine *Penthouse*. (USA)
441 Double page initiale pour une nouvelle qui a paru dans le magazine *Penthouse*. Illustration en couleur. (USA)
442 Double page introduisant l'histoire d'un disc jockey spécialisé dans la musique rock. Extrait du magazine *Penthouse*. Titre et texte en jaune sur fond violet foncé. (USA)
443, 444 Double page complète et détail de l'illustration parues dans le magazine *Penthouse*. Premières pages d'un article sur les cascadeurs. (USA)

**Magazine Illustrations
Zeitschriften-Illustrationen
Illustrations de périodiques**

445

Magazine Illustrations
Zeitschriften-Illustrationen
Illustrations de périodiques

446

445, 446 Illustration in actual size and complete double spread from a feature in *Penthouse* magazine on religious themes presented on Broadway. (USA)
447 Full-colour spread opening a story about a band in *Penthouse.* Beige frame. (USA)
448 Double spread of a flower and pixie world in pastel shades from PR magazine. (JPN)
449 Double spread from *Lithopinion.* It relates to an interview with a ninety-year-old lithographer. Chiefly brown and sepia shades. (USA)

445, 446 Illustration in Originalgrösse und vollständige Doppelseite aus einem Artikel in *Penthouse* über am Broadway präsentierte religiöse Themen. (USA)
447 Mehrfarbige Doppelseite als Eröffnung einer Erzählung über ein Orchester. (USA)
448 Doppelseite über eine Blumen- und Feenwelt in Pastelltönen aus dem Magazin PR. (JPN)
449 Doppelseite aus *Lithopinion* im Zusammenhang mit einem Interview mit einem 90jährigen Lithographen. Vorwiegend Braun- und Sepia-Töne. (USA)

445, 446 Illustration en grandeur originale et double page complète extraites d'un article de *Penthouse* sur les spectacles religieux présentés au Broadway. (USA)
447 Double page introduisant l'histoire d'un groupe de musiciens. Encadrement beige. (USA)
448 Double page illustrant un monde des fleurs et des fées, tirée de PR. Teintes pastel. (JPN)
449 Double page tirée de *Lithopinion.* L'article correspondant est consacré à une interview avec un lithographe de quatre-vingt-dix ans. Teintes prédominantes brunes et sépia. (USA)

447

448

449

450

451

452

453

450 Full-page illustration from an article in *Penthouse* magazine on fake oil shortages intended to drive up prices. Full colour. (USA)
451 Colour illustration from an article on impotence in *Viva* magazine. (USA)
452 Page opening an article from a series in *Penthouse* on the Vietnam veterans. Black-and-white drawing in a brown frame. (USA)
453 Page opening an article on drugs from the series on Vietnam veterans in *Penthouse*. Black-and-white drawing on grey stock. (USA)
454 Full-page illustration from a story about a sensualist in *Viva* magazine. (USA)

450 Ganzseitige Illustration aus einem Artikel in *Penthouse* über vorgetäuschte Ölknappheit, um die Preise hochzutreiben. Mehrfarbig. (USA)
451 Farbillustration aus einem Artikel über Impotenz im Magazin *Viva*. (USA)
452 Einleitende Seite eines Artikels aus einer Serie in *Penthouse* über Vietnam-Veteranen. Schwarzweisse Zeichnung in braunem Rahmen. (USA)
453 Einleitende Seite eines Artikels über Drogen aus der Serie über Vietnam-Veteranen in *Penthouse*. Schwarzweisse Zeichnung auf grauem Papier. (USA)
454 Ganzseitige Illustration aus einer Erzählung über einen Sensualisten in *Viva*. (USA)

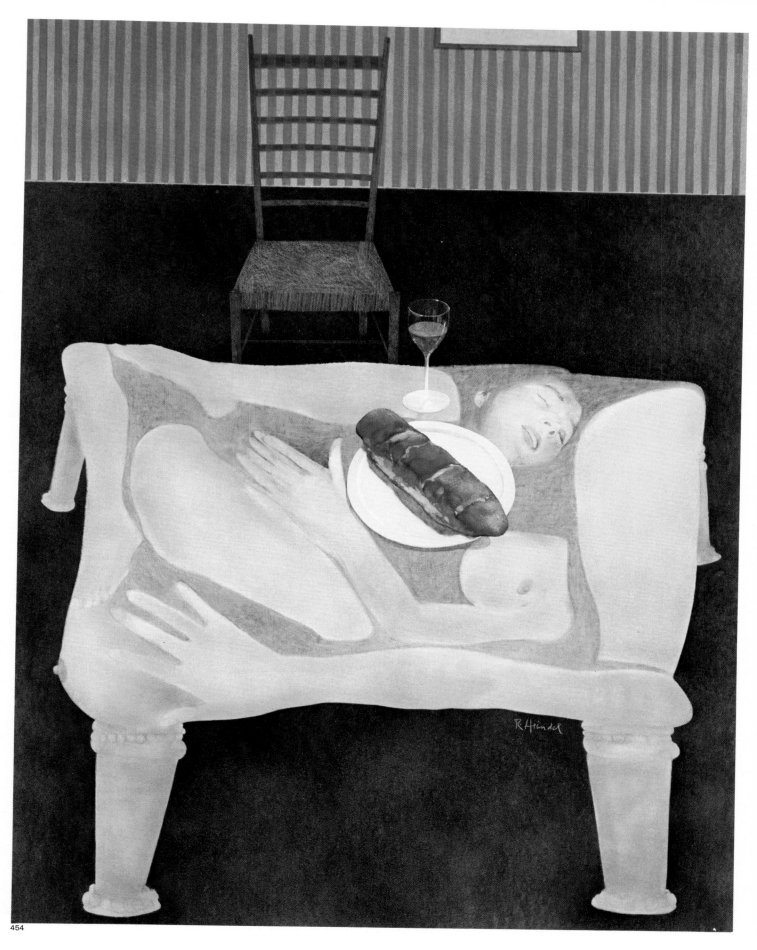

454

450 Illustration pleine page tirée de *Penthouse*. L'article oriente sur les informations d'une pénurie d'huile falsifiées pour faire hausser les prix. Polychrome. (USA)
451 Illustration polychrome d'un article sur l'impotence, paru dans le magazine *Viva*. (USA)
452 Page initiale d'un article extrait d'une série de *Penthouse* sur les vétérans du Vietnam. Dessin en noir et blanc, encadrement brun. (USA)
453 Page introduisant un article sur les drogues. Extrait d'une série sur les vétérans du Viet-nam parue dans *Penthouse*. Dessin en noir et blanc sur papier gris. (USA)
454 Illustration pleine page tirée d'un article de *Viva* sur un sensualiste. (USA)

ARTIST / KÜNSTLER / ARTISTE:

450 Dickran Palulian
451 Barbara Nessim
452 Paul Giovanopoulos
453 Bill Greer
454 Robert Hindel

ART DIRECTOR:

450, 452, 453 Joe Brooks
451, 454 Art Kane

PUBLISHER / VERLEGER:

450–454 Penthouse

456

455–458 Full-page illustrations and a double spread from two of the parts of a major feature on the Watergate scandal in *New York* magazine. Fig. 455: Anthony Ulasewicz receives instructions to make payments to a Watergate conspirator; Fig. 456: Haldeman listens to the Presidential tapes; Fig. 457: E. Howard Hunt interviews Dita Beard in hospital. (USA)

455–458 Ganzseitige Illustrationen und eine Doppelseite aus einer Reihe Artikel über Watergate in *New York*. Abb. 455: Anthony Ulasewicz erhält Anweisungen für Zahlungen an einen Watergate-Verschwörer; Abb. 456: Haldeman hört die Tonbänder des Präsidenten ab; Abb. 457: E. Howard Hunt interviewt Dita Beard im Spital. (USA)

455–458 Illustrations sur pages entières et page double parues dans deux articles successifs d'une série importante que le magazine *New York* a consacrée au scandale de Watergate Fig. 455: Anthony Ulasewicz reçoit des ordres pour faire des paiements aux conspirateurs de Watergate; fig. 456: Haldeman en train d'écouter les bandes magnétiques présidentielles; fig. 457: E. Howard Hunt lors d'une interview avec Dita Beard à l'hôpital. (USA)

457

ARTIST / KÜNSTLER / ARTISTE:

455, 458 Melinda Bordelon
456 Roger Hane
457 Julian Allen

DESIGNER / GESTALTER / MAQUETTISTE:

455 Walter Bernard/Milton Glaser
457 Walter Bernard/Tom Bentkowski

ART DIRECTOR / DIRECTEUR ARTISTIQUE:

455–458 Walter Bernard/Milton Glaser

PUBLISHER / VERLEGER / EDITEUR:

455–458 The New York Magazine

458

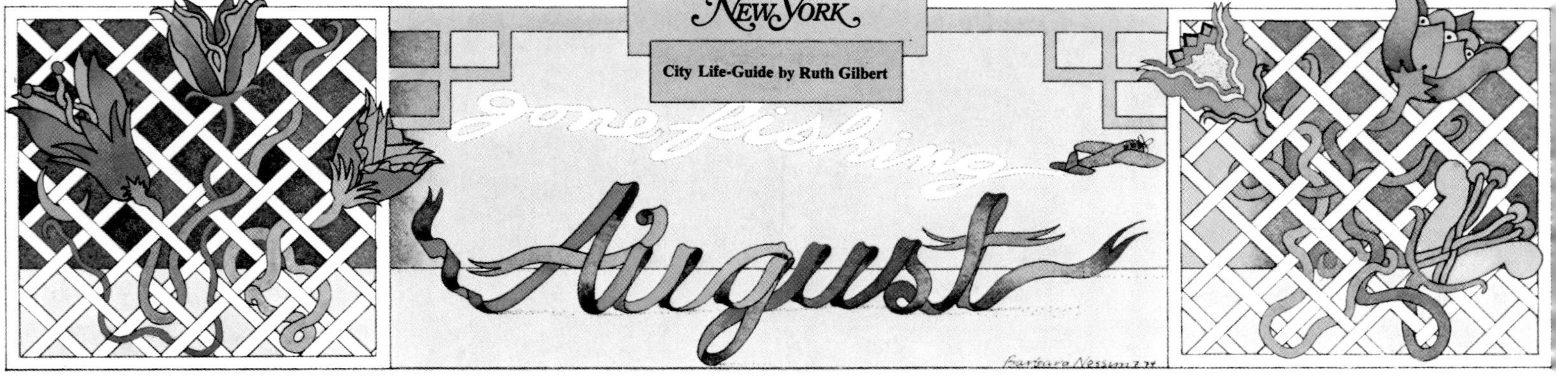

459

459, 460 Heading and complete calendar from a series of monthly poster guides to city life in New York bound into *New York* magazine. Full colour. (USA)
461 Double spread from an article on the Forest Hills tennis tournament, with vignettes of the leading players, in *New York.* (USA)
462 Full-page portrait of Bob Dylan from an article on him in *New York.* Monochrome. (USA)
463 Full-page colour portrait of Derek Sanderson from an article on hockey in *New York.* (USA)
464 Full-page colour portrait of Joel Grey from an article in *New York* magazine on Broadway, where Grey was playing the role of the Dauphin in a piece about Joan of Arc. (USA)
465 Black-and-white portrait of the pop singer Stevie Wonder from *New York.* Full page. (USA)

459, 460 Überschrift und vollständiger Kalender aus einer Serie von monatlichen Poster-Führern durch das New Yorker Stadtleben, die in *New York* eingebunden wurden. Farbig. (USA)
461 Doppelseite aus einem Artikel über die Forest-Hills-Tennisturniere, mit Vignetten der führenden Spieler, in *New York.* (USA)
462 Ganzseitiges Porträt von Bob Dylan aus einem Artikel über ihn in *New York.* (USA)
463 Ganzseitiges Farbporträt von Derek Sanderson aus einem Hockey-Artikel in *New York.* (USA)
464 Ganzseitiges Farbporträt von Joel Grey aus einem Artikel in *New York* bezüglich eines Broadway-Stückes über Jeanne d'Arc. (USA)
465 Schwarzweiss-Porträt des Pop-Sängers Stevie Wonder in *New York.* Ganzseitig. (USA)

459, 460 Entête et calendrier d'information complet. D'une série d'affiches mensuelles avec le programme des événements culturels à New York. Encart du magazine *New York.* Couleur. (USA)
461 Double page accompagnant un article sur un championnat de tennis à Forest Hills, avec des vignettes des meilleurs joueurs. Extrait du magazine *New York.* (USA)
462 Portrait pleine page de Bob Dylan d'un article sur lui dans *New York.* Monochrome. (USA)
463 Portrait pleine page de Derek Sanderson d'un article sur le hockey dans *New York.* (USA)
464 Portrait sur page entière de Joel Grey. L'article correspondant du magazine *New York* est consacré au Broadway où Grey joue le rôle du Dauphin dans une pièce sur Jeanne d'Arc. (USA)
465 Portrait en noir et blanc du chanteur pop Stevie Wonder, d'un article dans *New York.* (USA)

ARTIST / KÜNSTLER / ARTISTE:

459 Barbara Nessim
460 Jerry Joyner
461 David Levine
462 Milton Glaser
463 John O'Leary
464 James McMullan
465 Christian Piper

DESIGNER / GESTALTER:

459 Walter Bernard
461 Walter Bernard/Paul Richer
463–465 Tom Bentkowski

ART DIRECTOR:

459–462, 464, 465 Walter Bernard/Milton Glaser
463 Walter Bernard

PUBLISHER / VERLEGER / EDITEUR:

459–465 The New York Magazine

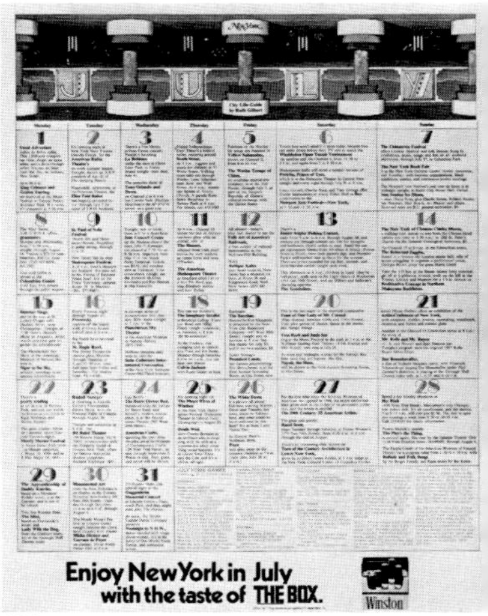

460

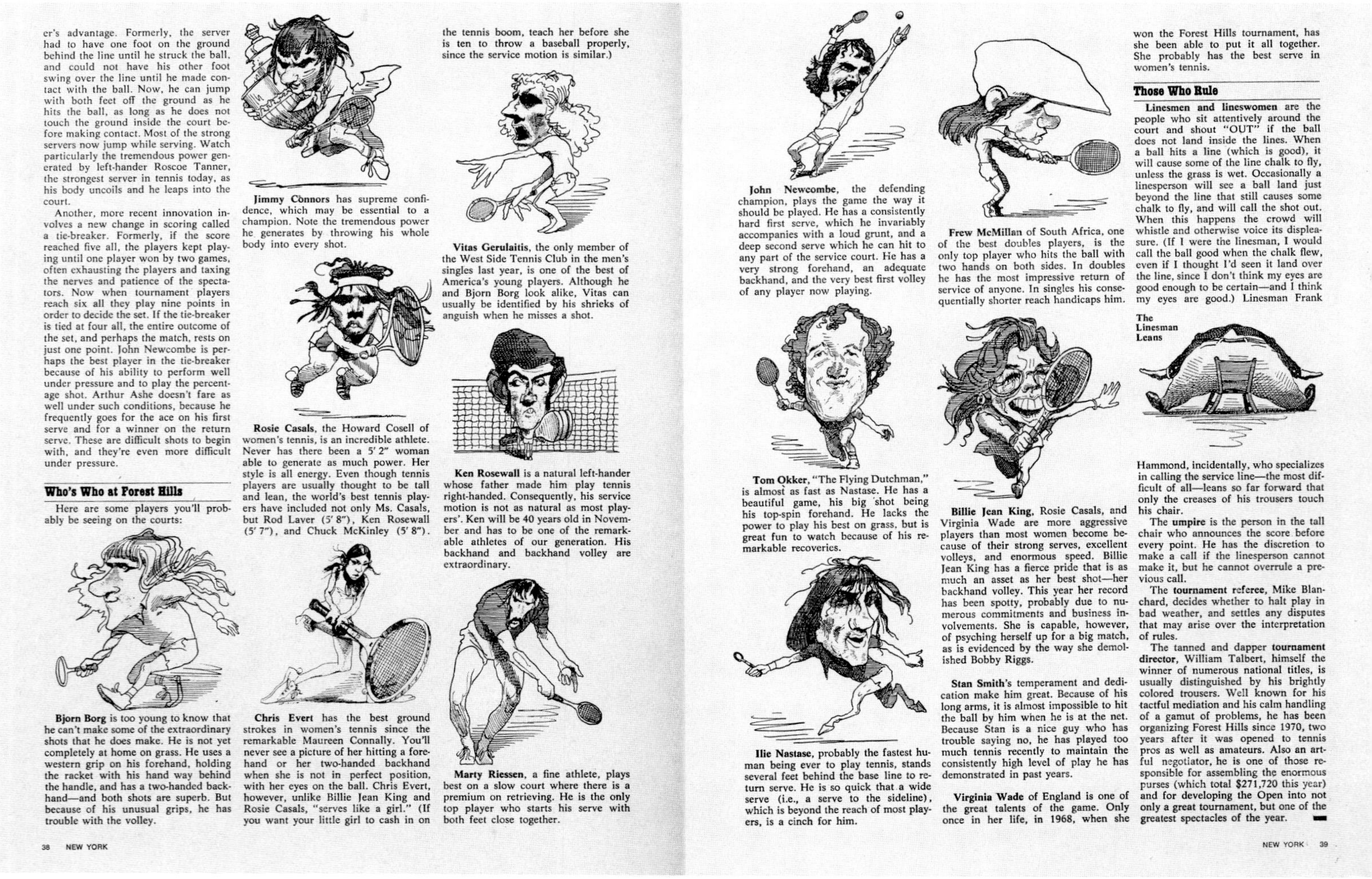

er's advantage. Formerly, the server had to have one foot on the ground behind the line until he struck the ball, and could not have his other foot swing over the line until he made contact with the ball. Now, he can jump with both feet off the ground as he hits the ball, as long as he does not touch the ground inside the court before making contact. Most of the strong servers now jump while serving. Watch particularly the tremendous power generated by left-hander Roscoe Tanner, the strongest server in tennis today, as his body uncoils and he leaps into the court.

Another, more recent innovation involves a new change in scoring called a tie-breaker. Formerly, if the score reached five all, the players kept playing until one player won by two games, often exhausting the players and taxing the nerves and patience of the spectators. Now when tournament players reach six all they play nine points in order to decide the set. If the tie-breaker is tied at four all, the entire outcome of the set, and perhaps the match, rests on just one point. John Newcombe is perhaps the best player in the tie-breaker because of his ability to perform well under pressure and to play the percentage shot. Arthur Ashe doesn't fare as well under such conditions, because he frequently goes for the ace on his first serve and for a winner on the return serve. These are difficult shots to begin with, and they're even more difficult under pressure.

Who's Who at Forest Hills

Here are some players you'll probably be seeing on the courts:

Bjorn Borg is too young to know that he can't make some of the extraordinary shots that he does make. He is not yet completely at home on grass. He uses a western grip on his forehand, holding the racket with his hand way behind the handle, and has a two-handed backhand—and both shots are superb. But because of his unusual grips, he has trouble with the volley.

Jimmy Connors has supreme confidence, which may be essential to a champion. Note the tremendous power he generates by throwing his whole body into every shot.

Rosie Casals, the Howard Cosell of women's tennis, is an incredible athlete. Never has there been a 5′ 2″ woman able to generate as much power. Her style is all energy. Even though tennis players are usually thought to be tall and lean, the world's best tennis players have included not only Ms. Casals, but Rod Laver (5′ 8″), Ken Rosewall (5′ 7″), and Chuck McKinley (5′ 8″).

Chris Evert has the best ground strokes in women's tennis since the remarkable Maureen Connally. You'll never see a picture of her hitting a forehand or her two-handed backhand when she is not in perfect position, with her eyes on the ball. Chris Evert, however, unlike Billie Jean King and Rosie Casals, "serves like a girl." (If you want your little girl to cash in on the tennis boom, teach her before she is ten to throw a baseball properly, since the service motion is similar.)

Vitas Gerulaitis, the only member of the West Side Tennis Club in the men's singles last year, is one of the best of America's young players. Although he and Bjorn Borg look alike, Vitas can usually be identified by his shrieks of anguish when he misses a shot.

Ken Rosewall is a natural left-hander whose father made him play tennis right-handed. Consequently, his service motion is not as natural as most players'. Ken will be 40 years old in November and has to be one of the remarkable athletes of our generation. His backhand and backhand volley are extraordinary.

Marty Riessen, a fine athlete, plays best on a slow court where there is a premium on retrieving. He is the only top player who starts his serve with both feet close together.

38 NEW YORK

John Newcombe, the defending champion, plays the game the way it should be played. He has a consistently hard first serve, which he invariably accompanies with a loud grunt, and a deep second serve which he can hit to any part of the service court. He has a very strong forehand, an adequate backhand, and the very best first volley of any player now playing.

Tom Okker, "The Flying Dutchman," is almost as fast as Nastase. He has a beautiful game, his big shot being his top-spin forehand. He lacks the power to play his best on grass, but is great fun to watch because of his remarkable recoveries.

Ilie Nastase, probably the fastest human being ever to play tennis, stands several feet behind the base line to return serve. He is so quick that a wide serve (i.e., a serve to the sideline), which is beyond the reach of most players, is a cinch for him.

Frew McMillan of South Africa, one of the best doubles players, is the only top player who hits the ball with two hands on both sides. In doubles he has the most impressive return of service of anyone. In singles his consequentially shorter reach handicaps him.

Billie Jean King, Rosie Casals, and Virginia Wade are more aggressive players than most women become because of their strong serves, excellent volleys, and enormous speed. Billie Jean King has a fierce pride that is as much an asset as her best shot—her backhand volley. This year her record has been spotty, probably due to numerous commitments and business involvements. She is capable, however, of psyching herself up for a big match, as is evidenced by the way she demolished Bobby Riggs.

Stan Smith's temperament and dedication make him great. Because of his long arms, it is almost impossible to hit the ball by him when he is at the net. Because Stan is a nice guy who has trouble saying no, he has played too much tennis recently to maintain the consistently high level of play he has demonstrated in past years.

Virginia Wade of England is one of the great talents of the game. Only once in her life, in 1968, when she won the Forest Hills tournament, has she been able to put it all together. She probably has the best serve in women's tennis.

Those Who Rule

Linesmen and lineswomen are the people who sit attentively around the court and shout "OUT" if the ball does not land inside the lines. When a ball hits a line (which is good), it will cause some of the line chalk to fly, unless the grass is wet. Occasionally a linesperson will see a ball land just beyond the line that still causes some chalk to fly, and will call the shot out. When this happens the crowd will whistle and otherwise voice its displeasure. (If I were the linesman, I would call the ball good when the chalk flew, even if I thought I'd seen it land over the line, since I don't think my eyes are good enough to be certain—and I think my eyes are good.) Linesman Frank Hammond, incidentally, who specializes in calling the service line—the most difficult of all—leans so far forward that only the creases of his trousers touch his chair.

The Linesman Leans

The **umpire** is the person in the tall chair who announces the score before every point. He has the discretion to make a call if the linesperson cannot make it, but he cannot overrule a previous call.

The **tournament referee**, Mike Blanchard, decides whether to halt play in bad weather, and settles any disputes that may arise over the interpretation of rules.

The tanned and dapper **tournament director**, William Talbert, himself the winner of numerous national titles, is usually distinguished by his brightly colored trousers. Well known for his tactful mediation and his calm handling of a gamut of problems, he has been organizing Forest Hills since 1970, two years after it was opened to tennis pros as well as amateurs. Also an artful negotiator, he is one of those responsible for assembling the enormous purses (which total $271,720 this year) and for developing the Open into not only a great tournament, but one of the greatest spectacles of the year.

NEW YORK 39

461

462

463

464

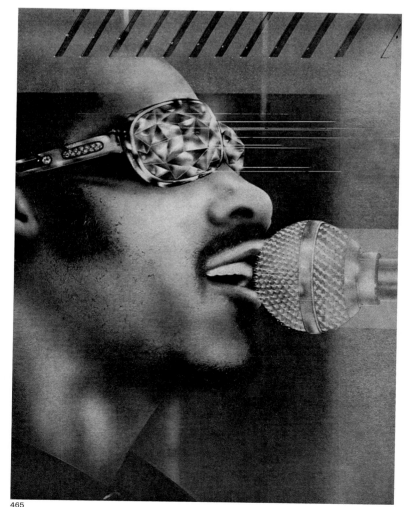

465

466

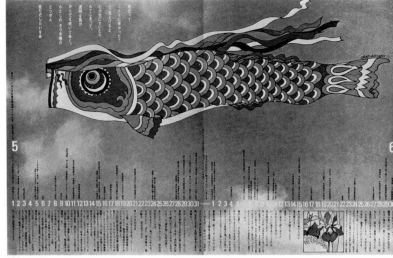

467

468

469

Magazine Illustrations
Zeitschriften-Illustrationen
Illustrations de périodiques

466 Double spread opening an article on the presence of lead in canned milk in *Essence* magazine. Black and white. (USA)
467 Double-spread calendar from a series in PR magazine. Fish in bright reds, yellow, green and white on a blue ground. (JPN)
468 Opening spread of a feature published in *Atlanta* magazine on the blandishments of swindlers. Full colour. (USA)
469 Double spread opening an article in *Atlanta* magazine on the subject of motivating salesmen. Bright colours, green suit. (USA)
470 Illustration from an article in *New York* magazine on the female assessment of the male and his shortcomings. (USA)
471 Full-page illustration from an article in *New York* on the independent and eccentric character of the State of New Jersey. (USA)

466 Einleitende Doppelseite eines Artikels über den Bleigehalt von Konservenmilch in der Zeitschrift *Essence*. Schwarzweiss. (USA)
467 Doppelseitiger Kalender aus einer Serie im Magazin PR. Fisch in lebhaften Rottönen, Gelb, Grün und Weiss auf blauem Grund. (JPN)
468 Einleitende Doppelseite eines im Magazin *Atlanta* veröffentlichten Artikels über die Schmeicheleien von Schwindlern. Mehrfarbig. (USA)
469 Einleitende Doppelseite eines in *Atlanta* veröffentlichten Artikels über die Motivation von Handelsreisenden. Lebhafte Farben, grüner Anzug. (USA)
470 Illustration aus einem Artikel in *New York* über das weibliche Urteil bezüglich der Schwächen des Mannes. (USA)
471 Ganzseitige Illustration aus einem Artikel in *New York* über den unabhängigen und exzentrischen Charakter des Staates New Jersey. (USA)

466 Double page introduisant un article sur les résidus de plomb contenus dans le lait en boîte. Extrait du magazine *Essence*. Noir et blanc. (USA)
467 Calendrier sur page double extrait d'une série qui a paru dans PR magazine. Poisson en couleurs vives (rouge, jaune et vert) sur fond bleu. (JPN)
468 Page double introduisant un article sur les cajoleries des escrocs, paru dans le magazine *Atlanta*. En couleur. (USA)
469 Page double introduisant un article dans le magazine *Atlanta* sur la justification de l'engagement de représentants. Couleurs vives, habit vert. (USA)
470 Illustration du magazine *New York* pour un article sur les imperfections de l'homme et le jugement féminin sur l'homme. (USA)
471 Illustration pleine page du magazine *New York*, pour un article sur le caractère indépendant et eccentrique de l'état de New Jersey. (USA)

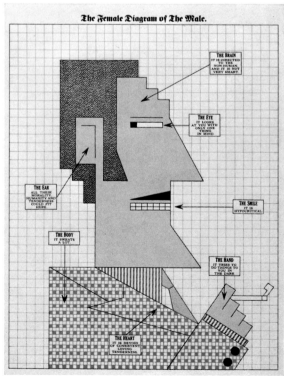

470

471

ARTIST / KÜNSTLER / ARTISTE:

466 Walter Velez
467 Taro Yoshida
468, 469 Gene Wilkes
470, 471 Seymour Chwast

DESIGNER / GESTALTER / MAQUETTISTE:

470, 471 Walter Bernard

ART DIRECTOR / DIRECTEUR ARTISTIQUE:

466 Alexander Mapp
467 Taro Yoshida
468, 469 Suzanne Anderson
470 Walter Bernard
471 Walter Bernard/Milton Glaser

PUBLISHER / VERLEGER / EDITEUR:

466 Hollingsworth Group
467 Toa Kosan
468, 469 Atlanta Magazine
470, 471 The New York Magazine

472

473

474

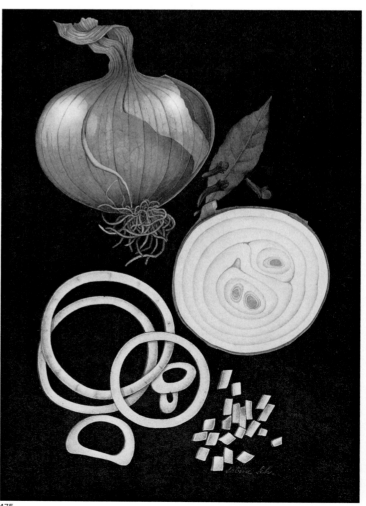

475

472 Colour illustration of "the world's most complicated recipe" accompanying a cookery competition in *Tages-Anzeiger-Magazin*. (SWI)
473–475 Full-page colour illustrations from culinary articles in *Tages-Anzeiger-Magazin* on the garlic and leek family (Fig. 473), on peas, beans and lentils (Fig. 474) and on the onion (Fig. 475). (SWI)
476 Double spread with brightly coloured illustrations from a feature in *Human Behavior* magazine on a new psychological training. (USA)
477, 478 Complete cover and detail of the artwork for an issue of *Avant-Garde* containing an article on the art of Roy Carruthers. (USA)

472 Farbillustration des «kompliziertesten Rezeptes der Welt» im Rahmen eines Kochwettbewerbes im *Tages-Anzeiger-Magazin*. (SWI)
473–475 Ganzseitige Farbillustrationen aus kulinarischen Artikeln im *Tages-Anzeiger-Magazin* über Knoblauch und die Lauch-Familie (Abb. 473), über Erbsen, Bohnen, Linsen (Abb. 474) und über Zwiebeln (Abb. 475). (SWI)
476 Doppelseite mit bunten Illustrationen aus einem Artikel in der Zeitschrift *Human Behavior* über ein neues Psychologie-Training. (USA)
477, 478 Vollständiger Umschlag und Illustrationsausschnitt aus einer Ausgabe von *Avant-Garde*, die einen Artikel über die Kunst des Graphikers Roy Carruthers enthält. (USA)

472 Illustration en couleur de «la recette la plus compliquée du monde entier». D'un concours culinaire dans le *Tages-Anzeiger-Magazin*. (SWI)
473–475 Illustrations sur pages entières (en couleur) extraites d'une série d'articles parus dans le supplément hebdomadaire du *Tages-Anzeiger*. Fig. 473: référence à l'ail et le poireau, fig. 474: aux petits pois, aux haricots et aux lentilles, fig. 475: aux oignons. (SWI)
476 Page double avec illustrations en couleurs. Article du magazine *Human Behavior* sur une nouvelle méthode d'éducation psychologique. (USA)
477, 478 Couverture complète et détail de l'illustration d'un numéro d'*Avant-garde* contenant un article sur l'art de Roy Carruthers. (USA)

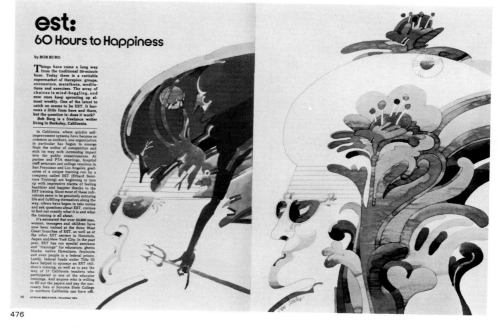

476

477

ARTIST / KÜNSTLER / ARTISTE:

472–475 Sabine Schroer
476 Don Weller
477, 478 Roy Carruthers

ART DIRECTOR / DIRECTEUR ARTISTIQUE:

472 Paul Kälin
473–475 Albert Kälin
476 Annemarie Clarke
477, 478 Herb Lubalin

AGENCY / AGENTUR / AGENCE – STUDIO:

476 Weller Institute
477, 478 Lubalin, Smith, Carnase, Inc.

PUBLISHER / VERLEGER / EDITEUR:

472–475 Tages Anzeiger AG
476 Human Behavior
477, 478 Avant-Garde

Magazine Illustrations
Zeitschriften-Illustrationen
Illustrations de périodiques

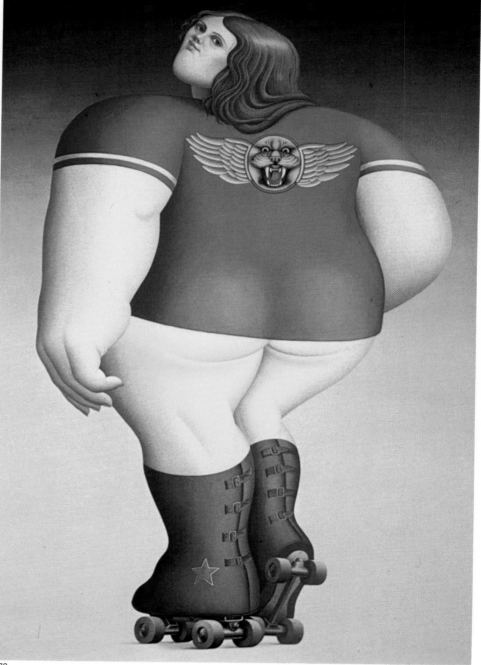

478

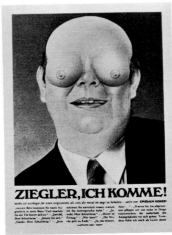

480

ARTIST / KÜNSTLER / ARTISTE:

479 Tadanori Yokoo
480, 481 Noss + Sickert
482 Eraldo Carugati/Kerrig Pope (Design)
483 Rainer C. Friz

ART DIRECTOR / DIRECTEUR ARTISTIQUE:

479 Tadanori Yokoo
480, 481, 483 Rainer Wörtmann
482 Art Paul

AGENCY / AGENTUR / AGENCE – STUDIO:

482 Stephens, Biondi, De Cicco, Inc.

PUBLISHER / VERLEGER / EDITEUR:

479 Shueisha
480, 481, 483 Heinrich Bauer Verlag
482 Playboy Enterprises

479 Full-page illustration from an article on old customs in the Japanese version of *Playboy* magazine. (JPN)
480 Full-page colour illustration from a story in *Playboy*. (USA)
481 Full-page illustration from a story in *Playboy*. Full colour. (USA)
482 Colour illustration opening a story about oil workers in the German edition of *Playboy*. (GER)
483 Colour illustration opening an article on the interest taken by managers in moral aspects of employee behaviour. From the German *Playboy*. (GER)

479 Ganzseitige Illustration aus einem Artikel über alte Bräuche in der japanischen Ausgabe von *Playboy*. (JPN)
480 Ganzseitige Farbillustration aus einer Erzählung in *Playboy*. (USA)
481 Ganzseitige Illustration aus einer Erzählung in *Playboy*. Mehrfarbig. (USA)
482 Farbillustration zu einer Geschichte über Öl-Arbeiter, erschienen im deutschen *Playboy*. (GER)
483 Farbillustration als Eröffnung eines Artikels über das Interesse der Manager für Aspekte des moralischen Verhaltens von Angestellten. Aus dem deutschen *Playboy*. (GER)

479 Illustration pleine page d'un article sur les coutumes d'autrefois. Extrait de l'édition japonaise de *Playboy*. (JPN)
480 Illustration pleine page pour une nouvelle parue dans *Playboy*. (USA)
481 Illustration sur page entière pour un récit paru dans *Playboy*. (USA)
482 Illustration polychrome introduisant un article sur les employés de l'industrie pétrolière. Extrait de l'édition allemande de *Playboy*. (GER)
483 Illustration polychrome introduisant un article sur les managers et l'intérêt qu'ils portent aux aspects moraux de la conduite des employés. (GER)

479

Magazine Illustrations

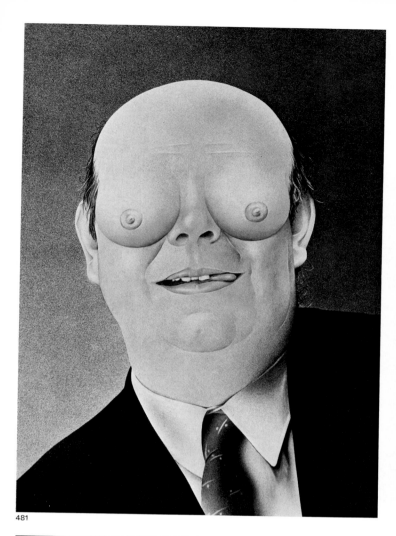

481

ILLUSTRATION BY ERALDO CARUGATI

482

483

484

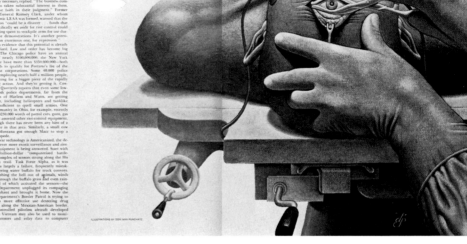

485

486

484 Full-page black-and-white illustration for an article in the magazine *Coast* about splitting California into two states. (USA)
485 Double spread from *Playboy*. The article is about government surveillance of citizens, and the "eye" is visible through the punched hole on the left. (USA)
486 Double-spread illustration opening a story in the Japanese *Playboy*. (JPN)
487 Cover of a cultural magazine published in Berne, *der Löwe* (the Lion). Pen drawing. (SWI)
488 Illustration from *Playboy* magazine. Full colour. (USA)

484 Ganzseitige Schwarzweiss-Illustration aus einem Artikel der Zeitschrift *Coast* über den Vorschlag, Kalifornien in zwei Staaten zu teilen. (USA)
485 Doppelseite aus *Playboy* über die Beaufsichtigung von Bürgern durch die Regierung. Das «Auge» ist durch das Loch in der linken Seite sichtbar. (USA)
486 Doppelseitige Illustration als Eröffnung einer Geschichte im japanischen *Playboy*. (JPN)
487 Umschlag der Kulturzeitschrift *der Löwe*, in Bern herausgegeben. Federzeichnung. (SWI)
488 Illustration aus *Playboy*. Mehrfarbig. (USA)

484 Illustration pleine page en noir et blanc pour un article dans le magazine *Coast* sur un éventuel partage en deux de l'état de Californie. (USA)
485 Page double de *Playboy*. L'article est consacré à la surveillance des citoyens par le gouvernement. «L'œil» est visible à travers le trou découpé à gauche. (USA)
486 Illustration sur page double introduisant une nouvelle dans l'édition japonaise de *Playboy*. (JPN)
487 Couverture du magazine culturel *der Löwe* (le lion), publié à Berne. Dessin à la plume. (SWI)
488 Illustration de *Playboy*. En couleur. (USA)

ARTIST / KÜNSTLER / ARTISTE:

484 Seymour Chwast
485 Don Ivan Punchatz
486 Tadanori Yokoo
487 Roland Topor
488 Christian Piper

ART DIRECTOR:

484 Don Owens
485, 488 Art Paul
486 Tadanori Yokoo
487 Roland Gfeller-Corthésy

PUBLISHER / VERLEGER:

484 Macro/Comm Corp.
485, 488 Playboy Enterprises
486 Shueisha
487 Lisbet Kornfeld Verlag

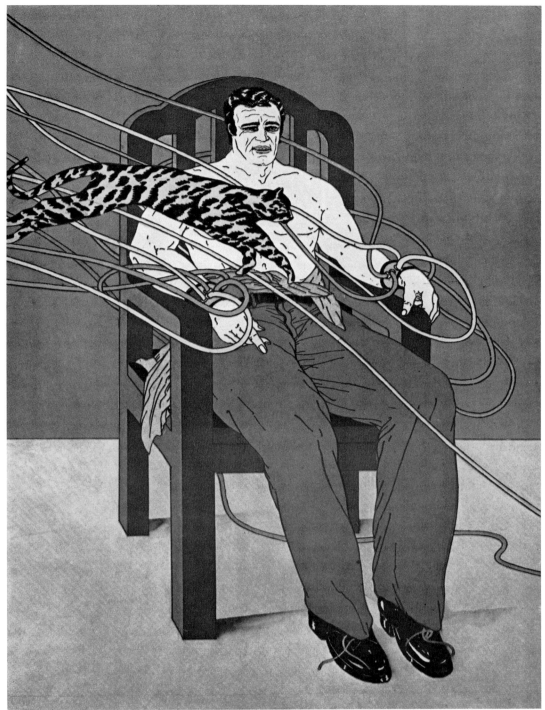

488

487

Magazine Illustrations
Zeitschriften-Illustrationen
Illustrations de périodiques

489 Full-page illustration from an article in *Ms* magazine on the rise of men's clubs in America. Full colour, predominantly brown shades. (USA)
490 Double-spread illustration from a feature in *Audience* magazine. (USA)
491 Double spread opening a story in the German *Playboy* entitled "Torture for the Boss". Illustrations in colour. (GER)
492 Double-spread colour illustration from the Japanese *Playboy*. (JPN)

489 Ganzseitige Illustration aus einem Artikel in der Zeitschrift *Ms* über den Aufstieg der Männerclubs in Amerika. Mehrfarbig, vorwiegend Brauntöne. (USA)
490 Doppelseitige Illustration aus einem Artikel in der Zeitschrift *Audience*. (USA)
491 Einleitende Doppelseite einer Geschichte im deutschen *Playboy* mit dem Titel «Folter für den Chef». Farbige Illustrationen. (GER)
492 Doppelseitige Farbillustration aus dem japanischen *Playboy*. (JPN)

489 Illustration pleine page se référant au nombre accru de clubs d'hommes aux Etats-Unis. Article paru dans le magazine *Ms*. En couleur, teintes prédominantes brunes. (USA)
490 Illustration sur page double figurant dans un article du magazine *Audience*. (USA)
491 Page double introduisant une nouvelle intitulée «La torture pour le chef», parue dans l'édition allemande de *Playboy*. Illustrations en couleur. (GER)
492 Illustration sur page double de l'édition japonaise de *Playboy*. En couleur. (JPN)

489

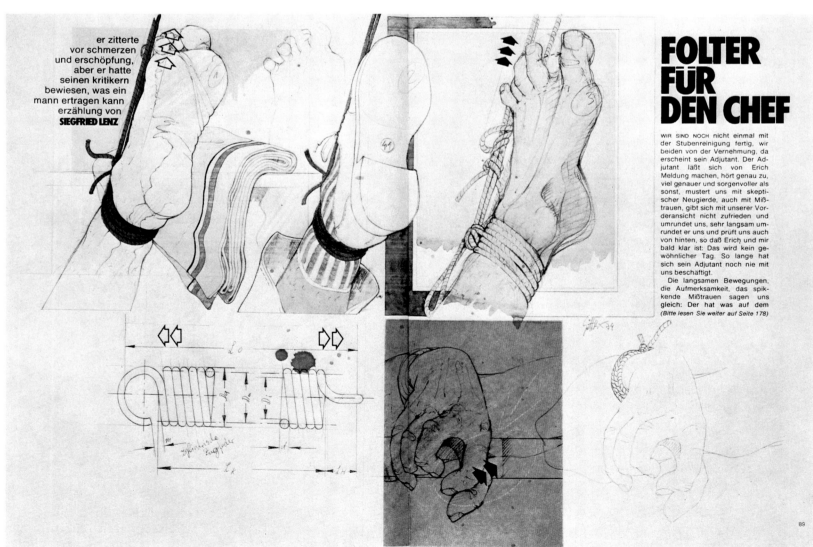

er zitterte
vor schmerzen
und erschöpfung,
aber er hatte
seinen kritikern
bewiesen, was ein
mann ertragen kann
erzählung von
SIEGFRIED LENZ

FOLTER FÜR DEN CHEF

WIR SIND NOCH nicht einmal mit der Stubenreinigung fertig, wir beiden von der Vernehmung, da erscheint sein Adjutant. Der Adjutant läßt sich von Erich Meldung machen, hört genau zu, viel genauer und sorgenvoller als sonst, mustert uns mit skeptischer Neugierde, auch mit Mißtrauen, gibt sich mit unserer Voransicht nicht zufrieden und umrundet uns, sehr langsam umrundet er uns und prüft uns auch von hinten, so daß Erich und mir bald klar ist: Das wird kein gewöhnlicher Tag. So lange hat sich sein Adjutant noch nie mit uns beschäftigt.

Die langsamen Bewegungen, die Aufmerksamkeit, das spikkende Mißtrauen sagen uns gleich: Der hat was auf dem (Bitte lesen Sie weiter auf Seite 178)

491

490

ILLUSTRATED BY CHRISTIAN PIPER

492

163

493

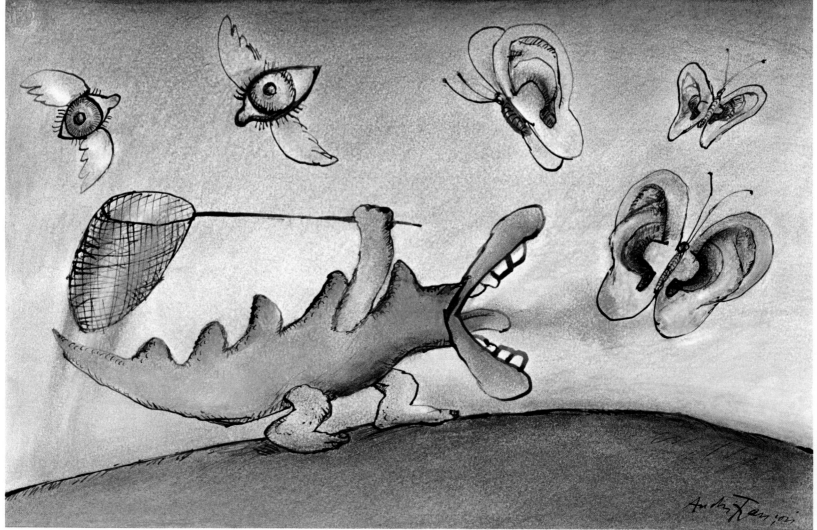

494

493 Colour illustration for an article in *record*, a magazine for young people, about the free fashions of modern youth. (FRA)
494 Double spread from *record*, intended for use as a poster, showing the "Publicity Beast, a great devourer of eyes and ears". (FRA)
495 Black-and-white illustration for a story published in *Club International*. (GBR)
496 Portrait in yellow-green shades from an article on Gandhi in *record* magazine. (FRA)

493 Farbillustration zu einem Artikel in *record*, einer Zeitschrift für junge Leute, über die freien Moden der modernen Jugend. (FRA)
494 Doppelseite aus *record*, als Poster zu benützen, welches das «Biest Werbung, ein grosser Verzehrer von Augen und Ohren» zeigt. (FRA)
495 Schwarzweiss-Illustration einer im *Club International* veröffentlichten Geschichte. (GBR)
496 Porträt in gelbgrünen Tönen aus einem Artikel über Gandhi in der Jugendzeitschrift *record*. (FRA)

493 Illustration polychrome pour un article paru dans *record*, un magazine de la jeune génération, ici avec référence à la mode libre des jeunes gens. (FRA)
494 Page double publiée dans le magazine *record*. Elle est destinée à être employée en tant qu'affiche décorative. (FRA)
495 Illustration en noir et blanc pour un récit paru dans le magazine *Club International*. (GBR)
496 Portrait en teintes jaunes et vertes illustrant un article sur Gandhi dans le magazine *record*. (FRA)

495

496

ARTIST / KÜNSTLER / ARTISTE:

493 Louis de Boynes
494 André François
495 Owen Wood
496 Etienne Delessert

ART DIRECTOR:

493, 494, 496 Etienne Delessert
495 Steve Ridgeway

PUBLISHER / VERLEGER:

493, 494, 496 Bayard Presse
495 Paul Raymond Publications

Magazine Illustrations
Zeitschriften-Illustrationen
Illustrations de périodiques

497

498

497, 498 Drawings in full colour illustrating statements by children as to what animal they would most like to be, from *Femme pratique* magazine. (FRA)
499 Double-spread illustration in *Coast* magazine, from an article on the use of computers in psychiatry. Black and white. (USA)
500 Opening spread of an article about violence in *Shock!* magazine. Black and white, purple shirts. (GER)

497, 498 Farbige Zeichnungen als Illustration zur Aussage von Kindern über das Tier, das sie am liebsten sein möchten. Aus einer französischen Zeitschrift. (FRA)
499 Doppelseitige Illustration aus einem Artikel in der Zeitschrift *Coast* über den Gebrauch von Computern in der Psychiatrie. Schwarzweiss. (USA)
500 Einleitende Doppelseite zu einem Artikel über Gewalttätigkeit aus der Zeitschrift *Shock!* Schwarzweiss, Hemden violett. (GER)

497, 498 Dessins en couleur illustrant des déclarations faites par des enfants sur leurs préférences au cas où ils auraient le choix d'être un animal. D'un article publié dans *Femme pratique*. (FRA)
499 Illustration sur page double du magazine *Coast*, pour un article discutant les avantages et inconvénients des ordinateurs employés dans la psychiatrie. (USA)
500 Page double initiale du magazine *Shock!* introduisant un article sur la violence. Noir et blanc, chemises violettes. (GER)

ARTIST / KÜNSTLER / ARTISTE:

497, 498 André Dahan
499 Jack Unruh
500 Günter Blum

ART DIRECTOR / DIRECTEUR ARTISTIQUE:

497, 498 Yvan de la Girauniere
499 Don Owens
500 Noelle Thieux

AGENCY / AGENTUR / AGENCE – STUDIO:

499 Coast Magazine

PUBLISHER / VERLEGER / EDITEUR:

497, 498 Magazine Femme pratique
499 Macro/Comm. Corp.
500 Shock (Hans Gamber)

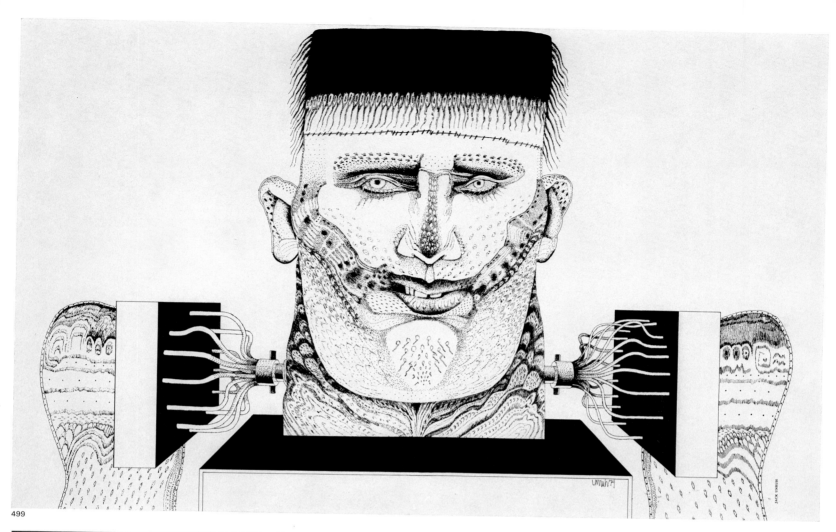

499

Einer von uns beiden

Wer dominiert hier über wen?
Keine Frage - es ist ohnehin alles
nur sinnlose Gewalt. Aber einer
fand bestimmt kein kreatives Ventil,
und einer leidet unter destruktiver
Psychose. Warum? COLIN WILSON
erforscht dieses dunkle Reich
zwischenmenschlicher Beziehungen.

500

501

502

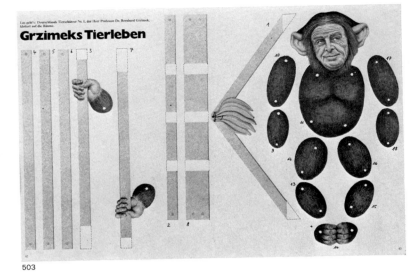

503

ARTIST / KÜNSTLER / ARTISTE:

502, 503 Günter Blum
504 Hans Arnold
505 Daniel Guerrier
501, 506 Vlasta Zabransky
507 Heinz Stieger

ART DIRECTOR / DIRECTEUR ARTISTIQUE:

507 Taussig

PUBLISHER / VERLEGER / EDITEUR:

501–507 Pardon Verlagsgesellschaft mbH

504

Magazine Illustrations

168

505

506

501, 504 Covers of a special section of the magazine *Pardon* entitled "The Truth". (GER)
502, 503 Cover and spread from an issue of *Pardon*
with a cut-out model of the popular zoologist,
Prof. Grzimek. Full colour. (GER)
505 Colour page with a cartoon of a mixed relay
race, from *Pardon* magazine. (GER)
506 Cartoon from *Pardon* referring to an announcement about abolition of the censorship at the
time of the Greek Junta. (GER)
507 Black-and-white drawing serving as subject
for a verse competition in *Pardon*. (GER)

501, 504 Umschläge einer Beilage der Zeitschrift
Pardon mit dem Titel «Die Wahrheit». (GER)
502, 503 Umschlag und Doppelseite einer Ausgabe von *Pardon* mit einem Modell zum Aus-
schneiden des populären Zoologen Prof. Grzimek.
Mehrfarbig. (GER)
505 Farbseite mit einem Cartoon über einen ge-
mischten Staffellauf, aus *Pardon*. (GER)
506 Cartoon aus *Pardon*, das Bezug nimmt auf die
Ankündigung der Zensur-Abschaffung zur Zeit der
Militärjunta in Griechenland. (GER)
507 Schwarzweiss-Zeichnung als Thema für einen
Gedichte-Wettbewerb in *Pardon*. (GER)

501, 504 Couverture d'un supplément spécial du
magazine *Pardon*, intitulé «La vérité». (GER)
502, 503 Couverture et page double d'un numéro
de *Pardon* avec une maquette découpée du
prof. Grzimek, le célèbre zoologue. En couleur. (GER)
505 Page en couleur avec une caricature sur une
course de relais pour hommes et femmes. (GER)
506 Caricature parue dans *Pardon*. Elle se réfère à
un avis en faveur de l'abolition de la censure que
la Junte grècque a introduite après la prise du
pouvoir. (GER)
507 Dessin noir-blanc qui a servi de sujet pour un
concours de poésie dans *Pardon*. (GER)

507

169

ARTIST / KÜNSTLER / ARTISTE:
508–511 Bruno Caruso

ART DIRECTOR / DIRECTEUR ARTISTIQUE:
508–511 Giuseppe Orlandi

PUBLISHER / VERLEGER / EDITEUR:
508–511 S. F. Flaccovio

508

509

510

511

508–511 From an issue of the cultural and tourist publication *Sicilia* which was illustrated throughout by the same artist. Fig. 508: Detail of a full-page coloured drawing of the octopus of Villa Igiea; Fig. 509: detail of a pen drawing of a model among cushions; Fig. 510: cover of the issue, with face and map of the island in colour; Fig. 511: contents page, with map of Palermo and margin in sepia shades. (ITA)

508–511 Aus einer Ausgabe der Kultur- und Touristik-Zeitschrift *Sicilia*, die durchwegs vom selben Künstler illustriert wurde. Abb. 508: Ausschnitt einer ganzseitigen Farbillustration des Kraken der Villa Igiea; Abb. 509: Ausschnitt einer Federzeichnung eines Modells zwischen Kissen; Abb. 510: Umschlag der Ausgabe mit Gesicht und Karte der Insel in Farben; Abb. 511: Seite des Inhaltsverzeichnisses, Karte von Palermo und Rand in Sepiatönen. (ITA)

508–511 Illustrations extraites d'un numéro de *Sicilia*, une publication culturelle et touristique. Toutes les illustrations de ce numéro ont été réalisées par le même artiste. Fig. 508: détail d'un dessin sur page entière représentant le poulpe de la Villa Igiea, en couleur; fig. 509: détail d'un dessin à la plume d'un modèle au milieu de coussins; fig. 510: couverture du numéro dont ces illustrations ont été extraites, visage et carte de l'île en couleur; fig. 511: sommaire, plan de Palerme et marge en teintes sépia. (ITA)

512

513

Five ways to look at one elephant

514

ARTIST / KÜNSTLER / ARTISTE:

512, 513 Bruno Caruso
514, 515 Milton Glaser
516 Charles Santore

ART DIRECTOR / DIRECTEUR ARTISTIQUE:

512, 513 Giuseppe Orlandi
514, 515 Henry Wolf
516 Pam Hoffman

AGENCY / AGENTUR / AGENCE – STUDIO:

514, 515 Henry Wolf Productions

PUBLISHER / VERLEGER / EDITEUR:

512, 513 S. F. Flaccovio
514, 515 Children's Television Workshop
516 Triangle Publishing, Inc.

Magazine Illustrations

512, 513 Pages from the issue of *Sicilia* illustrated in Figs. 508–511. Fig. 512: octopus fisher (flesh and grey shades); Fig. 513: Proserpina (yellow hair, green grass, pink ground). (ITA)
514 A study in elephants—and in perspective—from *Sesame Street*. Full colour. (USA)
515 Double spread entitled "Crazy World", with the instructions to "find the things you think are wrong", from the children's magazine *Sesame Street*. (USA)
516 Full-page illustration from an article in *Seventeen* magazine on the sexual pressures to which modern girls are exposed. Full colour. (USA)

512, 513 Seiten aus der in den Abb. 508–511 illustrierten Ausgabe von *Sicilia*. Abb. 512: Kraken-Fischer (Fleisch- und Grautöne); Abb. 513: Proserpina (gelbes Haar, grünes Gras). (ITA)
514 Eine Studie über Elefanten – und Perspektive – aus *Sesame Street*. Mehrfarbig. (USA)
515 Doppelseite mit dem Titel «Verrückte Welt», mit der Weisung, «jene Dinge zu finden, die man als falsch empfindet». Aus der Kinderzeitschrift *Sesame Street*. (USA)
516 Ganzseitige Illustration aus einem Artikel in der Zeitschrift *Seventeen* über den sexuellen Druck, dem die heutigen jungen Mädchen ausgesetzt sind. Mehrfarbig. (USA)

512, 513 Pages d'un numéro de *Sicilia* (voir figs. 508–511). Fig. 512: pêcheur de poulpes (teintes chair et gris); fig. 513: Proserpina (cheveux jaunes, pré vert, fond rose). (ITA)
514 Etude sur les éléphants – et la perspective – publié dans *Sesame Street*. (USA)
515 Page double intitulée «Le monde dérangé» avec des instructions pour trouver «les objets qui ne sont pas justes». Extrait du magazine pour enfants *Sesame Street*. (USA)
516 Illustration pleine page figurant dans un article du magazine *Seventeen* sur les jeunes filles d'aujourd'hui et leurs problèmes sexuels. (USA)

516

515

517

This Magazine is in two parts. Part 2 is a report on Fashions of The Times.

The New York Times Magazine
AUGUST 25, 1974 | SECTION 6 | PART 1

Whatever happened to Father? | CONTENTS: PAGE 2

520

518

519

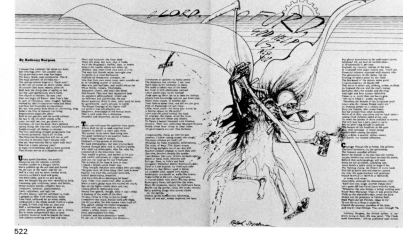

522

523

ARTIST / KÜNSTLER / ARTISTE:

517 518 John Holmes
519 Marshall Arisman
520 Seymour Chwast
521 Christian Piper
522 Ralph Steadman
523 Cathy Hull/Joyce MacDonald/Stavrinos/ Harmo
524 Antonio

DESIGNER / GESTALTER / MAQUETTISTE:

517, 518 John Pym

ART DIRECTOR / DIRECTEUR ARTISTIQUE:

517, 518 Jeanette Collins
519–524 Ruth Ansel

PUBLISHER / VERLEGER / EDITEUR:

517, 518 Times Newspapers Ltd.
519–524 The New York Times

Magazine Illustrations / Zeitschriften-Illustrationen
Illustrations de périodiques

517, 518 Illustration and complete page from a story in a supplement of *The Times*. (GBR)
519 An unexpected skeleton from an article on the automobile in *The New York Times*. (USA)
520 Cover of an issue of *The New York Times Magazine* containing an article on fathers. (USA)
521 Black-and-white illustration from *The New York Times Magazine*. (USA)
522 Double spread with verses for the New Year, from *The New York Times Magazine*. (USA)
523 Double spread on fashions, accessories and household utensils, from *The New York Times Magazine*. Black and white. (USA)
524 Fashion spread (black and white) from *The New York Times Magazine*. (USA)

517, 518 Illustration und vollständige Seite aus einer Erzählung in einer Beilage der *Times*. (GBR)
519 Ein ungewöhnliches Skelett aus einem Artikel über das Auto in *The New York Times*. (USA)
520 Umschlag einer Ausgabe des *New York Times Magazine* mit einem Artikel über Väter. (USA)
521 Schwarzweiss-Illustration aus *The New York Times Magazine*. (USA)
522 Doppelseite mit einem Gedicht zum Neujahr aus *The New York Times Magazine*. (USA)
523 Doppelseite über Mode, Accessoires und Haushaltartikel aus *The New York Times Magazine*. Schwarzweiss. (USA)
524 Mode-Doppelseite (schwarzweiss) aus *The New York Times Magazine*. (USA)

517 518 Illustration et page d'une nouvelle parue dans un supplément du *Times*. (GBR)
519 Un squelette inattendu dans un article sur la voiture dans *The New York Times*. (USA)
520 Couverture d'une édition de *The New York Times Magazine* avec un article sur les pères. (USA)
521 Illustration en noir et blanc du supplément hebdomadaire du *New York Times*. (USA)
522 Page double avec un poème pour Nouvel An, publié dans le supplément hebdomadaire du *New York Times*. (USA)
523 Page double du supplément hebdomadaire du *New York Times*. L'article correspondant est consacré à la mode, aux accessoires de mode et aux ustensiles de ménage. Noir-blanc. (USA)
524 Double page d'un supplément mode (noir et blanc) du *New York Times Magazine*. (USA)

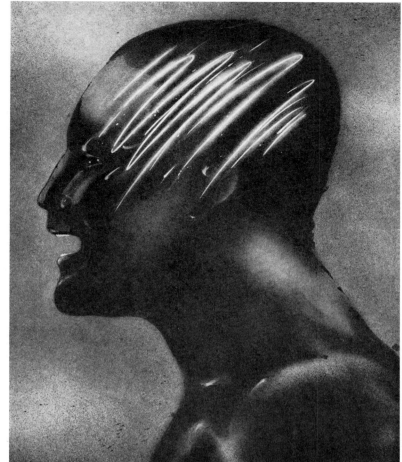

521

Fashion

By Patricia Peterson

As black as magic

Opposite page: Wild mysterious black keynotes winter fashion. A big black cape of soft mohair (big sketch and at right in inset) ties at the neck and swoops on over everything. $150. Hitch, Ltd. Bendel's. Shirt and pants of ebony satin, polyester for practicality (at left in inset), add to an evening's drama. By Calvin Klein. Shirt, $60; pants, $56. Saks Fifth Avenue.

This page: A billowing smock over a full shirt (at left in inset at top), both in a jersey blend, are by Liz Claiborne for Youth Guild. $90. Bloomingdale's. A Chanel-like suit (at right in inset) with longer jacket is hand-crocheted of deepest black bouclé. Designed by Joan Voss. The jacket is $115; the skirt, $110. On the third floor at Bloomingdale's.

The New York Times Magazine/November 24, 1974   69

524

525

526

527

528

529

530

525, 526 Detail of the illustration and complete page opening a prize-winning story published in *The Times*. Black and white. (GBR)
527 Illustration for an article in *The Times* on the laws applying to rape. (GBR)
528 Heading for a special report on sport in *The Times*. (USA)
529 Illustration from an article on American politics in *The New York Times*. (USA)
530 Pen drawing illustrating an article on the Op-Ed page of *The New York Times*. (USA)

525, 526 Illustrationsausschnitt und vollständige Seite als Eröffnung einer preisgekrönte in *The Times* veröffentlichten Geschichte. Schwarzweiss. (GBR)
527 Illustration zu einem Artikel in *The Times* über die Notzuchtgesetze. (GBR)
528 Titel eines Spezialberichtes über Sport in *The Times*. (USA)
529 Illustration aus einem Artikel über amerikanische Politik in *The New York Times*. (USA)
530 Federzeichnung als Illustration zu einem Artikel in *The New York Times*. (USA)

525, 526 Détail de l'illustration et page complète introduisant un récit primé publié da *Times*. Noir et blanc. (GER)
527 Illustration pour un article du *Times* sur les lois appliquées au cas de viol. (GBR)
528 Entête pour un rapport spécial consacré au sport, publié dans le *Times*. (GBR)
529 Illustration pour un article sur la politique américaine, dans le *New York Times*. (U
530 Dessin à la plume illustrant un article paru à la page Op-Ed (face à l'éditorial) d *York Times*. (USA)

ARTIST / KÜNSTLER / ARTISTE:

525, 526 Wayne Anderson
527 Bill Sanderson/Adrian Morris (design)
528 Rod Springett/Klaus Wuttke
529, 530 Jean Claude Suares

ART DIRECTOR / DIRECTEUR ARTISTIQUE:

525–527 Jeanette Collins
528 Valerie Sargent
529, 530 Steve Haller

AGENCY / AGENTUR / AGENCE – STUDIO:

528 Springett, Wuttke Ltd.

PUBLISHER / VERLEGER / EDITEUR:

525–528 Times Newspapers Ltd.
529, 530 The New York Times

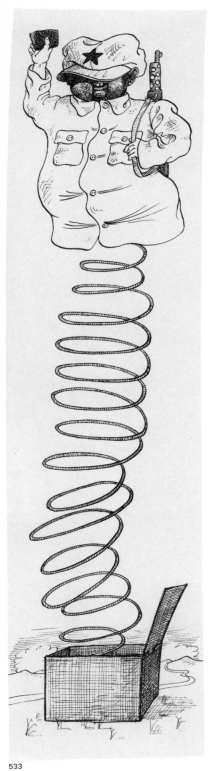

531–535 Drawings, all in black and white, published as free illustrations to (usually controversial) articles on the Op-Ed (opposite editorial) page of *The New York Times*. The articles were on the following subjects: "Chicken" (Fig. 531); "The Battle against Inflation" (Fig. 532); "Chez Mao", a visit to China (Fig. 533); "Highways" (Fig. 534); "The American Dilemma" (Fig. 535). (USA)

531–535 Zeichnungen, alle schwarzweiss, als freie Illustrationen zu (meist aktuellen) Artikeln auf der Op-Ed (dem Editorial gegenüberliegenden) Seite der *New York Times*. Die Artikel bezogen sich auf folgende Themen: «Chicken» (Abb. 531); «Der Kampf gegen die Inflation» (Abb. 532); «Bei Mao», ein China-Besuch (Abb. 533); «Autobahnen» (Abb. 534); «Das amerikanische Dilemma» (Abb.535). (USA)

531–535 Dessins en noir et blanc qui accompagnent en tant qu'illustrations libres les articles sur des questions brûlantes du jour, publiés à la page Op-Ed (face à l'éditorial) du *New York Times*. Les articles correspondants étaient consacrés aux sujets suivants: «Capon» (fig. 531), «La lutte contre l'inflation» (fig. 532), «Chez Mao», une visite en Chine (fig. 533), «Autoroutes» (fig. 534) et «L'embarras américain» (fig. 535). (USA)

533

534

ARTISTE:

de Suares

ARTISTIQUE:

R:

535

MISS·klang

537

Ver·MISS·elle

538

MISS·geburt

539

ARTIST / KÜNSTLER / ARTISTE:

536 Jean Claude Suares
537–540 Oskar Weiss
541 Stane Jagodic
542 Jerry Gersten
543 Hedda Johnson/Herb Lubalin/Marvin Mattelson/Marie Michal/Jerome Snyder
544, 545 Tom C. Haygood

ART DIRECTOR / DIRECTEUR ARTISTIQUE:

536 Steve Heller
541 Stane Bernik
542, 543 Herb Lubalin
544, 545 Tom C. Haygood

AGENCY / AGENTUR / AGENCE – STUDIO:

537–540 Oskar Weiss
542, 543 Lubalin, Smith, Carnase, Inc.

PUBLISHER / VERLEGER / EDITEUR:

536 The New York Times
537–540 Weltwoche-Verlag AG
541 Mestna Galeria
542, 543 International Typeface Corp.
544, 545 San Antonio Light

540

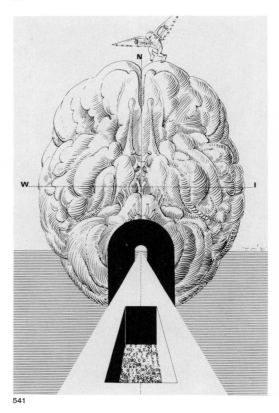

541

536

536 Illustration from an article on the Op-Ed page of *The New York Times* (see preceding spread) on "Rare and Endangered Wildlife". (USA)
537–540 Three of a series of twelve cartoons and page showing their use in the weekly *Die Weltwoche*. They presented the winners of various "Miss" elections in the form of German wordplays. Black and white. (SWI)
541 Cartoon from a Slovenian daily: "A fateful leap."
542, 543 Page and double spread from *U&lc.*, a journal of typographics published by the International Typeface Corporation. Black and white. (USA)
544 Illustration from a review of Solzhenitsyn's *The Gulag Archipelago* in a Sunday issue of *The San Antonio Light*. (USA)
545 Cartoon on the subject of world hunger from a daily, *The San Antonio Light*. (USA)

Newspaper Illustrations
Zeitungs-Illustrationen
Illustrations de journaux

546

547

546, 547 Full-page illustrations in full colour from an annual report of the Empresa Brasileira de Correios e Telégrafos, a mail and telegraph company. (BRA)
548, 549 Full-page illustrations from an annual report of The Ansul Company. They refer to the various fields (fire protection, agricultural and animal-feed chemicals) in which the company operates. (USA)

546, 547 Ganzseitige Farbillustrationen aus einem Jahresbericht der Empresa Brasileira de Correios e Telégrafos, eine Post- und Telegraphen-Gesellschaft. (BRA)
548, 549 Ganzseitige Illustrationen aus einem Jahresbericht der Ansul Company. Sie beziehen sich auf die verschiedenen Gebiete (Feuerschutz, Ackerbau- und Tierfutter-Chemikalien), auf denen die Firma tätig ist. (USA)

546, 547 Illustrations pleines pages du rapport annuel d'une compagnie brasilienne de télé-communication. En couleur. (BRA)
548, 549 Illustrations sur pages entières d'un rapport annuel de l'Ansul Company. Elles se réfèrent aux différents domaines de production (produits pour la protection contre le feu, produits chimiques pour l'agriculture et les animaux). (USA)

ARTIST / KÜNSTLER / ARTISTE:

546, 547 Gian Calvi
548, 549 Leon Travanti

DESIGNER / GESTALTER / MAQUETTISTE:

546, 547 Elber Duarte

ART DIRECTOR / DIRECTEUR ARTISTIQUE:

546, 547 Gian Calvi

AGENCY / AGENTUR / AGENCE – STUDIO:

546, 547 Casa do Desenho
548, 549 Sebstad & Lutrey

**Annual Reports
Jahresberichte
Rapports annuels**

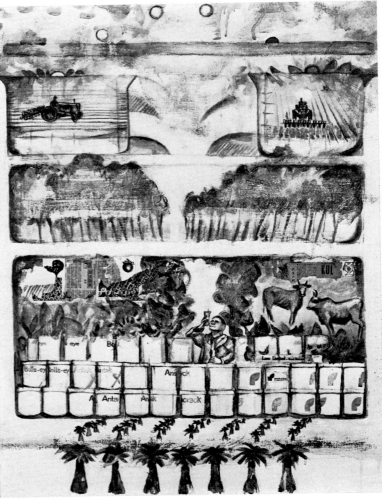

548

550 Cover of an annual report of R.H. Macy & Co., Inc., a department-store enterprise. (USA)
551–553 Cover, colour page (a loan as a partnership) and first page of an annual report in the form of a cheque book for the Alison Mortgage Investment Trust. (USA)
554–556 Cover (black and white) and two double spreads (blue, orange, grey and black figures) from an annual report of the financial and merchandising company *Aristar*. (USA)
557 Double spread from an annual report of The Flying Tiger Corporation, air and rail transport, showing various aspects of development (curves in greens and buff). (USA)
558 Cover of an annual report of Thermo Electron Corp., thermodynamic engineers. Figure yellow, green, blue, grey and black. (USA)

550 Umschlag eines Jahresberichtes von R.H. Macy & Co., Inc., einer Warenhauskette. (USA)
551–553 Umschlag, Farbseite (ein Darlehen als Partnerschaft) und erste Seite eines Jahresberichtes in Form eines Checkheftes, für die Alison Mortgage Investment Trust. (USA)
554–556 Umschlag (schwarzweiss) und zwei Doppelseiten (blaue, orange, graue und schwarze Figuren) aus einem Jahresbericht der Finanz- und Handelsgesellschaft *Aristar*. (USA)
557 Doppelseite aus einem Jahresbericht der Flying Tiger Corporation, Luft- und Schienentransport. Es werden verschiedene Aspekte der Entwicklung gezeigt. Linien in grünen und braungelben Tönen. (USA)
558 Umschlag eines Jahresberichtes der Thermo Electron Corp. Figur mehrfarbig. (USA)

Annual Report August 3, 1974

550

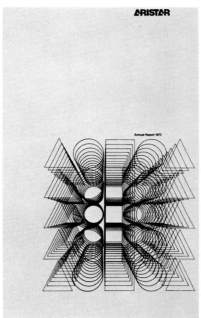

554

550 Couverture du rapport annuel d'une chaine de grands magasins. (USA)
551–553 Couverture, page (un prêt, c'est une forme d'association) et première page du rapport annuel sous forme de carnet de chèques de l'Alison Mortgage Investment Trust. (USA)
554–556 Couverture (noir et blanc) et deux pages doubles (figures en bleu, orange, gris et noir) du rapport annuel d'une compagnie de financement et de commerce. (USA)
557 Double page d'un rapport annuel de la Flying Tiger Corporation (transports aériens et ferroviaires), présentant divers aspects du développement (courbes en vert et chamois). (USA)
558 Couverture du rapport annuel d'une entreprise du domaine de la thermodynamique. Figure en jaune, vert, bleu, gris et noir. (USA)

ARTIST / KÜNSTLER / ARTISTE:

551–553 Don Weller
554 Aaron Marcus
555, 556 Sam Shoulberg/Ken Cooke
557 Rusty Kay
558 Barbara Pfeffer

DESIGNER / GESTALTER / MAQUETTISTE:

554 Eugene J. Grossman
555, 556 Alfred Zurchew
558 Len Fury

ART DIRECTOR / DIRECTEUR ARTISTIQUE:

550 Sheldon Seidler/Bill Mihalik
551–553 Dennis S. Juett
554–556 Eugene J. Grossman
557 Robert Runyan
558 Len Fury

AGENCY / AGENTUR / AGENCE – STUDIO:

550 Sheldon Seidler, Inc.
551–553 Dennis S. Juett & Associates
554–556 Anspach Grossman Portugal, Inc.
557 Robert Miles Runyan & Associates
558 Corporate Annual Reports, Inc.

Annual Reports
Jahresberichte
Rapports annuels

551

When the loan is made, it is not the
end of a transaction but the beginning
of a close business relationship.

552

553

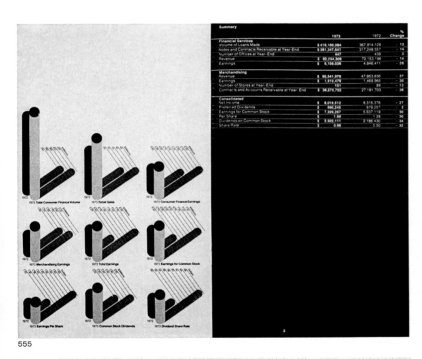

555

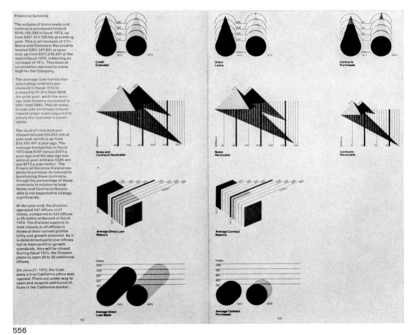

556

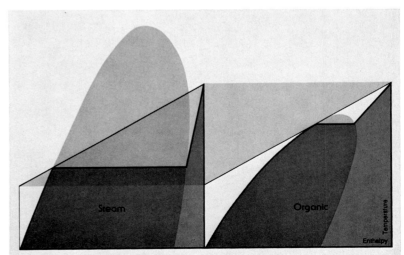

557

558

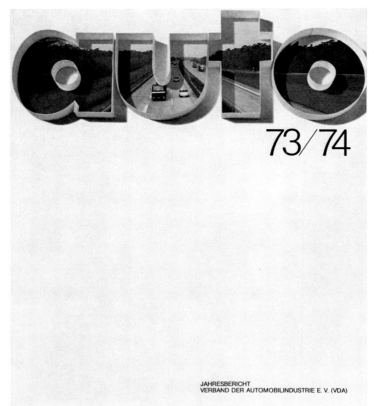

559

560

563

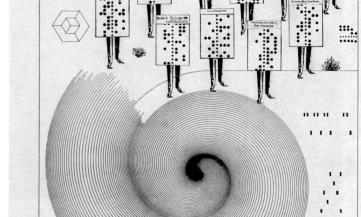

564

559, 560 Cover of an annual report of an automobile industry association (colour photograph inside letters) and page from the report comparing production figures for the years (green and yellow columns). (GER)
561 Cover of an annual report of Imasco Limited (consumer products and services). Polychrome symbols in embossed squares. (CAN)
562 Double spread on gatefold pages (illustrating "the search for perfection" and "a need for balance") from an annual report of *Compucorp*. Monochrome. (USA)
563, 564 Two black-and-white pages from an annual report of The New York Times Company, here referring to the sports magazines and dailies it publishes. (USA)
565 Cover of an annual report of the Cummins Engine Company, Inc. Blue and red, year in black and white. (USA)
566 Annual report cover for the Federal National Mortgage Association. (USA)

559, 560 Umschlag eines Jahresberichtes einer Automobilhersteller-Vereinigung (Farbphoto in den Buchstaben) und Seite aus dem Bericht mit Produktionszahlen für die verschiedenen Jahre (grüne und gelbe Kolonnen). (GER)
561 Umschlag eines Jahresberichtes der Imasco Limited (Konsumgüter und Serviceleistungen). Mehrfarbige Symbole in geprägten Quadratfeldern. (CAN)
562 Aufklappbare Doppelseite («die Suche nach Perfektion» und «ein Bedürfnis nach Ausgewogenheit» werden dargestellt) aus einem Jahresbericht der *Compucorp*. (USA)
563, 564 Zwei Schwarzweiss-Seiten aus einem Jahresbericht der New York Times Company, die sich hier auf die von ihr verlegten Sport- und Tageszeitungen bezieht. (USA)
565 Umschlag eines Jahresberichtes der Cummins Engine Company, Inc. Blau und rot, Jahr schwarzweiss. (USA)
566 Umschlag des Jahresberichtes eines Hypothekar-Instituts. (USA)

561

ARTIST / KÜNSTLER / ARTISTE:

559, 560 Creative Team Nacke & Flink
561 Ernst Roch
562 Bill Imhof/Lamb & Hall (Photo)
563, 564 Colos
565 Paul Rand
566 Lee O. Warfield III

ART DIRECTOR / DIRECTEUR ARTISTIQUE:

561 Ernst Roch
562 Dennis S. Juett
563, 564 Andrew Kner/Louis Silverstein
566 Lee O. Warfield III

Annual Reports / Jahresberichte
Rapports annuels

AGENCY / AGENTUR / AGENCE – STUDIO:

559, 560 Creative Team Nacke & Flink
561 Design Collaborative
562 Abert, Newhoff & Burr
566 Beveridge & Assoc., Inc.

562

565

566

559, 560 Couverture du rapport annuel d'une association de l'industrie auto-mobile et page du rapport comparant les chiffres d'affaires actuels à ceux des années précédentes (colonnes en vert et jaune). (USA)
561 Couverture du rapport annuel d'Imasco Ltd. (biens de consommation et services publics). Symboles polychromes dans des carrés gaufrés. (CAN)
562 Illustration sur les deux pages repliées (recherches de perfectionnement, le besoin d'équilibre) d'un rapport annuel de Compucorp. Monochrome. (USA)
563, 564 Deux pages en noir et blanc d'un rapport annuel du New York Times Co. avec référence aux magazines de sport et aux journaux qu'elle publie. (USA)
565 Couverture d'un rapport annuel de la Cummins Engine Co., Inc. Bleu et rouge, indication de l'année en noir et blanc. (USA)
566 Couverture d'un rapport annuel d'une association hypothécaire. (USA)

567

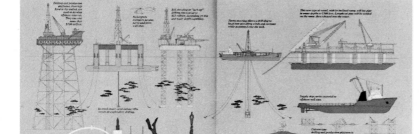

568

House Organs / Hauszeitschriften
Journaux d'entreprises

ARTIST / KÜNSTLER / ARTISTE:

567 Wynn Medinger
568, 569 Tre Tryckare
570 Alan E. Cober

ART DIRECTOR / DIRECTEUR ARTISTIQUE:

567 Gottschalk + Ash, Ltd.
568–570 Harry O. Diamond

AGENCY / AGENTUR / AGENCE – STUDIO:

567 Gottschalk + Ash, Ltd.

567 Double spread from *Habitat*, a bilingual publication of Central Mortgage and Housing Corporation. The article is about Le Vaudreuil, an experimental town in France. Hexagonal figure in two blues, grey and black. (CAN)
568, 569 Double spread, with detail, from *The Lamp*, house organ of the Exxon Corporation. It shows some of the equipment used in offshore drilling. (USA)
570 Full-page illustration from a special issue of Exxon Corporation's *The Lamp* devoted to the ocean. It is taken from an article on the communication systems of marine creatures. (USA)

567 Doppelseite aus *Habitat*, einer zweisprachigen Publikation der Central Mortgage and Housing Corporation. Der Artikel handelt von Le Vaudreuil, einer experimentellen Stadt in Frankreich. Hexagone in zwei verschiedenen Blautönen, Grau und Schwarz. (CAN)
568, 569 Doppelseite, mit Detail, aus *The Lamp*, Hauszeitung einer amerikanischen Ölgesellschaft. Gezeigt werden einige Geräte, die bei Bohrarbeiten benutzt werden. (USA)
570 Ganzseitige Illustration aus einer Spezialausgabe von *The Lamp*, die dem Meer gewidmet war. Aus einem Artikel über Kommunikationssysteme von Meerbewohnern. (USA)

567 Page double de *Habitat*, une publication bilingue d'une entreprise de financement et de logement. L'article correspondant est consacré aux expériences faites en France dans la ville du Vaudreuil. Figure hexagonale en bleu, gris et noir. (CAN)
568, 569 Page double et détail du journal d'entreprise *The Lamp* de l'Exxon Corporation. Elle présente quelques pièces d'équipement utilisées pour le forage maritime. (USA)
570 Illustration pleine page d'un numéro spécial de *The Lamp*, consacré à la mer. L'article correspondant se réfère au système de communication des créatures marines. (USA)

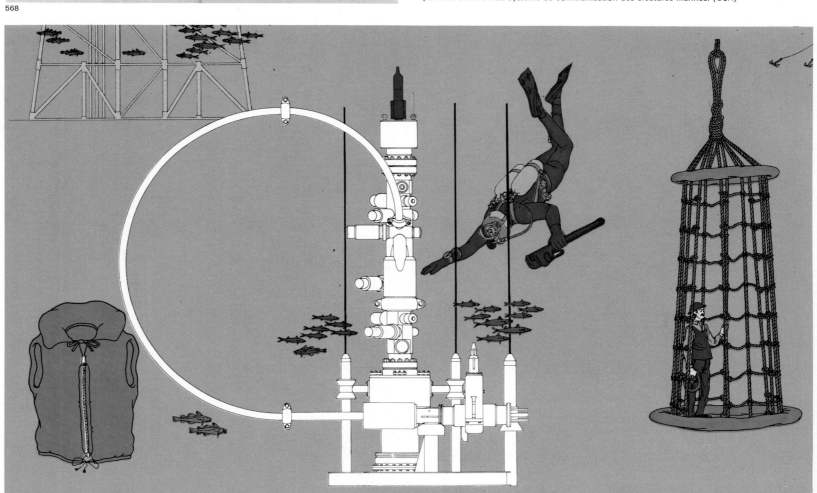

569

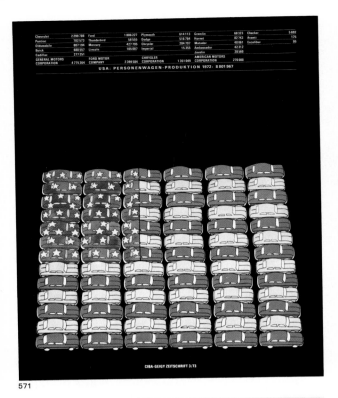

571

572

ARTIST / KÜNSTLER / ARTISTE:

571, 572 Mario Grasso
573 Fernanda Fedi
574 Delima Medeiros
575 J.F. Foat
576–578 Alan E. Cober
579 Werner Munkenhirn
580 W. Chris Gorman

ART DIRECTOR:

575 J.F. Foat
579 Alicia Landon
580 W. Chris Gorman

AGENCY / AGENTUR / AGENCE:

571, 572 Ciba-Geigy, Zentrale Werbung
575 Design Studio, Pfizer Ltd.
576–578 Johnson & Simpson
579 Corporate Annual Reports, Inc.
580 W. Chris Gorman Assoc., Inc.

573

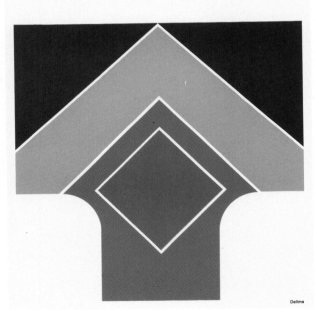

574

House Organs
Hauszeitschriften
Journaux d'entreprises

190

575

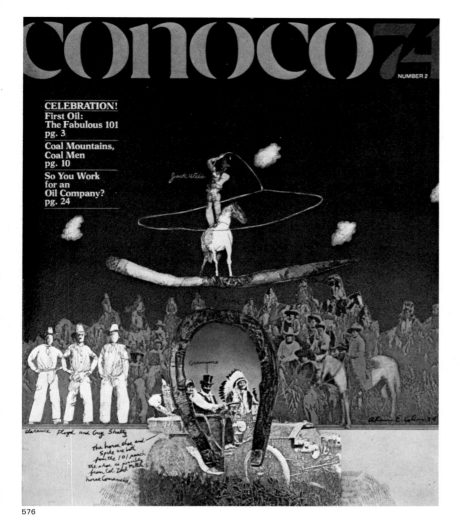

576

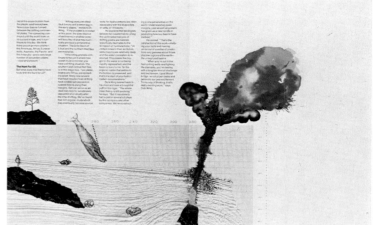

578

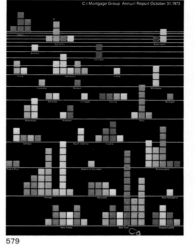

579

580

577

571 Cover of an issue of *Ciba-Geigy Zeitschrift* containing an article devoted to the production of private cars in the USA. (SWI)
572 Cover of *Ciba-Geigy Zeitschrift* referring to the problems of food production. Green frame and leaves, yellow apple, green caterpillar, red sun. (SWI)
573, 574 Covers of *Esso Rivista*, house organ of Esso Italia. Fig. 573: blues, yellows and greens on grey-green ground. (ITA)
575 Double spread from an article in *Rostrum*, house magazine of Pfizer Limited, on the subject of women's shoe fashions through the ages. (GBR)
576–578 Cover, page and spread from an issue of *Conoco*, organ of the Continental Oil Company, with articles on the Wild West and work for an oil company. Full colour. (USA)
579 Polychrome cover of a C. I. Mortgage Group annual report. (USA)
580 Programme cover for a conference of Atomic Industrial Forum, Inc. Blue X's. (USA)

571 Umschlag einer Ausgabe der *Ciba-Geigy-Zeitschrift* mit einem Artikel über die Produktion von Privatautos in den Vereinigten Staaten. (SWI)
572 Umschlag der *Ciba-Geigy-Zeitschrift*, der sich auf die Nahrungsmittelproduktion bezieht. Grüner Rahmen und Blätter, gelber Apfel, grüne Raupe, rote Sonne. (SWI)
573, 574 Umschläge der *Esso Rivista*, Hauszeitschrift der Esso Italia. Abb. 573: verschiedene Blau-, Gelb- und Grüntöne auf graugrünem Hintergrund. (ITA)
575 Doppelseite aus einem Artikel in *Rostrum*, Hauszeitschrift einer pharmazeutischen Firma, über Damenschuhmode damals und heute. (GBR)
576–578 Titelblatt, Seite und Doppelseite aus dem Hausorgan der Continental Oil Company mit Artikeln über den Wilden Westen und Arbeit bei einer Ölgesellschaft. Farbig. (USA)
579 Mehrfarbiger Umschlag des Jahresberichtes eines Hypothekar-Instituts. (USA)
580 Programm-Umschlag einer Konferenz der Atomic Industrial Forum, Inc. (USA)

571 Couverture d'un numéro du *Ciba-Geigy-Zeitschrift* avec un article sur la fabrication de voitures privées aux Etats-Unis (SWI)
572 Couverture du *Ciba-Geigy-Zeitschrift* avec référence au problème de la production alimentaire. Encadrement et feuilles verts, pomme jaune, chenille verte, soleil rouge. (SWI)
573, 574 Couverture d'*Esso Rivista*, journal d'entreprise d'*Esso Italia*. Fig. 573: teintes bleues, jaunes et vertes sur fond gris vert. (ITA)
575 Page double d'un article de *Rostrum*, journal d'entreprise de *Pfizer*, sur la mode de la chaussure pour femmes, vue à travers les siècles. (USA)
576–578 Page de couverture et page double de *Conoco*, journal d'entreprise de la Continental Oil Co.: le Far West et le travail dans une compagnie pétrolière. (USA)
579 Couverture polychrome du rapport annuel de C. I. Mortgage Corp. (USA)
580 Couverture du programme pour une conférence de l'industrie nucléaire. (USA)

ARTIST / KÜNSTLER / ARTISTE:

581 Simms Taback
582 Don Kindschi/Fritz Gottschalk (Design)
583, 584, 586, 587 Ronald Searle
585 Georges Lemoine

ART DIRECTOR / DIRECTEUR ARTISTIQUE:

581 Peter Adler
582 Gottschalk + Ash Ltd.
585, 586 Jacques Tribondeau

AGENCY / AGENTUR / AGENCE – STUDIO:

581 Adler, Schwartz & Connes, Inc.
582 Gottschalk + Ash Ltd.
583, 584, 587 Jerrild + Associates

583

584

581 Cover of the Cooper Union alumni magazine referring to the renovation of the institution's foundation building. Blue background. (USA)
582 Cover of a periodical published by the Canada Labour Relations Board. The letters *di* signify "decisions" and "information". Two greens and white. (CAN)
583, 584, 587 Three full-page illustrations, all in full colour, from the *Price Waterhouse & Co. Review*. They accompany an article on the subject of cross-frontier mergers and on the various methods of avoiding the taxation risks which these frequently involve. (USA)
585, 586 Covers of *Pétrole Progrès,* house organ of the French *Esso* company. They relate to oil as a source of light plastics and synthetic rubbers (Fig. 585) and to the 25th anniversary of the magazine with its 100th issue (Fig. 586). Both are in full colour. (FRA)

581 Umschlag der Altstudenten-Zeitschrift der Cooper Union, die Bezug nimmt auf das renovierte Gebäude dieser Institution. Blauer Hintergrund. (USA)
582 Umschlag einer Publikation der Canada Labour Relations Board. Die Buchstaben *di* bedeuten «decisions» (Entscheidungen) und «information». Grüntöne und Weiss. (CAN)
583, 584, 587 Drei ganzseitige Illustrationen, alle mehrfarbig, aus der *Price Waterhouse & Co. Review*. Sie begleiten einen Artikel über Fusionen über Landesgrenzen hinweg und über die verschiedenen Methoden, die Steuerrisiken zu vermeiden, die solche Fusionen mit sich bringen. (USA)
585, 586 Umschläge von Ausgaben der Hauszeitschrift von Esso Frankreich, *Pétrole Progrès,* die über Öl als Grundlage für die Herstellung von leichten Kunststoffen und synthetischem Gummi (Abb. 585), sowie über den 25. Geburtstag der Zeitschrift und ihre 100. Ausgabe (Abb. 586) berichten. Farbig. (FRA)

585

586

581

582

581 Couverture du magazine des anciens membres de la *Cooper Union* avec référence à la rénovation de la maison de fondation de l'institution. (USA)
582 Couverture du périodique publié par le Canada Labour Relations Board. Les lettres *di* signifient «décision» et «information». Deux teintes vertes et blanc. (CAN)
583, 584, 587 Trois illustrations pleines pages, toutes en couleur, d'une revue d'entreprise. Les articles correspondants sont consacrés à la fusion avec des entreprises d'autres pays et les différentes possibilités pour éviter les risques fiscaux que de telles opérations entraînent. (USA)
585, 586 Couverture de *Pétrole Progrès,* journal d'entreprise de l'Esso France. Elles se réfèrent à l'huile en tant que base pour la production de matières plastiques légères et de caoutchouc synthétique (fig. 585) et au 25e anniversaire du magazine célébré lors de la publication du no. 100 (fig. 586). (FRA)

House Organs
Hauszeitschriften
Journaux d'entreprises

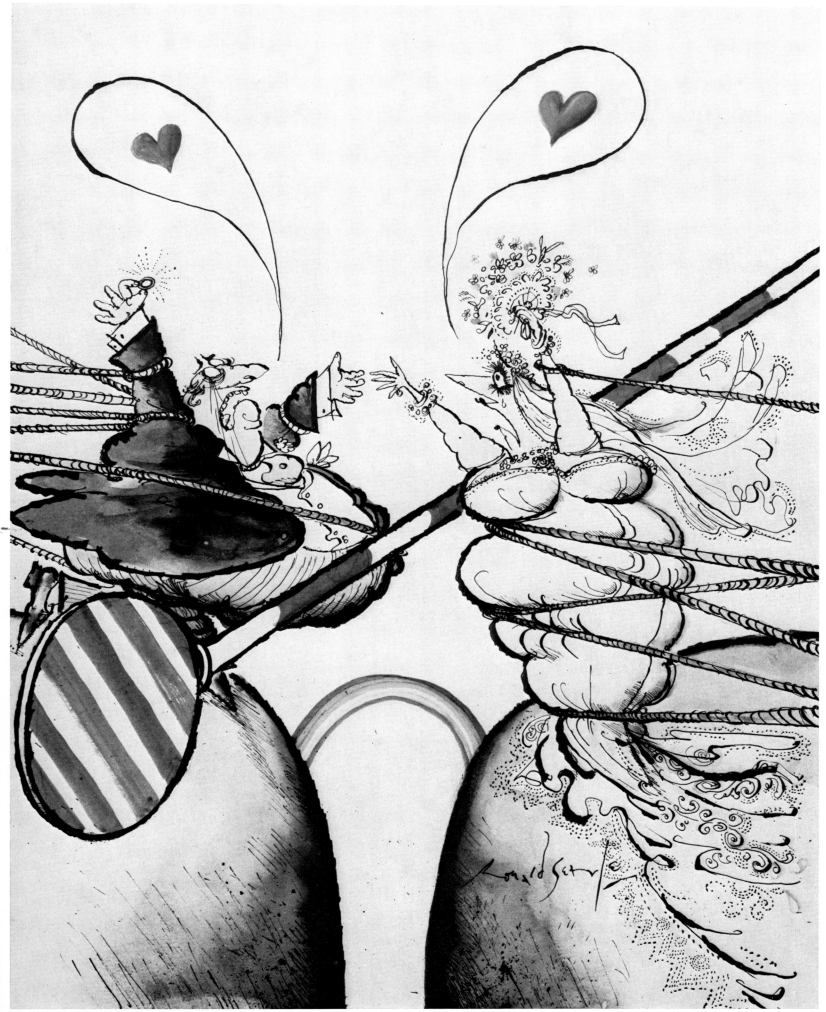

588

House Organs
Hauszeitschriften
Journaux d'entreprises

590

589

591

ARTIST / KÜNSTLER / ARTISTE:

588 Deanna Glad
589 Eduard Prüssen
590–592 André Amstutz
593, 594 Marcus Hodel

ART DIRECTOR / DIRECTEUR ARTISTIQUE:

588 Elin Waite
589 Eduard Prüssen
590–592 Guy Challis
593, 594 Jacques Hauser

AGENCY / AGENTUR / AGENCE – STUDIO:

588 Westways Magazine
593, 594 Hoffmann-La Roche, Werbeabteilung

588 Cover of *Westways* magazine, organ of the Automobile Club of Southern California. Polychrome quilted and appliqué rendering of a building in Venice. (USA)
589 Linocut from *Donkey Post*, a designer's small self-promotion magazine. (GER)
590–592 Three full-colour covers of *Guinness Time*, magazine of the Guinness Park Royal Brewery, here alluding to various sports. (GBR)
593 Drawing from the *Roche* house magazine *Hexagon*, illustrating an article on the confrontation of medicine and death. (SWI)
594 Double-spread black-and-white illustration for an article on causality in the *Roche* magazine *Hexagon*. (SWI)

588 Umschlag von *Westways*, dem Organ des südkalifornischen Automobilclubs. Farbwiedergabe in Quilt- und Appliquéarbeit eines Gebäudes in Venedig. (USA)
589 Linolschnitt aus *Donkey Post*, der kleinen Eigenwerbungs-Zeitschrift eines Designers. (GER)
590–592 Drei Farbumschläge von *Guinness Time*, der Zeitschrift einer Brauerei, hier im Zusammenhang mit verschiedenen Sportarten. (GBR)
593 Zeichnung aus *Hexagon*, Hauszeitschrift von *Roche*, als Illustration eines Artikels über die Konfrontation von Medizin und Tod. (SWI)
594 Doppelseite, schwarzweiss, als Illustration eines Artikels über die Kausalität in der Zeitschrift *Hexagon*. (SWI)

588 Couverture du magazine *Westways*, journal d'entreprise du Club Automobile de la Californie du Sud. Représentation d'une maison de Venise en utilisant une combinaison de quilt et d'appliqués. Polychrome. (USA)
589 Lino pour *Donkey Post*, le magazine autopromotionnel d'un designer. (GER)
590–592 Trois couvertures polychromes de *Guinness Time*, le magazine de la brasserie *Guinness*, ici avec allusion aux différentes activités sportives. (GBR)
593 Design pour *Hexagon*, journal d'entreprise de *Roche*, sur la médecine confrontée à la mort. (SWI)
594 Illustration sur page double en noir et blanc pour un article de *Hexagon* sur la causalité. (SWI)

593

592

594

595

596

597

ARTIST / KÜNSTLER / ARTISTE:

595, 596 Cathy Hull/Jules Perlmutter (Design)
597, 598 Enrico Baj
599–601 Raymond Côme

ART DIRECTOR / DIRECTEUR ARTISTIQUE·

597, 598 Giorgio Soavi
599–601 Henri Van Hoof

**House Organs / Hauszeitschriften
Journaux d'entreprises**

598

599

LE SYSTEME VESTIBULAIRE™

LE LABYRINTHE

INTRODUCTION

600

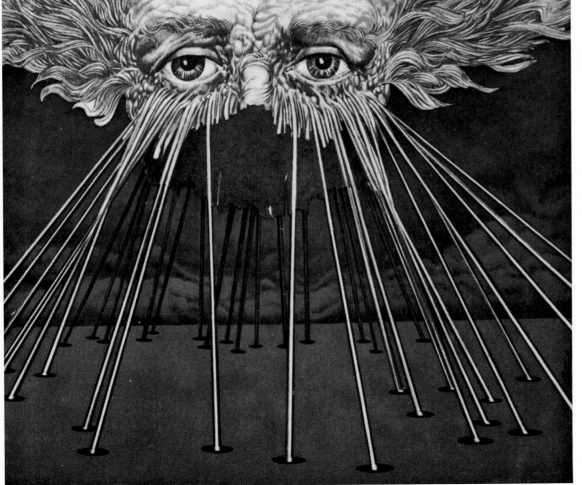

601

595, 596 Pages in black and blue opening chapters on schizophrenia and organic syndromes in the book *Abnormal Psychology* by Davison and Neale, published by John Wiley & Sons, Inc. (USA)
597, 598 Double-spread illustration in colour and full-page black-and-white drawing from a large book by Dino Buzzati, *Il deserto dei Tartari*, published as a gift by *Olivetti*. (ITA)
599–601 Two illustrations and one complete page from an issue of *essentialia*, house magazine of the pharmaceutical company UCB. Fig. 599 (black and dark red) illustrates an article on environment and sleep, Fig. 600 (blue, green and black) opens a feature on the vestibular apparatus of the ear, and Fig. 601 (black and dark red) relates to the treatment of high blood pressure. (BEL)

595, 596 Seiten in Schwarz und Blau als Einleitung zu Kapiteln über Schizophrenie und organische Syndrome aus dem Buch *Abnormal Psychology* von Davison and Neale. Herausgeber John Wiley & Sons, Inc. (USA)
597, 598 Doppelseitige Illustration in Farbe und ganzseitige Schwarzweiss-Zeichnung aus einem Buch von Dino Buzzati, *Il deserto dei Tartari*, herausgegeben als Geschenk von *Olivetti*. (ITA)
599–601 Zwei Illustrationen und eine ganze Seite aus einer Ausgabe von *essentialia*, Hausmagazin einer pharmazeutischen Gesellschaft. Abb. 599 (schwarz, rot) illustriert einen Artikel über Umgebung und Schlaf, Abb. 600 (blau, grün, schwarz) bezieht sich auf den Vorhof des menschlichen Ohres und Abb. 601 (schwarz, rot) auf die Behandlung von hohem Blutdruck. (BEL)

595, 596 Pages en noir et bleu introduisant les chapitres sur la schizophrénie et les syndromes organiques dans le livre *Abnormal Psychology*, par Davison et Neale. (USA)
597, 598 Illustration sur page double (en couleur) et dessin pleine page en noir et blanc d'une importante publication-cadeau d'*Olivetti*, *Il deserto dei Tartari* par Dino Buzzati. (ITA)
599–601 Deux illustrations et page complète d'un numéro d'*essentialia*, journal d'entreprise d'UCB, fabrique de produits pharmaceutiques. Fig. 599: pour un article sur l'environnement et le sommeil (noir/rouge foncé); fig. 600: introduisant un article sur la fonction de la cavité du tympan de l'oreille (bleu/vert/noir); fig. 601: sur le traitement de la tension arteriélle (noir/rouge foncé). (BEL)

602

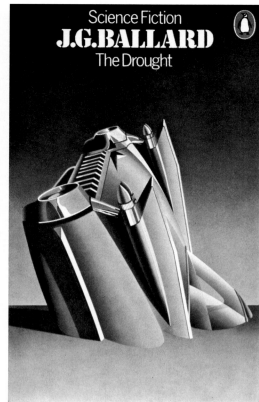

603

604

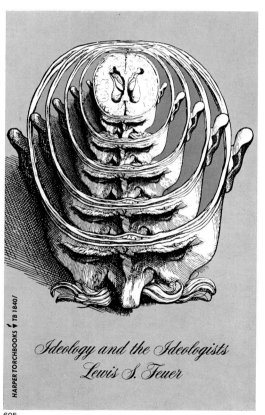

605

607

606

602, 603 Covers in full colour for two *Penguin* science-fiction paperbacks. (GBR)
604 Cover of a book of short stories (Furrows of Time) published as a *Fischer* paperback. Beige and blue. (GER)
605 Cover of a *Harper* paperback. Black drawing on yellow with red title. (USA)
606 Cover of a *Semester* paperback on Czechoslovakia. Flat colours on green ground. (SWE)
607 Cover of a fiction paperback (The White Bird and Other Stories). Full colour. (POL)
608, 609 Detail of the drawing and complete cover (black on brown stock) of a book about a rural community. (USA)
610–612 Complete cover and details of the artwork for two *Grote ABC* paperbacks forming part of a series of the work of Hermann Hesse. (NLD)

602, 603 Umschläge von zwe Zukunftsromanen aus der *Penguin*-Taschenbuchreihe. Mehrfarbig. (GBR)
604 Umschlag eines Buches mit Kurzgeschichten aus der *Fischer*-Taschenbuchreihe. Beige und blau. (GER)
605 Umschlag eines *Harper*-Taschenbuches. Schwarze Zeichnung auf Gelb mit rotem Titel. (USA)
606 Umschlag eines Taschenbuches über die Tschechoslowakei. Flach aufgetragene Farben auf grünem Grund. (SWE)
607 Umschlag eines Taschenbuch-Romanes («Der weisse Vogel und andere Geschichten»). Mehrfarbig. (POL)
608, 609 Ausschnitt und Umschlag (schwarz auf braunem Papier) eines Buches über eine Landgemeinde. (USA)
610–612 Vollständiger Umschlag und Illustrationsausschnitte aus zwei *Grote-ABC*-Taschenbüchern als Teil einer Reihe über die Arbeit Hermann Hesses. (NLD)

602, 603 Couvertures en couleur pour deux livres de poche *Penguin*, d'une série de science-fiction. (GBR)
604 Couverture d'une collection de nouvelles publiée dans la série des livres de poche *Fischer*. Beige, bleu. (GER)
605 Couverture d'un livre de poche *Harper*. Dessin noir sur fond jaune, titre rouge. (USA)
606 Couverture d'un livre de poche *Semester* sur la Tchécoslovaquie. Couleurs à plat sur fond vert. (SWE)
607 Couverture d'un livre de poche (L'oiseau blanc et d'autres histoires). En couleur. (POL)
608, 609 Détail du dessin et couverture complète (noir sur papier brun) d'un livre sur une communauté rurale. (USA)
610–612 Couverture et détails des illustrations de deux livres de poche *Grote ABC*, faisant partie d'une série consacrée à l'œuvre de Hermann Hesse. (NLD)

Paperbacks
Taschenbücher
Livres brochés

610

611

608

609

612

199

613

614

HERMANN HESSE
TREATISE ON THE
STEPPENWOLF

An artist's revelation in forty-five paintings by Jaroslav Bradac

ARTIST / KÜNSTLER / ARTISTE:

613–615 Jaroslav Bradác
616 Fred Bauer
617 Stellan Kristenson
618 Tom Carnase

ART DIRECTOR / DIRECTEUR ARTISTIQUE:

617 Stellan Kristenson
618 Alan Peckolick

AGENCY / AGENTUR / AGENCE – STUDIO:

618 Lubalin, Smith, Carnase Inc.

PUBLISHER / VERLEGER / EDITEUR:

613–615 Wildwood House Ltd.
616 Artemis Verlag
617 GLA Förlag
618 Watson-Guptill Publications

613–615 Cover painting in actual size, complete cover and double spread, also in full colour, from en edition of Hermann Hesse's *Treatise on the Steppenwolf* illustrated with forty-five paintings. The Czechoslovakian artist also made an animated sequence on the same subject for the film *Steppenwolf.* (GBR)
616 Cover of a large children's book by a Swiss author. Red sun and predominantly blue scarecrow on a yellow background. (SWI)
617 Cover of a large map for holiday-makers showing parts of Sweden and Denmark. Polychrome, flat colours on yellow ground. (SWE)
618 Cover of the annual recording the work included in The One Show, New York, 1974. Red gold on black, white copy. (USA)

613–615 Umschlagbild in Originalgrösse, vollständiger Umschlag und farbige Doppelseite aus einer mit 45 Bildern illustrierten Ausgabe von Hermann Hesses *Abhandlung über den Steppenwolf.* Der tschechische Künstler zeichnete ebenfalls eine Filmsequenz über dasselbe Thema für den Film *Steppenwolf.* (GBR)
616 Umschlag eines grossen Kinderbuches von Max Bolliger. Rote Sonne und vorwiegend blaue Vogelscheuche auf gelbem Hintergrund. (SWI)
617 Umschlag einer grossen Karte für Ferienreisende, die Teile von Schweden und Dänemark zeigt. Farbig, flach aufgetragene Farben auf gelbem Hintergrund. (SWE)
618 Umschlag des Jahrbuches, das die in The One Show, New York, ausgestellten Arbeiten enthält. Dies ist die jährliche, nun international gewordene Ausstellung des Art Directors Club. Rotgold auf Schwarz, weisse Schrift. (USA)

616

617

615

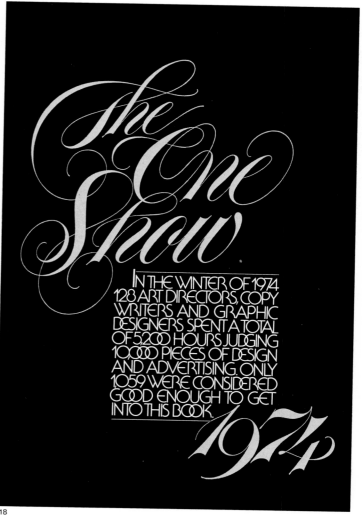
618

613–615 Peinture de couverture en grandeur nature, couverture complète et page double (en couleur) d'un *Traité du Loup des Steppes* de Hermann Hesse, publication illustrée par quarante-cinq peintures. L'artiste tchécoslovaque a réalisé aussi une séquence sur le même sujet pour le film sur *Le Loup des Steppes*. (GBR)

616 Couverture d'un livre d'enfant grand format réalisé par un artiste suisse. Soleil rouge, épouvantail en teintes prédominantes bleues sur fond jaune. (SWI)

617 Couverture d'une carte géographique grand format pour les villégiateurs, présentant différentes régions de la Suède et du Danemark. Couleurs à plat sur fond jaune. (SWE)

618 Couverture du répertoire annuel qui réunit toutes les créations exposées dans le One Show, New York, 1974. Rouge sur noir, typo blanc. (USA)

Book Covers
Buchumschläge
Couvertures de livres

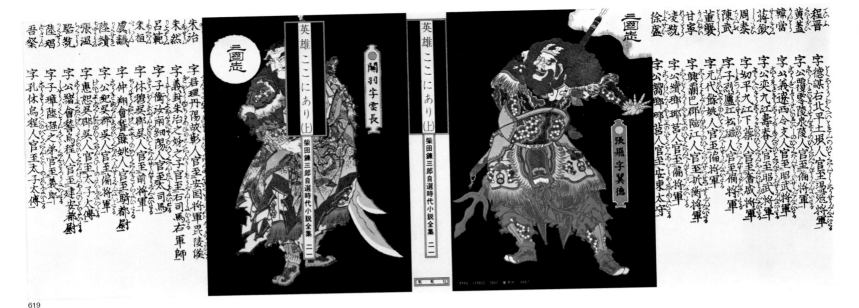

619

619–621 Three polychrome covers for books from a series published by Shuei-Sha. The titles are: *Here is the Hero, Detective Dobu, The Abnormal Door/Blood Flute.* (JPN)
622–624 Complete polychrome covers of two ''creative expression'' books for children and of a book about making and reading maps, all published by Scholastic Book Services. (USA)

619–621 Drei mehrfarbige Umschläge aus einer von Shuei-Sha herausgegebenen Buchreihe. Die Titel lauten: *Hier ist der Held, Detektiv Dobu, Die Zauber-Türe/Blut-Flöte.* (JPN)
622–624 Vollständige, mehrfarbige Umschläge zweier Bücher aus einer Reihe, die Kinder zum schöpferischen Ausdruck ermuntern soll, und Umschlag eines Buches des gleichen Verlages über das Herstellen und Lesen von Landkarten. (USA)

619–621 Trois couvertures polychromes pour une série de publications de la maison d'édition Shuei-sha. Les titres signifient: *Voici le héros, Détective Dobu, Porte mystérieuse/Flûte de sang.* (JPN)
622–624 Couvertures polychromes de deux volumes sur l'expression créative, publications destinées aux enfants, et d'un livre sur la cartographie et l'interprétation des cartes, tous publiés par Scholastic Book Services. (USA)

620

621

Book Covers
Buchumschläge
Couverture de livres

622

623

624

ARTIST / KÜNSTLER / ARTISTE:

619–621 Tadanori Yokoo
622 Seymour Chwast
623 Frank Bozzo
624 John Alcorn

DESIGNER / GESTALTER / MAQUETTISTE:

622, 624 Doug Gervasi
623 Skip Sorvino

ART DIRECTOR / DIRECTEUR ARTISTIQUE:

619–621 Tadanori Yokoo
622, 624 Skip Sorvino/Phil Slater
623 Skip Sorvino

PUBLISHER / VERLEGER / EDITEUR:

619–621 Shuei-Sha
622–624 Scholastic Book Services

Chinesische Märchen

Buddhistische Märchen

625

626

627

625 Cover of a Swiss edition of a detective story by James Jones. Polychrome. (SWI)
626 Cover of a book of Chinese tales. Yellow bird with brown, blue and green on black. (SWI)
627 Cover of a book of Buddhist tales. Yellow lion with brown, blue and green on black. (SWI)
628–631 Artwork and complete covers of two books from a series of stories of mystery and horror translated into German from English (Figs. 628/631) and French (Figs. 629/630). (GER)
632 Vignette for a book cover. (GER)
633 Complete cover (full colour on black) of a book containing six old-fashioned horror stories by an American author and artist. (SWI)

625 Umschlag einer Schweizerausgabe einer Detektivgeschichte von James Jones. Mehrfarbig. (SWI)
626 Umschlag eines Buches mit chinesischen Geschichten. Gelber Vogel mit Braun, Blau und Grün auf Schwarz. (SWI)
627 Umschlag eines Buches mit buddhistischen Geschichten. Gelber Löwe mit Braun, Blau und Grün auf Schwarz. (SWI)
628–631 Illustration und vollständige Umschläge zweier Bücher aus einer Serie von Geister- und Schauergeschichten, ins Deutsche aus dem Englischen (Abb. 628/631) und aus dem Französischen (Abb. 629/630) übersetzt. (GER)
632 Vignette für einen Buchumschlag. (GER)
633 Vollständiger Umschlag (mehrfarbig auf Schwarz) eines Buches mit altmodischen Schauergeschichten, erzählt von einem amerikanischen Künstler. (SWI)

625 Couverture de l'édition suisse d'un roman policier par James Jones. Polychrome. (SWI)
626 Couverture d'un livre de contes chinoises. Oiseau jaune avec brun, bleu et vert sur noir. (SWI)
627 Couverture d'un livre de contes Bouddhistes. Lion jaune avec brun, bleu et vert sur noir. (SWI)
628–631 Illustration et couvertures complètes pour deux livres d'une série de contes d'épouvante, traduits en allemand de l'anglais (fig. 628/631) et du français (figs. 629/630). (GER)
632 Vignette pour une couverture de livre. (GER)
633 Couverture (polychrome sur noir) d'un livre contenant six contes d'épouvante d'un auteur et artiste américain. (SWI)

ARTIST / KÜNSTLER / ARTISTE:

625–627 Oskar Weiss
628, 631 Ute Osterwalder
629, 630 Hans & Ulrich Osterwalder
632 Eduard Prüssen
633 Edward Gorey

ART DIRECTOR:

625–627 Oswald Dubacher
632 Hans Peter Willberg

628

629

630

631

AGENCY / AGENTUR / AGENCE:

628–631 Osterwalder's Office

PUBLISHER / VERLEGER / EDITEUR:

625–627 Ex Libris Verlag
628–631 Insel Verlag
632 Ehrenwirth Verlag
633 Diogenes Verlag

632

633

Book Covers
Buchumschläge
Couverture de livres

634

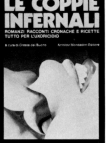

635

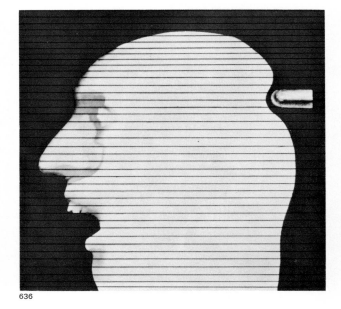

636

634, 635 Artwork and complete cover of a collection of stories (The Infernal Couples) about uxoricide. (ITA)
636 Artwork for the cover of a book from the same series as Figs. 634/635, here containing five detective stories by Ellery Queen. (ITA)
637 Complete cover of a children's book (The Islet of the Green Boot). Polychrome illustrations. (CSR)
638 Cover of a novel (Two Letters). Black and white. (POL)
639 Cover of a collection of stories by a well-known author. Black and white. (POL)
640 Cover of a book (Diary of a Master of TV). Black on red, white title. (ITA)
641 Cover of a work of science fiction. (NLD)

634, 635 Illustration und vollständiger Umschlag einer Geschichtensammlung («Die teuflischen Paare»). (ITA)
636 Illustration eines Buchumschlages aus der gleichen Reihe wie Abb. 634/635. Das Buch enthält fünf Detektiv geschichten. (ITA)
637 Umschlag eines Kinderbuches. («Das Inselchen des grünen Schuhs».) Mehrfarbige Illustrationen. (CSR)
638 Umschlag für einen Roman («Zwei Briefe»). Schwarzweiss. (POL)
639 Umschlag einer Geschichtensammlung eines bekannten Autors. Schwarzweiss. (POL)
640 Umschlag eines Buches («Tagebuch eines Fernseh-Maestros»). Schwarz auf Rot, weisser Titel. (ITA)
641 Umschlag eines Buches mit Zukunftsromanen. (NLD)

634, 635 Illustration et couverture complète d'une collection de contes (Le couple infernal) sur l'uxoricide. (ITA)
636 Illustration de couverture pour un livre figurant dans la même série que les figs. 634/635, ici pour une collection de cinq romans policier par Ellery Queen. (ITA)
637 Couverture d'un livre d'enfant (L'îlot de la bottine verte). Illustrations en couleur. (CSR)
638 Couverture d'une nouvelle (Deux lettres). Noir et blanc. (POL)
639 Couverture d'une collection de contes par un auteur bien connu. Noir et blanc. (POL)
640 Couverture d'un livre (Le journal d'un maître de la TV). Noir sur rouge, titre blanc. (ITA)
641 Couverture d'une publication de science-fiction. (NLD)

ARTIST / KÜNSTLER / ARTISTE:

634–636 Ferenc Pintér
637 Kveta Pacovská
638, 639 Andrzey Darowski
640 Gianni Parlacino
641 Roger Wolfs

ART DIRECTOR:

634–636 Bruno Binosi
640 Gianni Parlacino
641 Nick Hiemstra

AGENCY / AGENTUR / AGENCE:

634–636 Servizio Grafico Editoriale
641 H.B.M. Design

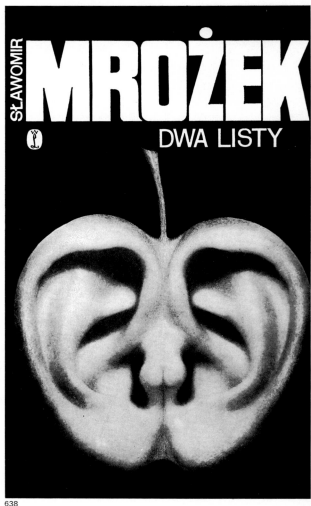

638

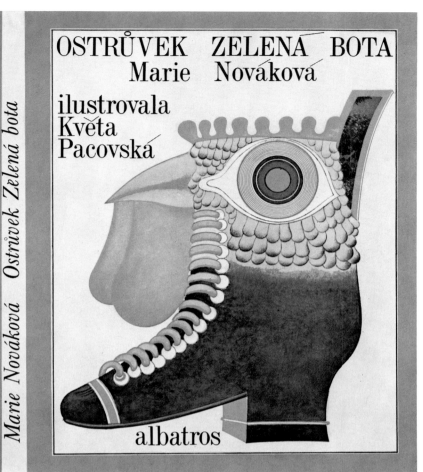

OSTRŮVEK ZELENÁ BOTA
Marie Nováková

ilustrovala
Květa
Pacovská

albatros

Marie Nováková   Ostrůvek Zelená bota

637

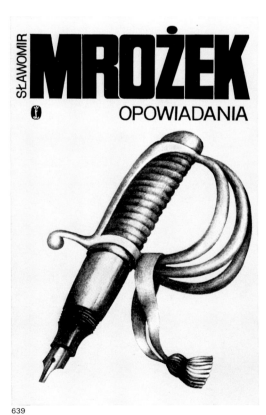

SŁAWOMIR
MROŻEK
OPOWIADANIA

639

GIAN PAOLO CRESCI

UNA ESPERIENZA
PER CHI INSEGNA OGGI
IL DIARIO DI LAVORAZIONE
IL TESTO DEI DIALOGHI

EDA

DE SETA
DIARIO DI
UN MAESTRO
IN TV

640

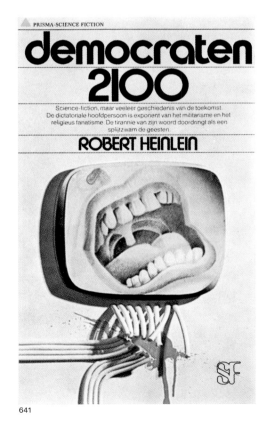

PRISMA-SCIENCE FICTION

democraten 2100

Science-fiction, maar veeleer geschiedenis van de toekomst.
De dictatoriale hoofdpersoon is exponent van het militarisme en het
religieus fanatisme. De tirannie van zijn woord doordringt als een
splijtzwam de geesten.

ROBERT HEINLEIN

641

PUBLISHER / VERLEGER / EDITEUR:

634–636 Arnoldo Mondadori, Editore
637 Albatros
638, 639 Wydawnictwo Literackie
640 Edizioni EDA
641 Avla Editions

4

Calendars

Trade Marks and Symbols

Letterheads

Packaging

Gramophone Record Covers

Kalender

Schutzmarken

Briefköpfe

Packungen

Schallplatten-Umschläge

Calendriers

Marques et emblèmes

En-têtes

Emballages

Pochettes de disques

642

643

644

645

642–647 Four of the twelve motifs and one complete sheet of a calendar issued by *Sony* and entitled "A year of music anyway you want it". The pop compositions by two artists illustrate various categories of music—here, in the order of the illustrations, a black singer (figure in pink, old rose and blue); an orchestral conductor (face and hands in dusty brown); circus music (fair-ground colouring and atmosphere); folk and Western music (green, yellow and orange shades); and gospel music. (USA)

642–647 Vier von zwölf Motiven und ein vollständiges Blatt aus einem *Sony*-Kalender betitelt: «Ein Jahr Musik für jeden Geschmack.» Die in Zusammenarbeit von zwei Künstlern entstandenen Pop-illustrationen repräsentieren verschiedene Arten von Musik. In der Reihenfolge der Bilder: eine schwarze Sängerin (hell- und altrosa, blau); einen Orchesterdirigenten (Gesicht und Hände in staubigem Braun); Zirkus-Musik (mit Zirkus-Farben und -Atmosphäre); Folk- und Western-Musik (Grün-, Gelb- und Orangetöne); und Gospel-Musik. (USA)

642–647 Quatre motifs et feuillet complet d'un calendrier publié par *Sony*, sous le titre «A chacun sa musique pendant une année». Les illustrations pop réalisées par deux artistes présentent les différentes catégories musicales – ici, par ordre des illustrations, une chanteuse noire (figure en rouge, rose pâle et bleu); un chef d'orchestre (visage et mains brun poussiéreux); musique de cirque (couleurs vives évoquant l'atmosphère du cirque); musique populaire et western (teintes verte, jaune et orange); gospel music. (USA)

Calendars / Kalender / Calendriers

646

ARTIST / KÜNSTLER / ARTISTE:

642–644 Stanislaw Zagorski
645–647 John O'Leary

DESIGNER / GESTALTER / MAQUETTISTE:

642–647 J. Cavallo/G. Segnini/B. Venezia

ART DIRECTOR / DIRECTEUR ARTISTIQUE:

642–647 John Channell

AGENCY / AGENTUR / AGENCE – STUDIO:

642–647 Group One Creative Graphic Inc.

Die Einbandstoffe
von Zanders

JANUAR
16
DONNERSTAG

Elefantenhaut   Elanta   Efalin   Efanta-Karton

648

ARTIST / KÜNSTLER / ARTISTE:

648 Hansjürgen Hölzer
649, 650 Maryella Warren
651–655 Shelley Kopel

DESIGNER / GESTALTER / MAQUETTISTE:

648 Klaus Winterhager
651–655 Emil Micha

ART DIRECTOR / DIRECTEUR ARTISTIQUE:

649, 650 Tom Gould
651–655 Andrew Kner

AGENCY / AGENTUR / AGENCE – STUDIO:

649, 650 Marc Friedberg, Marketing

649

**Calendars
Kalender
Calendriers**

648 Stiff wall calendar for *Zanders* papers. The colours on the elephant's legs are those available in the various materials supplied by the company for book bindings. GER)
649, 650 Example of a drawing (printed black on tinted stock) and complete sheet of a spirally bound calendar issued as self-promotion for an artist. The purposes for which the drawings were used are also indicated (this one was an illustration for a magazine). (USA)
651–655 Cover, three motifs and complete spread of a black-and-white teachers' planning calendar issued by the College and School Service of *The New York Times*. Each motif refers to some event noted on the date page and shows a paper sculpture incorporating snippets of the newspaper itself. (USA)

648 Calendrier mural pour les papiers *Zanders*. Les différentes couleurs offertes par cette papéterie pour les reliures sont représentées sur les pieds de l'éléphant. (GER)
649, 650 Exemple d'un dessin (imprimé en noir sur papier teint) et feuillet complet d'un calendrier autopromotionnel d'un artiste. Sur chaque feuillet on trouve les indications concernant l'emploi du dessin (celui-ci a été réalisé pour une revue). (USA)
651–655 Couverture, trois motifs et page double d'un calendrier de bureau pour professeurs (noir et blanc) publié par le service d'instruction de la *New York Times*. Chaque motif se réfère à un événement noté sur cette page et présente une sculpture en papier incorporant de petits morceaux du journal même. (USA)

648 Wandkalender der Zanders Feinpapiere GmbH. Die Elefantenbeine zeigen, in welchen Farben die Firma ihre verschiedenen Einbandstoffe für Bücher liefert. (GER)
649, 650 Beispiel einer Zeichnung (schwarzer Druck auf farbigem Papier) und komplettes Blatt aus dem Eigenwerbungs-Kalender einer Illustratorin, mit Angaben über die Verwendung der verschiedenen Zeichnungen. (Diese erschien in einer Zeitschrift). (USA)
651–655 Titelblatt, drei Motive und vollständige Doppelseite aus dem Planungskalender für Lehrer, herausgegeben vom «College and School Service» der *New York Times*. Jede Papierplastik enthält Schnitzel der Zeitung und bezieht sich auf ein im Kalenderteil erwähntes Ereignis. In Schwarzweiss. (USA)

651

652

653

654

650

655

656

657

658

659

656–659 Three motifs and one complete sheet from a large calendar issued by the Stuttgart Tourist Office. It shows views of Stuttgart and its environs painted in a "primitive" style—here an outlying village, a modern complex and fun on "Swabian Sunday". (GER)
660 Illustration of Toby from the *Punch* Canine Calendar. Full colour. (GBR)
661, 662 Artwork and complete sheet from a large calendar issued by a South African winegrowers' co-operative and showing maps of the main wine-growing areas. (SAF)

656–659 Drei Motive und ein vollständiges Blatt eines grossen, vom Stuttgarter Verkehrsamt herausgegebenen Kalenders mit Ansichten von Stuttgart und Umgebung im naiven Stil gemalt. Hier ein Dorf in Stadtnähe; modernes Stadtbild; «Schwäbischer Sonntag». (GER)
660 Illustration von Toby aus dem Hundekalender von *Punch*. Mehrfarbig. (GBR)
661, 662 Bild und vollständiges Blatt aus einem grossen Kalender mit Karten von Weinbaugebieten. Herausgegeben von der Genossenschaft südafrikanischer Weinbauern. (SAF)

656–659 Trois motifs et l'un des feuillets d'un calendrier grand format publié par l'office de tourisme de la ville de Stuttgart. Il présente quelques aspects de la ville et ses alentours: un village de la banlieue, un complexe moderne et un «dimanche souabe». (GER)
660 Illustration de Toby tirée du calendrier canin de *Punch*. En couleurs. (GBR)
661, 662 Illustration et feuillet complet d'un calendrier grand format publié par une société de viticulteurs de l'Afrique du sud avec des cartes des régions vignobles. (SAF)

ARTIST / KÜNSTLER / ARTISTE:

656–659 Josef Wahl/Frieder Grindler (Design)
660 Michael ffolkes
661, 662 Janice Ashby/Tobie Beele/Veronica Dutzle

ART DIRECTOR / DIRECTEUR ARTISTIQUE:

661, 662 Janice Ashby

AGENCY / AGENTUR / AGENCE – STUDIO:

661, 662 Janice Ashby Design Studio

660

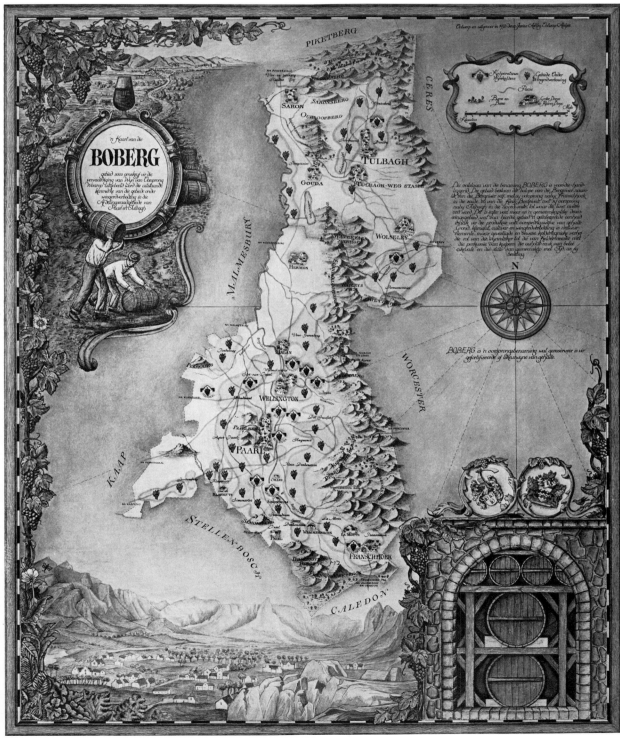

661

662

663, 664 Artwork and complete loose sheet of a calendar for Washington University Mortar Board, listing the events of the month. Black on yellow stock. (USA)

665–670 Five of the imaginative illustrations and one complete spread from a Hermann Hesse calendar issued by Farrar, Straus and Giroux. Quotations from Hesse's works and from writings about him appear on the date page. The treatment moves chronologically through Hesse's life. Fig. 665 relates to his horoscope and boyhood, Fig. 666 to his inner voice, Fig. 667 to the cosmic soul, Fig. 668 to the bird that flies to God, Fig. 669/670 to the poet as an old man and the escape from bondage. (USA)

663, 664 Detail und vollständiges Blatt des Kalenders einer Washingtoner Studentenvereinigung mit Angaben über die Ereignisse des Monats. Schwarz auf gelbem Papier. (USA)

665–670 Fünf der phantasievollen Illustrationen und ein vollständiges Blatt aus dem Hermann-Hesse-Kalender eines New Yorker Verlagshauses. Zitate aus Hesse's Werken und Auszüge aus Schriften über ihn erscheinen im Kalenderteil. Die Texte folgen Hesse's Leben chronologisch. Abb. 665 bezieht sich auf sein Horoskop und seine Kindheit, Abb. 666 auf seine innere Stimme, Abb. 667 auf die kosmische Seele, Abb. 668 auf den Vogel, der zu Gott fliegt, Abb. 669/670 auf den Dichter als alten Mann und seine Befreiung aus irdischen Fesseln. (USA)

663, 664 Illustration et feuillet volant du calendrier d'un club d'étudiants de l'Université de Washington avec un programme des événements. Noir sur papier jaune. (USA)

665–670 Cinq illustrations fantastiques et double page complète du calendrier «Hermann Hesse» publié par Farrar, Strauss & Giroux. On utilise des quotations de Hermann Hesse, soit de son œuvre complet, soit de la littérature secondaire. Les textes sont arrangés par ordre chronologique. Fig. 665 se réfère à son horoscope et sa jeunesse; fig. 666 à ses pensées intimes; fig. 667 à l'âme cosmique; fig. 668 à l'oiseau qui s'envole vers Dieu; figs. 669/670 au poète âgé et à sa libération des liens. (USA)

665

666

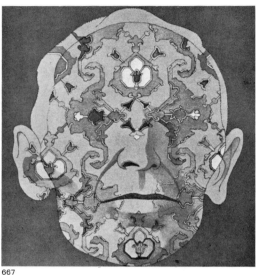

667

668

663

664

669

670

ARTIST / KÜNSTLER / ARTISTE:

663, 664 Bobbye Cochran
665–670 Milton Glaser

DESIGNER / GESTALTER / MAQUETTISTE:

663, 664 Bobbye Cochran/Dennis Gillaspy

ART DIRECTOR / DIRECTEUR ARTISTIQUE:

663, 664 Stan Gellman

AGENCY / AGENTUR / AGENCE – STUDIO:

663, 664 Stan Gellman Graphic Design
665–670 Milton Glaser, Inc.

Calendars / Kalender / Calendriers

671

672

ARTIST / KÜNSTLER / ARTISTE:

671, 672 Georges Lemoine
673–675 Gerd Grimm
676–678 Mabey Trousdell, Inc.

ART DIRECTOR:

671, 672 Georges Lemoine
673–675 Gerd Grimm
676–678 Mabey Trousdell, Inc.

AGENCY / AGENTUR / AGENCE:

673–675 Brose und Partner
676–678 Trousdell Mabey, Inc.

671, 672 Illustration and complete laminated calendar issued and sold by the artist. (FRA)
673–675 Two motifs and one complete sheet from a calendar for *Reval* cigarettes. Fig. 673 combines artwork and photography; Fig. 675: green figure. (GER)
676–678 Three sheets from a 1973 calendar issued by Mabey Trousdell Inc. recapitulating major events of 1972—here Nixon's visit to China, the shooting of Wallace and the assassination of Israeli athletes at the Munich Olympics. (USA)

671, 672 Illustration und vollständiger, laminierter Kalender von Georges Lemoine. (FRA)
673–675 Zwei Motive und vollständiges Blatt eines Kalenders für *Reval*-Zigaretten. Abb. 673 kombiniert Illustration und Photo; Fig. 675: Mann in Grün. (GER)
676–678 Drei Blätter aus einem Kalender für 1973, der an wichtige Ereignisse des Jahres 1972 erinnerte – Nixons Chinareise, die Schüsse auf Wallace und die Ermordung israelischer Athleten an der Olympiade in München. (USA)

671, 672 Illustration et calendrier sur papier couché publié et vendu par l'artiste. (USA)
673–675 Deux motifs et l'un des feuillets complets d'un calendrier pour les cigarettes *reval*. La fig. 673 combine le dessin et la photographie; la fig. 675: figure verte. (GER)
676–678 Trois feuillets du calendrier 1973 de Mabey Trousdell Inc. présentant les événements importants de l'année 1972 – la visite du Président Nixon en Chine; les coups de fusils sur Wallace; l'assassinat des athlètes israéliens lors des Jeux Olympiques à Munich. (USA)

674

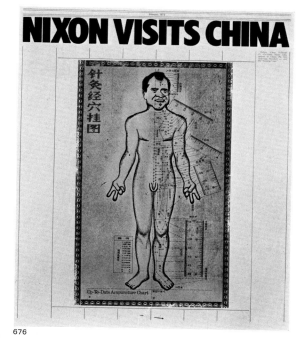

NIXON VISITS CHINA

676

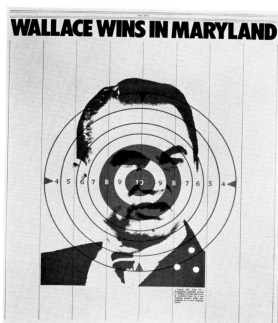

WALLACE WINS IN MARYLAND

677

673

675

Calendars
Kalender
Calendriers

SPIRIT OF OLYMPICS IGNITED AT MUNICH

678

219

679

680

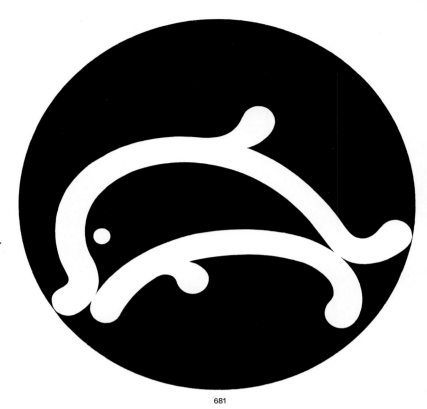

681

DESIGNER / GESTALTER / MAQUETTISTE:

679, 680 Design Research Unit
681, 686 Yusaku Kamekura
682 Edward Hughes
683 Tim Nielsen
684 Richard Nava
685 Stephan Geissbühler
687 Hayao Izuhara
688 CEI Compagnie de l'Esthétique Industrielle
689 Rosmarie Tissi
690 Linda Powell
691 Romano Chicherio/Cesare Bianch

686

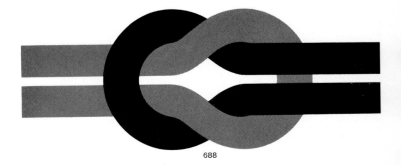

687

685

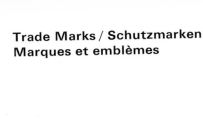

688

ART DIRECTOR / DIRECTEUR ARTISTIQUE:

681, 686 Yusaku Kamekura
682 Edward Hughes
684 Richard Nava
685 Eugene J. Grossman
687 Hayao Izuhara
691 Romano Chicherio

AGENCY / AGENTUR / AGENCE – STUDIO:

679, 680 Design Research Unit
682 Edward Hughes Design
683 Ken Parkhurst & Associates
684 Image Communications
685 Anspach Grossman Portugal, Inc.
688 CEI Compagnie de l'Esthétique Industrielle
689 Odermatt & Tissi
690 Westburg-Klaus Assoc., Inc.
631 Studio Grafico Romano Chicherio

682

683

684

679 Emblem designed for the Royal Garden Hotel, London. (GBR)
680 "Family" emblem for Britain's Countryside Commission. (GBR)
681 Symbol designed for the Japan Association for the International Ocean Exposition held in Okinawa in 1975. (JPN)
682 Symbol for Glenbrook Hospital. (USA)
683 Trade mark for Santa Fe Federal Savings, intended for offices in Indian and Spanish desert communities. (USA)
684 Trade mark for Intercontinental Apparel. (USA)
685 Trade mark for Blazer Financial Services. (USA)
686 Logotype for the Onkyo Corporation. (JPN)
687 Logotype for Bulldog, a doughnut shop. (JPN)
688 Red and blue emblem for the Association Méditerranéenne de Yachting. (FRA)
689 Trade mark inspired by old flour sack stamps for the Groba Bakery. (SWI)
690 Logotype for Medical Equipment & Design Associates, Inc. (USA)
691 Symbol for the tourist office of the Ticino. The "t" incorporates the Swiss cross. (SWI)

679 Signet des Royal Garden Hotel, London. (GBR)
680 «Familien»-Signet für die britische Countryside Commission. (GBR)
681 Signet der japanischen Vereinigung für die International Ocean Exposition, abgehalten in Okinawa im Jahre 1975. (JPN)
682 Symbol des Glenbrook Hospital. (USA)
683 Signet der Sparkasse Santa Fe Federal Savings für deren Büros in indischen und spanischen Wüstengemeinden. (USA)
684 Warenzeichen der Intercontinental Apparel. (USA)
685 Warenzeichen für Blazer Financial Services. (USA)
686 Schriftzug der Onkyo Corporation. (JPN)
687 Schriftzug eines Berliner-Pfannkuchen-Ladens namens Bulldog. (JPN)
688 Signet in Rot und Blau der Association Méditerranéenne de Yachting. (FRA)
689 Warenzeichen der Groba Grossbäckerei, inspiriert von den in Schablonenform gehaltenen Stempeln auf alten Mehlsäcken. (SWI)
690 Schriftzug für die Medical Equipment & Design Associates, Inc. (USA)
691 Symbol des Verkehrsbüros des Kantons Tessin. Das «t» beinhaltet das Schweizerkreuz. (SWI)

679 Emblème conçu pour le Royal Garden Hotel à Londres. (GBR)
680 Emblème pour la Countryside Commission en Grande Bretagne. (GBR)
681 Symbole réalisé pour une association japonaise qui organise une exposition internationale, consacrée à la mer et tous ses aspects, présentée à Okinawa en 1975. (JPN)
682 Symbole pour l'hôpital Glenbrook. (USA)
683 Marque pour les succursales d'une banque installées dans des villages indiens et espagnols qui se trouvent loin des grands centres commerciaux. (USA)
684 Marque pour Intercontinental Apparel. (USA)
685 Marque pour Blazer Financial Services. (USA)
686 Logo pour l'Onkyo Corporation. (JPN)
687 Logo pour Bulldog, un magasin spécialisé dans différentes sortes de beignets. (JPN)
688 Emblème en rouge et bleu pour l'Association Méditerranéenne de Yachting. (FRA)
689 Marque d'une boulangerie. Design inspiré par les vieilles estampes des sacs à farine. (SWI)
690 Logo pour les Medical Equipment & Design Associates, Inc. (USA)
691 Symbole pour l'office du tourisme du Tessin. Le «t» incorpore la croix suisse. (SWI)

689

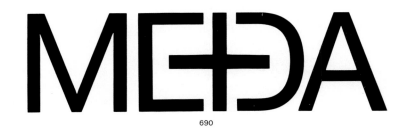

690

691

Trade Marks / Schutzmarken
Marques et emblèmes

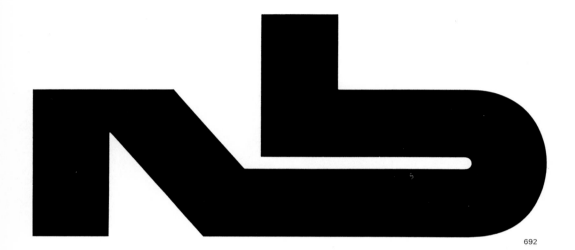

692

693

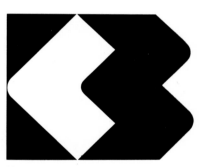

694

695

696

697

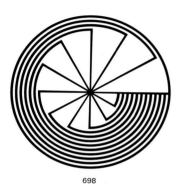

698

699

700

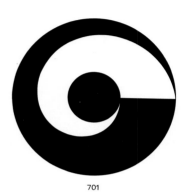

701

702

703

704

705

692 Trade mark for the Nobel Bozel company, which manufactures explosives. (FRA)
693 The "Pirelli Presenter", an articulated "tyreman" used as a sales presentation figure by Pirelli. (GBR)
694 Corporate trade mark for Consolidated Brands. (USA)
695 Symbol for a Design Year organized in Japan in 1973. (JPN)
696 Trade mark for the Chemical Research Company. (USA)
697 Symbol for the Japan Sporting Arms & Ammunition Manufacturers' Association. (JPN)
698 Trade mark (used as a positive or negative) for the Kjell Karlsen Entertainment AS. (NOR)
699 Symbol for the Cofremca Company. (FRA)
700 Trade mark for a printer, Schmid-Druck AG of Bienne. (SWI)
701 Symbol for a residential development, Ram Ridge Corporate Park I.E.C. Development Ltd. (USA)
702 Trade mark for Reed Paper Ltd. (CAN)
703 Company trade mark for Heinrich Baumann. (GER)
704 Trade mark for the bank Société Générale. (FRA)
705 Symbol for the Swiss society for the prevention of cruelty to animals. (SWI)

692 Warenzeichen der Firma Nobel Bozel, Herstellerin von Sprengstoffen. (FRA)
693 Der «Pirelli-Präsentator», ein gelenkiger «Pneumann», von Pirelli als Verkaufs- und Präsentationsfigur verwendet. (GBR)
694 Firmensignet der Consolidated Brands. (USA)
695 Symbol für ein Design-Jahr (1973) in Japan. (JPN)
696 Marke der Chemical Research Company. (USA)
697 Symbol der japanischen Sportwaffen- und Munitions-fabrikanten-Vereinigung. (JPN)
698 Marke (als Positiv und Negativ verwendet) der Kjell Karlsen Entertainment AS. (NOR)
699 Symbol der Firma Cofremca. (FRA)
700 Marke der Schmid-Druck AG, Biel. (SWI)
701 Symbol einer Immobiliengesellschaft, der Ram Ridge Corporate Park I.E.C. Development Ltd. (USA)
702 Marke der Reed Paper Ltd., Papierhersteller. (CAN)
703 Firmenmarke von Heinrich Baumann. (GER)
704 Marke der Grossbank Société Générale. (FRA)
705 Symbol der Schweizerischen Tierschutzgesellschaft, mit Fisch und Eule. (SWI)

692 Marque pour Nobel Bozel, une compagnie qui fabrique des matières explosibles. (FRA)
693 Le «bonhomme Pirelli» aux membres articulés qui est utilisé en tant que décoration pour les salles de vente. (ITA)
694 Marque pour Consolidated Brands. (USA)
695 Marque pour une «année d'art graphique» au Japon.(JPN)
696 Marque pour une compagnie de recherches chimiques. (US)
697 Symbole de l'association japonaise des fabricants d'armes sportives et de munition. (JPN)
698 Marque (utilisée en forme positive ou négative) pour le Kjell Karlsen Entertainment AS. (NOR)
699 Symbole pour la compagnie Cofremca. (FRA)
700 Marque pour l'imprimerie Schmid-Druck AG. (SWI)
701 Symbole d'une entreprise immobilière, la Ram Ridge Corporate Park I.E.C. Development Ltd. (USA)
702 Marque pour la papeterie Reed Paper Ltd. (CAN)
703 Symbole pour l'entreprise Heinrich Baumann. (GER)
704 Marque pour la Société Générale. (FRA)
705 Symbole pour la Société protectrice des animaux de la Suisse. (SWI)

Trade Marks / Letterheads
Schutzmarken / Briefköpfe
Marques et emblèmes / En-têtes

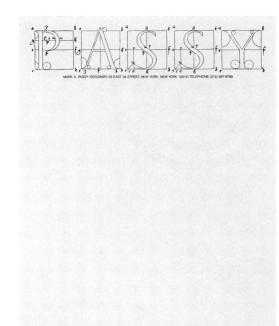

DESIGNER / GESTALTER / MAQUETTISTE:

706 G. S. Rosentswieg
707 Hannes Geissler
708 David Battle
709 Takenobu Igarashi
710 The Richards Group
711 Fritz Gottschalk
712 Paul Ibou
713 John Emery
714 Luis Huguet Aznar
715 Marjorie Katz
716 Armin Vogt
717 Mark Passy
718 Harrison Associates
719 Lou Dorfsman
720 Paul Rand
721 Peter Bradford
722 Ralph Coburn

ART DIRECTOR / DIRECTEUR ARTISTIQUE:

706 G. S. Rosentswieg
707 Horst Rickmann
708 David Battle
709 Takenobu Igarashi
710 Jack Summerford
711 Gottschalk & Ash Limited
713 Read Viemeister
714 Luis Huguet Aznar
715 Marjorie Katz
716 Armin Vogt
717 Mark Passy
719 Lou Dorfsman
720 Paul Rand
721 Peter Bradford/S. Richard Wurman

AGENCY / AGENTUR / AGENCE – STUDIO:

706 The Graphics Studio
708 David Battle Design
709 Igarashi Design Institute
710 The Richards Group, Inc.
711 Gottschalk & Ash Limited
713 Vie Design Studio, Inc.
714 Luis Huguet Aznar
715 Marjorie Katz Graphic Design
716 Armin Vogt Partner
717 Mark Passy
718 Harrison Associates
719 CBS/Broadcast Group
721 Peter Bradford & Associates

715

717

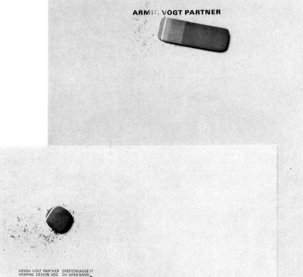

716

718

706

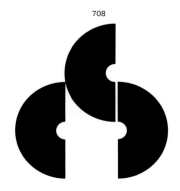

707

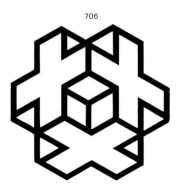

708

709

712

719

713

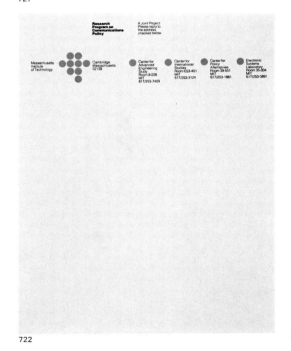

720

721

714

710

711

706 Trade mark for Total Financial Services, Inc. (USA)
707 Trade mark for Ozean Service & Reparatur GmbH. (GER)
708 Symbol for the Center Stage theatre. (USA)
709 Trade mark for Kaneshige-Kosan Inc. (JPN)
710 Symbol for the USA Film Festival. (USA)
711 Trade mark for Norstar Ski Corporation Ltd. (CAN)
712 Trade mark for Polytra SA, transit services. (BEL)
713 Symbol for the X-Line of Xenia city transport system. (USA)
714 Trade mark for *Cromoarte*, photoengravers. (SPA)
715 Stationery for Designer's Saturday, an exhibition programme organized by New York furniture manufacturers. (USA)
716 Stationery for a graphic design studio. Red eraser. (SWI)
717 Letterhead for a designer. Lettering by Dürer. (USA)
718 Letterhead for Harrison Associates, architects. ''H'' in red and yellow. (USA)
719 Notepaper head in full colour for a CBS cafeteria. (USA)
720 Letterhead for a *Cummins* promotion scheme. (USA)
721 Letterhead for a convention of the American Institute of Architects in bicentennial year 1976. Blue and red. (CAN)
722 Letterhead of an MIT research programme. Red spots. (USA)

706 Schutzmarke der Total Financial Services, Inc. (USA)
707 Signet der Ozean Service & Reparatur GmbH. (GER)
708 Symbol des Center Stage Theaters. (USA)
709 Signet der Kaneshige-Kosan Inc. (JPN)
710 Symbol des USA Film-Festivals. (USA)
711 Schutzmarke der Norstar Ski Corporation Ltd. (CAN)
712 Firmensignet der Polytra SA, Transportdienste. (BEL)
713 Symbol der X-Linie der Verkehrsbetriebe Xenia City. (USA)
714 Signet von *Cromoarte*, einem Clicheur. (USA)
715 Briefpapier für «Designer's Saturday», ein von Möbelfabrikanten organisiertes Ausstellungsprogramm. (USA)
716 Briefpapier für ein Graphiker-Atelier. (SWI)
717 Briefkopf eines Designers. Schrift von Dürer. (USA)
718 Briefkopf des Architekten-Teams Harrison Associates. «H» in Rot und Gelb. (USA)
719 Farbiges Notizpapier eines CBS-Cafeteria. (USA)
720 Briefkopf einer *Cummins*-Abteilung. Blau, schwarz. (USA)
721 Briefkopf für eine Architektentagung in 1976 zur 200-Jahrfeier der Vereinigten Staaten. Blau und rot. (USA)
722 Für ein Forschungsprogramm des MIT. Rote Punkte. (USA)

706 Marque pour Total Financial Services, Inc. (USA)
707 Marque pour Ozean Service & Reparatur GmbH. (GER)
708 Symbole pour le Center Stage Theater. (USA)
709 Marque pour la Kaneshige-Kosan, Inc. (JPN)
710 Symbole pour le festival américain du film. (USA)
711 Marque pour la Norstar Ski Corporation, Ltd. (CAN)
712 Marque pour les services de transport Polytra SA. (BEL)
713 Symbole pour la ligne X d'un service de transport. (USA)
714 Marque pour les photolithographes *Cromoarte*. (SPA)
715 Papier à lettre pour Designer's Saturday, un programme d'expositions organisé par des fabricants de meubles. (USA)
716 Papier à lettre pour un studio d'art graphique. (SWI)
717 En-tête pour un designer. Typo emprunté de Durer. (USA)
718 En-tête pour Harrison Associates, un groupe d'architectes. «H» en rouge et jaune. (USA)
719 En-tête d'un bloc-notes en couleur pour un café. (USA)
720 En-tête de la promotion de ventes de *Cummins*. (USA)
721 En-tête d'une convention de l'American Institute of Architects pour le bicentenaire en 1976. Bleu et rouge. (USA)
722 En-tête pour un programme de recherches MIT. (USA)

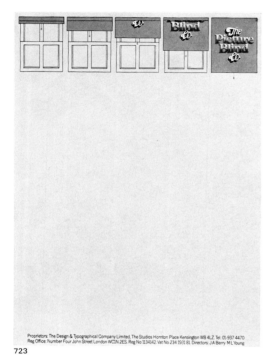

724

726

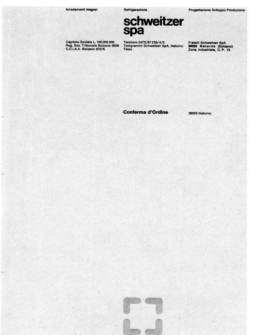

723

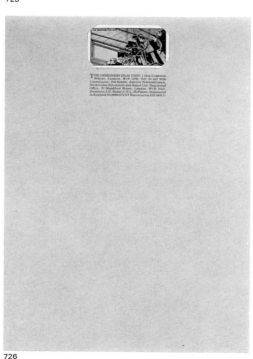

725

728

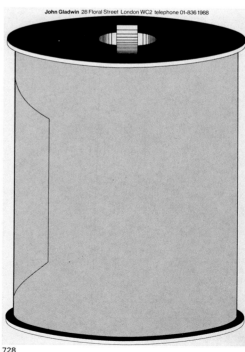

727

Letterheads
Briefköpfe
En-têtes

731

ARTIST / KÜNSTLER / ARTISTE:

728 Richard Escasany

DESIGNER / GESTALTER / MAQUETTISTE:

723 Malcolm Young/John Berry
724 Peter Eberle
725 Jan Lepair
726 Arnold Schwartzman
727 Alan Fletcher
728 Robin Hardy/Richard Escasany
729 R. Del Sordo/G. Berlinghieri
730 Milton Glaser
731, 732 Michael Doret
733 John George

ART DIRECTOR / DIRECTEUR ARTISTIQUE:

723 Malcolm Young/John Berry
725 Jan Lepair
726 Arnold Schwartzman
729 R. Del Sordo/G. Berlinghieri
731, 732 Peter Coutroulis
733 Rod Springett/Klaus Wuttke

729

732

733

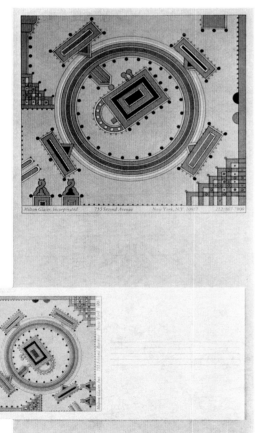

730

AGENCY / AGENTUR / AGENCE – STUDIO:

723 The Design & Typographical Company Ltd.
724 Studio Martinis
727 Pentagram Design Partnership
728 Hardy/Lodwick Limited
729 Studio Giob
730 Milton Glaser, Inc.
731, 732 Michael Doret, Inc.
733 Springett Wuttke Ltd.

734

735

738

739

ARTIST / KÜNSTLER / ARTISTE:

736 Gerry Keller
739 Les Mason/Sandi Clark
741 Hett, Friedemann

DESIGNER / GESTALTER / MAQUETTISTE:

734 Creative Team Nacke & Flink
735 Burton Kramer
736 Fritz Gottschalk/Gerry Keller
737 Shigeru Akizuki
738 Burton Kramer/Pat Valentine
739 Les Mason

ART DIRECTOR / DIRECTEUR ARTISTIQUE:

735, 738 Burton Kramer
736 Gottschalk + Ash Ltd.
739 Les Mason
741 Peter Selinka

AGENCY / AGENTUR / AGENCE – STUDIO:

734 Ted Bates
735, 738 Burton Kramer Associates Ltd.
736 Gottschalk + Ash Ltd.
739 Masius Wynne Williams & d'Arcy Mac Manus Pty., Ltd.
741 Peter Selinka, Werbeagentur

734 Conical metal container with black plastic cap for a *Mobil* synthetic lubricant. (GER)
735 Range of cubic and oblong folding boxes in different colours for floodlight bulbs, kits and projectors made by Noma Lites Canada Ltd. (CAN)
736 Range of folding boxes for a pharmaceutical product made by Syntex Ltd. Yellow "N" on black background, white print. (CAN)
737 Project for a folding box for a *Kanebo* toilet water. Black and grey "M". (JPN)
738 Carton for a "Moonvigil Kit", a multimedia teaching aid for the Ontario Educational Communications Authority, containing buttons, food units, etc., for a game to be played in a school TV programme. (CAN)
739 Package design for exclusive men's shoes made by Julius Marlow. (AUL)
740 Packet and carton for *Sano* cigarettes made by the US Tobacco Co. Beige, grey-brown, dark blue. (USA)
741 Package (full colour on magenta ground) containing a folder and a small pygmy hunting whistle, from a series sent to doctors by Dr. Karl Thomae GmbH to advertise a pharmaceutical against asthma. (GER)

Packaging / Packungen / Emballages

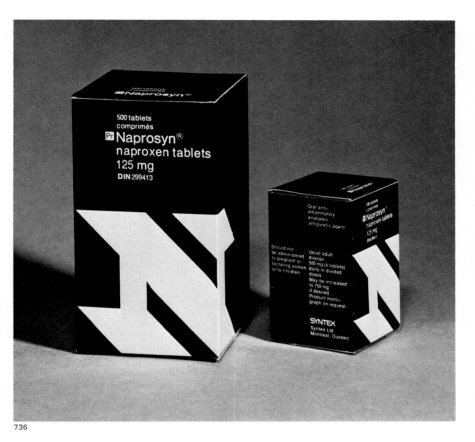

736

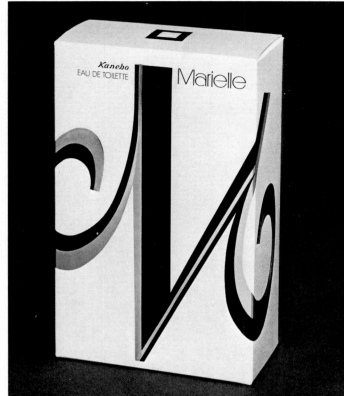

737

740

741

734 Metallbehälter mit schwarzem Plastikverschluss für ein synthetisches *Mobil*-Schmiermittel. (GER)
735 Auswahl kubischer und länglicher Faltschachteln in verschiedenen Farben für Flutlicht-Birnen, Ausrüstungen und Projektionsapparate, hergestellt von Noma Lites Canada Ltd. (CAN)
736 Serie von Faltschachteln für ein pharmazeutisches Produkt, hergestellt durch Syntex Ltd. Gelbes «N» auf schwarzem Hintergrund, weisse Schrift. (CAN)
737 Entwurf einer Faltschachtel für *Kanebo*-Toilettenwasser. «M» schwarz und grau. (JPN)
738 Schachtel für den «Moonvigil Kit», ein Multimedia-Lehrmittel für die Ontario Educational Communications Authority, das Knöpfe, Nahrungsmittel-Einheiten usw. enthält für ein Spiel im Schulfernsehen. (CAN)
739 Packungsentwurf für exklusive Herrenschuhe, hergestellt von Julius Marlow. (AUL)
740 Packung und Schachtel für *Sano*-Zigaretten. Beige, graubraun, dunkelblau. (USA)
741 Packung (mehrfarbig auf magentarotem Grund) mit Prospekt und Pygmäen-Schrillpfeife, aus einer an Ärzte versandten Serie der Dr. Karl Thomae GmbH für ein Mittel gegen Asthma. (GER)

734 Récipient conique en métal avec couvercle en plastique noir pour un lubrifiant synthétique *Mobil*. (GER)
735 Gamme de boîtes cubiques et oblongues en différentes couleurs pour des ampoules de projecteurs, des articles électriques et des appareils de projection. (CAN)
736 Gamme de boîtes pliantes pour un produit pharmaceutique de Syntex Ltd. «N» en jaune sur fond noir, typographie en blanc. (CAN)
737 Maquette pour une boîte pliante pour une eau de toilette de *Kanebo*. «M» en noir et gris. (JPN)
738 Carton contenant des boutons, des articles alimentaires, etc., pour un jeu présenté dans un programme scolaire télévisé Elément d'un programme d'enseignement. (CAN)
739 Emballage pour des souliers pour hommes, fabriqués par Julius Marlow. (AUL)
740 Paquet et carton pour les cigarettes *Sano* de la US Tobacco Co. Beige, brun gris et bleu foncé. (USA)
741 Emballage (polychrome sur fond magenta) contenant une brochure et un petit sifflet de chasse pygméen. Elément d'une série adressée aux médecins pour la promotion d'un produit contre l'asthme. (GER)

742

743

744

745

ARTIST / KÜNSTLER / ARTISTE:

742 Karin Welponer
746 Malcolm Smith
747 Sandi Clark
748 Les Mason/Sylvia Hennessey
749 Bill Kwan

DESIGNER / GESTALTER / MAQUETTISTE:

742 Karin Welponer
743, 744 Ernest Witzig
745 Studio Goossens
746–749 Les Mason

Packaging

ART DIRECTOR / DIRECTEUR ARTISTIQUE:

742 Karin Welponer
743 Michel Logoz
744 Peter Strickler
745 Francis Maurus
746–749 Les Mason

AGENCY / AGENTUR / AGENCE – STUDIO:

742 Nerdinger & Partner
743, 744 Roth & Sauter S.A.
745 Studio Goossens
746, 748 Les Mason Graphic Design
747 Hayes Advertising P.L.
749 Masius Wynne Williams & d'Arcy
    Mac Manus Pty., Ltd.

746

747

748

749

ARTIST / KÜNSTLER / ARTISTE:

753 Bill Kwan
756, 757 Doris Rosenquist/Ike Vern (Photo)

DESIGNER / GESTALTER / MAQUETTISTE:

750 Alan Zie Yongder
751 G. Marazzi e Staff
752 Urs Roos
753 Les Mason
754, 755 Gen Naito
756, 757 Irv Koons
758 John Downs/Dudley Davenport

ART DIRECTOR / DIRECTEUR ARTISTIQUE:

750 Alan Zie Yongder
751 G. Marazzi
752 Erich Hartmann
753 Les Mason
754, 755 Gen Naito
756, 757 Jack Yeager
758 James Black

AGENCY / AGENTUR / AGENCE – STUDIO:

750 LTZ Limited
751 G.M.D.
752 Gisler & Gisler
756, 757 Irv Koons Associates, Inc.
758 Leo Burnett/Moonink, Inc.

750

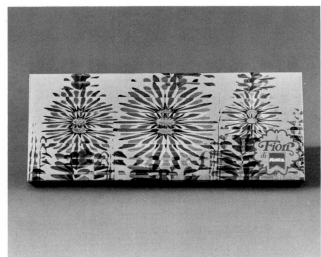

751

752

Packaging
Packungen
Emballages

753

754

755

756

757

758

750 Tins in two sizes for *Vecorn* oil made from maize. (JPN)
751 From a range of colourful cartons with flower motifs for *Motta* chocolates. (ITA)
752 Range of packages for several varieties of a popular type of Swiss cheese. (SWI)
753 Carton containing the ingredients for one litre of *Peters* natural ice cream. Red and black on yellow. (AUL)
754, 755 Can styling for *Kirin* lager beer. Gold, red and white, black lettering. (JPN)
756 Packs of 50 and 100 *Dixie* disposable kitchen cups. Cups in actual colours red ground. (USA)
757 Row of cartons for 100 *Dixie* disposable bathroom cups in the colours of the designs on the cups—blue, yellow, avocado and pink. (USA)
758 Packet of *Miyako* cigarettes, made under Japanese licence by Philip Morris, Inc. Red, pale beige, gold, black. (USA)

750 Dosen in zwei Grössen für *Vecorn*-Öl aus Mais. (JPN)
751 Aus einer Reihe von farbigen Schachteln mit Blumen-motiven für *Motta*-Pralinen. (ITA)
752 Serie von Packungen für einen Schweizerkäse in verschiedenen Varianten. (SWI)
753 Schachtel mit Zutaten für die Herstellung von einem Liter *Peters* Ice-Cream. Rot und Schwarz auf Gelb. (AUL)
754, 755 Dosengestaltung für *Kirin*-Lagerbier. Gold, Rot und Weiss, schwarze Schrift. (JPN)
756 Packungen von 50 und 100 *Dixie*-Wegwerfbechern. Becher farbig, roter Hintergrund. (USA)
757 Reihe von Schachteln für 100 *Dixie*-Wegwerfbecher fürs Badezimmer in den Farben der Bechermotive – blau, gelb, grün und rosa. (USA)
758 Packung von *Miyako*-Zigaretten japanischer Lizenzfabrikation. Rot, hellbeige, goldgelb, schwarz. (USA)

750 Boîtes en deux grandeurs pour une huile de maïs. (JPN)
751 D'une gamme de cartons en couleurs vives avec des motifs de fleurs pour les chocolats *Motta*. (ITA)
752 Gamme d'emballages pour les différentes sortes d'un fromage suisse bien connu. (SWI)
753 Carton contenant les ingrédients pour un litre de glace *Peters*. Rouge et noir sur fond jaune. (AUL)
754, 755 Différentes formes de boîtes pour la bière *Kirin*. Or, rouge et blanc, typo noir. (JPN)
756 Paquets pour 50 et 100 gobelets de cuisine. Gobelets en couleurs originales sur fond rouge. (USA)
757 Gamme de cartons pour 100 gobelets *Dixie* pour le bain, reproduits dans les couleurs respectives du design – bleu, jaune, avocado et rose. (USA)
758 Paquet pour les cigarettes *Mikado*, fabriquées sous licence japonaise par Philip Morris. Rouge, beige, or, noir. (USA)

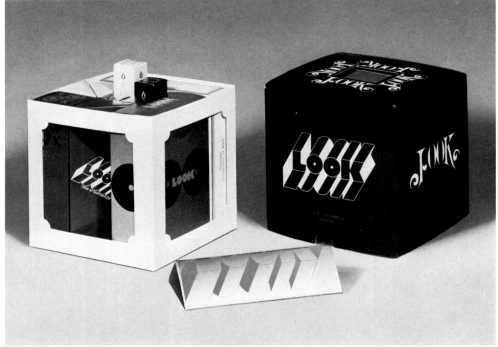

759

759 Set-up box in glossy black and white containing an assortment of fancy boxes of various sizes and colours to display the effects that can be obtained with *Chromolux* board in packaging applications. (GER)
760 Packages used in a sales motivation programme addressed to the *Westinghouse* industrial sales force. Tailor-made clothes were offered as prizes for sales successes, and each package contains literature on the sale drive together with objects connected with tailor-made clothing. White trade mark on blue. (USA)
761 Folding box for a modern *Terraillon* clock. Black and silver. (ITA)
762 From a range of set-up boxes and other packaging for *Robinson's* stores. Two blues and white. (USA)
763 Gift carton for a sweet wine marketed by Godo Shusei Ltd. (JPN)
764 Carton and prestige gift in the form of a limited-edition game for *Reuters*. Carton blue-black and silver, gift in perspex and aluminium with steel ball bearings. (GBR)
765 Packages for glasses made by Xlon Products Ltd. Black sleeves with white lettering, red trays containing the glasses. (GBR)

759 Schaubox in glänzendem Schwarzweiss mit einem Sortiment von Fantasieschachteln in verschiedenen Grössen, um die Wirkung des *Chromolux*-Kartons als Verpackungsmaterial zu demonstrieren. (GER)
760 Packungen, die im Verkaufs-Motivationsprogramm für das Verkaufspersonal von *Westinghouse* verwendet wurden. Als Preise für Verkaufserfolge wurden massgeschneiderte Anzüge offeriert. Jede Packung enthält Literatur über Verkaufstechnik, zusammen mit Gegenständen im Zusammenhang mit der Massschneiderei. (USA)
761 Faltschachtel für eine *Terraillon*-Uhr. Schwarz und Silber. (ITA)
762 Aus einer Reihe von Schachteln und anderen Packungen für *Robinson's* Warenhäuser. Zwei Blautöne und Weiss. (USA)
763 Geschenkschachtel für einen süssen Wein. (JPN)
764 Schachtel und Prestige-Geschenk in Form eines Spieles mit begrenzter Auflage für *Reuters*. Schachtel in Blau-Schwarz und Silber, Geschenk in Plexiglas und Aluminium mit Stahlkugellagern. (GBR)
765 Packungen für Gläser der Xlon Products Ltd. Schwarze Hülsen mit weisser Schrift, rote Ziehschubladen für die Gläser. (GBR)

762

763

759 Boîte-présentoir en noir brillant contenant une gamme de boîtes en grandeurs et couleurs variées pour démontrer les différents aspects des emballages en carton *Chromolux*. (GER)
760 Emballages figurant dans un programme de vente de *Westinghouse* pour les représentants industriels. Ils contiennent, outre un choix de vêtements offert à ceux qui remportent les commandes les plus importantes, des publications sur les campagnes de vente et des objets se rapportant aux vêtements. Marque blanche sur fond bleu. (USA)
761 Boîte pliante pour une pendule moderne. Noir sur argent. (ITA)
762 D'une gamme de boîtes et d'emballages pour les grands magasins *Robinson's*. Deux teintes bleues et blanc. (USA)
763 Boîte-cadeau pour un vin doux vendu par Godo Shusei Ltd. (JPN)
764 Carton et cadeau en forme d'un jeu dont le nombre d'exemplaires est limité. Carton en bleu-noir et argent, cadeau en plastique et aluminium avec des billes en métal. (GBR)
765 D'une gamme d'emballages pour une verrerie. Boîte en noir avec typo blanc, tiroir contenant les verres en rouge. (GBR)

Packaging / Packungen / Emballages

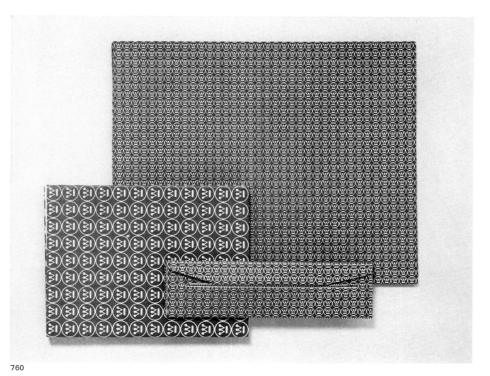

760

761

764

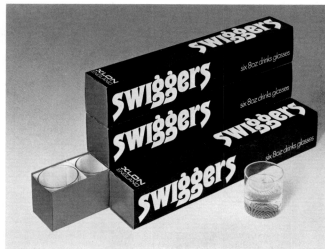

765

DESIGNER / GESTALTER / MAQUETTISTE:

759 Zanders Feinpapiere
760 Marini, Climes & Guip, Inc.
    (R. Radigan, J. Geyer, S. Klink, R. Gessay)
761 Alfredo Mastellaro
762 Douglas Boyd/Gordon Tani (Artist)
763 Shigeru Akizuki
764 Alan Fletcher
765 Collis Clements

ART DIRECTOR / DIRECTEUR ARTISTIQUE:

760 Vince Longo
761 Alfredo Mastellaro
762 Douglas Boyd
765 Collis Clements

AGENCY / AGENTUR / AGENCE – STUDIO:

760 Ketchum, MacLeod & Growe, Inc.
761 T.B.W.A./Studio Mastellaro
762 Douglas Boyd Design
764 Pentagram Design Partnership Ltd.
765 Clarke/Clements/Hughes

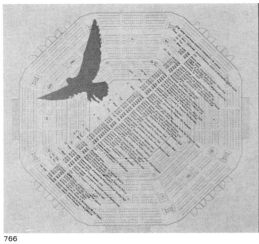

ARTIST / KÜNSTLER / ARTISTE:

767 Dave Willardson
768 Leo Monahan
769 Bill Jenkins
770 Patty Reynolds (Photo)
771–773 Richard Huebner

DESIGNER / GESTALTER / MAQUETTISTE:

766 Tadanori Yokoo
767, 768 Peter Whorf
769 Woody Pirtle
770 John Kosh
771–773 Catherine Deeter
774 David M. Seager

ART DIRECTOR / DIRECTEUR ARTISTIQUE:

767, 768 Peter Whorf
769 Woody Pirtle
770 Fabio Nicoli
771–773 Glenn Ross/Catherine Deeter
774 Bernard B. Sanders

766

767

768

AGENCY / AGENTUR / AGENCE – STUDIO:

769 The Richards Group, Inc.
771–773 Queens Litho Creative Dept.
774 Sanders & Noe, Inc.

PUBLISHER / VERLEGER / EDITEUR:

766 Santana Band
767, 768 ABC Records, Inc.
769 Capitol Records
770 A & M Records, Inc.
771–773 Playboy Records
774 National Association of Broadcasters

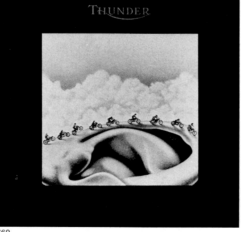

769

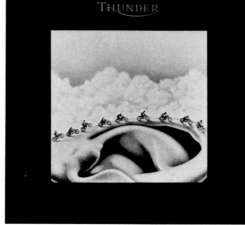

770

771

772

773

774

Record Covers / Schallplattenhüllen
Pochettes de disques

766 Two panels of a record cover for music by the Santana band, which toured Japan. Left-hand panel on yellow, right-hand panel on dull gold ground. (JPN)
767 Complete cover of an ABC record with music by a beat group. Full colour. (USA)
768 Cover of an ABC record with variations on a waltz by Beethoven. Cream to pale beige shades. (USA)
769 Cover of a *Capitol* record. Title in blue, ear in flesh shades, white clouds, pale blue sky. (USA)
770 Cover of a recording of songs by Hudson and Ford for A&M Records. Yellow and red lettering, blue plaque, green petrol can (a play on the word ''spirit''). (USA)
771–773 Four-record album for Playboy Records, used as a promotion kit. The parts can be unfolded to produce the girl shown in Fig. 771. Arms and legs are hinged and movable. Fig. 773 shows the cover (blue with red ribbon). (USA)
774 Cover of a record issued by the National Association of Broadcasters as part of a campaign to keep radio free. (USA)

766 Vorder- und Rückseite des Umschlags für eine Schall-platte der Santana-Band, die in Japan auf Tournee war. Links gelber, rechts mattgoldgelber Hintergrund. (JPN)
767 Vollständiger Umschlag einer ABC-Platte mit Musik einer Beat-Gruppe. Mehrfarbig. (USA)
768 Umschlag einer ABC-Schallplatte mit Variationen über einen Walzer von Beethoven. (USA)
769 Umschlag einer *Capitol*-Schallplatte. Titel in Blau, Ohr in Fleischtönen, weisse Wolken, hellblauer Himmel. (USA)
770 Umschlag einer Platte mit Songs von Hudson und Ford. Schrift gelb und rot, blaue Plakette, grüner Benzinbehälter. Das englische Wort «spirit» = «Geist» oder «Kraftstoff». (USA)
771–773 Vierer-Schallplatten-Album für Playboy Records, als Werbemittel verwendet. Die Teile sind beweglich und entfalten sich zur Mädchenfigur wie unter Abb. 771. Abb. 773 zeigt den Umschlag (blau mit rosa Band). (USA)
774 Umschlag einer Schallplatte, die Teil einer Kampagne für ein gebühren- und zensurfreies Radio war. (USA)

766 Deux encarts d'une pochette de disque du groupe Santana avec des enregistrements de sa tournée au Japon. Encart gauche en jaune, encart droite sur fond doré. (JPN)
767 Pochette pour l'enregistrement d'un groupe beat. (USA)
768 Pochette d'un disque ABC avec variations sur le thème d'une valse de Beethoven. Crème passant à beige. (USA)
769 Pochette d'un disque CBS. Titre en bleu, oreille cou-leur de chair, nuages blancs, ciel bleu pâle. (USA)
770 Pochette pour un enregistrement de songs de Hudson et Ford publié par A&M records. Typo jaune et rouge, plaque bleue, boîte de pétrol verte (jeu de mots sur «esprit»). (USA)
771–773 Album contenant quatre disques de *Playboy*. En repliant les encarts il apparaît une fille (reproduite en fig. 771) aux membres articulés. La fig. 773 présente le verso de la pochette (bleu avec ruban rouge). (USA)
774 Pochette de disque publié par la National Association of Broadcasters. Elle figure dans une campagne en faveur des emissions radiophoniques non-censurées. (USA)

775

ARTIST / KÜNSTLER / ARTISTE:

777 Christian Piper
779 M. Morchoisne
780 Basil Pao
782 Jirí Salamoun

DESIGNER / GESTALTER:

775, 776 Heinz Stieger
777 Basil Pao
778 Bruno Oldani
780 Peter Palombi
781 John & Barbara Casado

ART DIRECTOR:

775, 776 Oswald Dubacher
777, 780 Bob Defrin
781 Ed Trasher

Record Covers

776

777

778

920.421

Bobino 73

Jean Constantin

779

EDDIE HARRIS IS IT IN

780

MAMA KERSHAW'S BOY

781

A. FELIX SLOVÁČEK

klarinet (7b) (12)

sopránový saxofon
(1) (2) (5) (6) (9) (11) (13) (14)

altový saxofon
(3) (4) (7a) (7c) (10)

782

775, 776 Detail and complete polychrome cover of a record for children from a series based on puppet shows. (SWI)
777 Cover of a record made by black musicians about Negro solidarity. Polychrome snakes, black head, red ground. (USA)
778 Record cover for songs by a beat group, published by MAI A/S. (NOR)
779 Cover of a *Barclay* record of music by Jean Constantin. Black and white, blue lettering. (FRA)
780 Cover for an Eddie Harris recording (Atlantic Records). (USA)
781 Cover for recordings by a violinist (Warner Bros. Records). (USA)
782 Three-colour page of a yellow booklet enclosed in the sleeve of an MS recording of orchestral music. (CSR)

775, 776 Ausschnitt und vollständiger farbiger Umschlag einer Schallplatte für Kinder aus einer auf Marionettenspielen basierenden Serie. (SWI)
777 Umschlag einer von schwarzen Musikern bespielten Platte über Negersolidarität. Farbige Schlangen, schwarzer Kopf, roter Hintergrund. (USA)
778 Schallplattenumschlag für die Songs einer Beat-Gruppe, herausgegeben von MAI A/S. (NOR)
779 Umschlag einer *Barclay*-Schallplatte mit Musik von Jean Constantin. (FRA)
780 Umschlag einer Eddie Harris-Platte (Atlantic Records). (USA)
781 Umschlag einer Platte eines Violonisten (Warner Bros. Records). (USA)
782 Dreifarbige Seite einer gelben Broschüre als Umschlagbeilage einer MS-Schallplattenaufnahme von Orchestermusik. (CSR)

775, 776 Détail et pochette complète (en couleur) d'un disque pour enfants, faisant partie d'une série d'enregistrements de théâtres de marionnettes. (SWI)
777 Pochette d'un disque avec des enregistrements de chanteurs noirs consacrés à la solidarité des peuples noirs. Serpents polychromes, tête noire, fond rouge. (USA)
778 Pochette de disque pour un enregistrement d'un groupe de musique beat. (NOR)
779 Pochette pour un enregistrement *Barclay* de Jean Constantin. Noir et blanc, typo bleu. (FRA)
780 Pochette d'un disque d'Eddie Harris (Atlantic Records). (USA)
781 Pochette d'un disque d'un violoniste (Atlantic Records). (USA)
782 Page en trois couleurs d'une brochure contenue dans la pochette pour un enregistrement de musique d'orchestre. (CSR)

PUBLISHER / VERLEGER:

775, 776 Ex Libris
777 Atlantic Records
778 Mai A/S Plateselskapet
779 Barclay France
780 Warner Bros. Records
781 Atlantic Records
782 Supraphon

AGENCY / AGENTUR / AGENCE:

778 Bruno Oldani